Russell and Moore

RUSSELL AND MOORE

The Analytical Heritage

A. J. Ayer

Harvard University Press
Cambridge, Massachusetts
1971

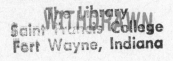

First published in 1971

Library of Congress Catalog Card Number 77-133216
SBN 674-78103-1

Printed in Great Britain

To

MARCELLE AND TONY QUINTON

Contents

Preface

In the Preface to my book, *The Origins of Pragmatism*, a study of the philosophy of Charles Sanders Peirce and William James, which was published in 1968, I said that my intention had been to combine this with a study of the philosophy of Bertrand Russell and G. E. Moore, and that I had not entirely given up the idea of producing the work on Russell and Moore at some later date. I should probably have carried out this project in any case, but the delay would have been longer had I not received an invitation from Harvard University to give the William James Lectures for 1970. This book is the result.

The book reproduces the lectures almost exactly in the form in which they were delivered. I have altered two paragraphs in which I found that I had made mistakes, and I have included in the eighth chapter an account of Moore's treatment of universals, which I omitted from the lecture to prevent it from being inordinately long. I should like to take this opportunity of thanking the members of the Philosophy Department at Harvard not only for paying me the honour of asking me to give the William James Lectures, but also for the kindness which they showed to me and to my wife during the semester that we spent in Cambridge.

As in the case of my work on Peirce and James, I have felt free to develop my own solutions to some of the problems which Russell and Moore raise, and I have again chosen for the most part to approach their philosophy directly, without entering into the question how far my interpretations agree with those of other commentators. On the occasions when I have consulted the works of other writers, I have made my acknowledgements in the text.

In several places I have made use of previously published work of my own. The essays from which I have quoted are: in the first chapter, 'An Appraisal of Bertrand Russell's Philosophy', which was first published in *Bertrand Russell, Philosopher of the Century* (George Allen & Unwin, 1967); in the seventh chapter, 'Metaphysics and Common Sense', which first appeared in an anthology entitled *Metaphysics*, edited by Professors W. E. Kenrick and Morris Lazerowitz (Prentice-Hall, 1966); and 'What Must There Be', which was originally delivered as a lecture to the Israel Academy of Sciences and Humanities and published in their 1969 *Proceedings*; in the eighth chapter, 'G. E. Moore on Propositions and Facts', which has been published in *G. E. Moore: Essays in Retrospect*, edited by Professors Alice Ambrose and Morris Lazerowitz (George Allen & Unwin, 1970); and in the ninth chapter, 'The Terminology of Sense-Data', which was first published in *Mind*, LIV, 216 (1945). The essay on 'The Terminology of Sense-Data' was reprinted in my *Philosophical Essays* (Macmillan, 1954) and the other essays are all included in my book *Metaphysics and Common Sense* (Macmillan, 1969, and, in the United States, Freeman Cooper, 1970). I have to thank the editors and publishers concerned for permission to reproduce passages from these works.

Finally, I wish to thank Mrs Guida Crowley for the trouble which she has taken in typing the manuscript and in other ways helping me to prepare this book for the press.

A. J. AYER

15 Lowell Street,
Cambridge, Mass.

Bertrand Russell

1 The Challenge of Scepticism

A. RUSSELL'S LIFE AND WORKS

By the turn of the century, at the time when Pragmatism was beginning to make its advance in the United States, British philosophy had fallen very largely under the spell of Hegel. The British Hegelians, of whom F. H. Bradley at Oxford and J. E. McTaggart at Cambridge were the most distinguished, were perhaps not very orthodox in their allegiance to Hegel, but with their belief in the Absolute, their characterisation of the material world as mere appearance and their denial of the reality of space and time, they committed themselves to metaphysics in a way that British philosophers have commonly fought shy of, both before and since. They were chiefly opposed by a school of Aristotelian realists, led by a man quite famous in his time but now almost wholly forgotten, the Professor of Logic at Oxford, J. Cook Wilson; but the achievements of this school, except in the way of Aristotelian scholarship, were not remarkable.

For the recovery of the empiricist outlook, which has traditionally marked the dominant strain in British philosophy, and for the flowering of this tradition in the first half of the present century, we have mainly to thank the University of Cambridge: and, among Cambridge philosophers, in the first instance, Bertrand Russell and G. E. Moore. The two men were contemporaries at Cambridge as undergraduates in the 1890s and had a varying influence upon each other. Russell, who was a year older than Moore and two years his senior as an undergraduate, had switched to philosophy from mathematics and it was he who persuaded Moore, originally a classical scholar, to study philosophy instead. On the other hand, it was Moore who converted Russell from the idealist position into which he had fallen, mainly under the influence of McTaggart's teaching and Bradley's writing, to a form of Platonic realism. The strength of Russell's attachment to idealist doctrine is reflected in his Kantian *Essay on the Foundations of Geometry*, the first of his philosophical books, which came out in 1897, and in the specimen of his Hegelian essays, written at about the same date, which he reprinted more than sixty years later in *My Philosophical Development*. By 1900, when he published *A Critical Exposition of the Philosophy of Leibniz*, he had renounced Hegel but was still under the influence of Kant, a philosopher for whom in later years he came to have little respect. The break with idealism was definitely made in 1903, with the publication of *The Principles of Mathematics*, which of all Russell's philosophical writings is the most realistic, in the Platonic sense of the term. After that, Moore's influence on Russell appears to have waned. I shall argue, later on, that the central point of Moore's mature philosophy is his acceptance of the common-sense view of the world; and while Russell thought it essential for philosophers to have a robust sense of reality, he never believed that this entailed having any great reverence for common sense. His own later influence on Moore is not easy to assess. Moore himself remarked, in his autobiographical introduction to *The Philosophy of G. E. Moore*, which appeared in 1942, that he had probably devoted more time to studying Russell's works than those of any other philosopher, but the effect of this study appears rather in his adaptation to his own purposes of some of Russell's technical vocabulary than in an adherence to Russell's views.

Of the two men Russell is much the more celebrated; but this is not only, or perhaps even mainly, because of his contribution to philosophy. Moore, as we shall see, is a philosopher's philosopher. At one time, owing to the respect and affection which members of the Bloomsbury circle felt for him, and the enthusiasm with which they received his *Principia Ethica*, his influence did extend to a wider circle, but this happened, as it were, despite himself: it did not divert him from the course of his quiet academic life. Russell, on the other hand, through his heritage, the range of his abilities, his needs and interests, moved upon a larger stage. He was born in 1872, just in time to have John Stuart Mill for an unreligious godfather. His father, Lord Amberley, was the son of the first Earl Russell, the famous liberal statesman who, as Lord John Russell, had introduced the first Reform Bill. His mother was the daughter of a less prominent Liberal politician, but still a member of the Whig aristocracy, the second Lord Stanley of Alderley. Both Russell's parents died before he was four years old. Russell's father had appointed two free-thinkers as his guardians, but his grandparents managed to get the will set aside and he and his elder brother passed into their care. His grandfather, who was born in 1792, died when Bertrand Russell was only six, but his grandmother, who lived until 1898, effectively took charge of his upbringing and had a very strong influence upon him. She was a very religious woman, which brought them into conflict in his adolescence, but the text which she inscribed on the flyleaf of the Bible that she gave him, 'Thou shalt not follow a multitude to do evil', was one of the guiding principles of his life. He wrote about his family in the Amberley Papers, which he edited in collaboration with Patricia Russell, his third wife, and published in 1937; and again, from a more personal angle, in the brilliant and revealing first volume of the three-volume autobiography which came out in the years 1967-9.

As the autobiography shows, Russell took a youthful interest in metaphysics and in questions of moral philosophy: but his first love, as I have said, was mathematics, and it was his desire to find some good reason to believe in the truth of mathematics that led him in his third year at Cambridge to make philosophy his principal study. The years from 1894, when he took his degree at Cambridge, to 1914, the outbreak of the First World War, were the most fruitful of his philosophical career; and this was also the period in which he mainly lived in an academic environment. He was a Fellow of Trinity College, Cambridge, from 1895 to 1901, and a lecturer in philosophy there from 1910 to 1916, when he was dismissed from Trinity because of his opposition to the war. In the intervening years he lived at different times in the neighbourhood of both Oxford and Cambridge and moved in university circles. These were the years of his collaboration with A. N. Whitehead, which produced their great work *Principia Mathematica*, of which the three volumes appeared between 1910 and 1913. He was a Visiting Professor at Harvard in 1914, when he gave the Lowell Lectures, but was prevented from accepting Harvard's offer of a professorship later in the war by the refusal of the British Government to give him a passport. Declining an invitation to return to Cambridge after the war, he chose instead to go to Peking as a Visiting Professor in 1920-1. After that he engaged only intermittently in university teaching. He gave the Tarner Lectures at Cambridge in 1926, and was a Special Lecturer at the London School of Economics in 1937 and at Oxford in 1938. He was Visiting Professor at the University of Chicago during 1937-8 and at the University of California during 1939-40, and in 1940 he also gave the William James Lectures at Harvard. His academic career in the United States was, however, cut short by the disgraceful episode of his being judicially pronounced unworthy, in his capacity as a free-thinker and as a humane and enlightened moralist, of occupying a chair at the City College of New York, and subsequently by his dismissal from the Barnes Institute in Philadelphia. In 1944, on his return to England, he was reappointed to a Fellowship and to a five-year lectureship at Trinity, and though the lectureship was not renewed and he did not thereafter reside in Cambridge, he remained a Fellow of Trinity until his death.

The tradition of Russell's family called him to public service, and even during the years, before the First World War, when he was concentrating on philosophy, his interest in politics was strong. For a brief period in 1894 he occupied a post at the British Embassy in Berlin: his first book, which was published in 1896, was a work on German Social Democracy: he was a member of the Fabian group and a friend of its leaders, Shaw and Wells and Beatrice and Sydney Webb: he was active in the movement for women's suffrage, and in 1907 stood unsuccessfully for Parliament as a candidate of the National Union of Women's Suffrage Societies. It was, however, his passionate opposition to the First World War that first brought politics into the forefront of his thought and also first brought him into serious conflict with authority. The occasion of his dismissal from Trinity in 1916 was his being prosecuted and fined for a pamphlet in which he had taken up the case of a conscientious objector; and in 1918 he was sent to prison for six months for libelling the American army: he had suggested that it might be most serviceable in putting down strikes. In prison he found the leisure to write his *Introduction to Mathematical Philosophy*.

In the period between the two wars, Russell earned his living mainly by writing books and articles of a more popular character on moral and social questions. He stood for Parliament as a Labour candidate, again unsuccessfully, in 1922 and 1923. The birth of his two elder children aroused his interest in primary education and in 1927, in conjunction with Dora Russell, his second wife, he founded a progressive school which he helped to run for several years. In retrospect, he judged that this experiment was not altogether successful. In 1931, on the death of his elder brother, he became the third Earl Russell. This gave him a political platform in the House of Lords, of which he took little advantage, preferring to exercise influence by his writing and speaking outside Parliament.

After the Second World War, Russell's energies were mainly concentrated on trying to prevent the outbreak of a third. He was one of the leaders of the Campaign for Nuclear Disarmament, a campaign in which his fourth wife, Edith Russell, also played a very active part.

Whatever sympathy he had ever felt for Communism had been destroyed in 1920 by a visit to Soviet Russia where he found, in his own words, nothing that he could like or admire, but his disapproval of British and above all American foreign policy in the 1950s and 1960s aligned him with the extreme left. Honours came to him in his old age – he was awarded the Order of Merit in 1949 and the Nobel Prize for Literature in 1950 – but this did not put an end to his conflict with authority. In 1961, at the age of eighty-nine, he was again sent to prison for a week, on the charge of incitement to civil disobedience, and his wife suffered the same penalty. Whatever view one may take of his political position, one's admiration must be commanded by the moral fervour, the persistent concern for humanity, the amazing intellectual and physical energy which drove him on. He died on 2 February 1970 in his ninety-eighth year.

The range of Russell's interests is reflected in the volume of his writing. He published over sixty books and an uncounted number of articles. His philosophical works cover logic, the philosophy of mathematics, the philosophy of science, the theory of knowledge, ontology, ethics and the history of philosophy. In addition, he wrote extensively on questions of political history, political science, morality, religion and education. His more popular books include expositions of contemporary physics. He wrote books about his visits to Russia and to China, and a book of memoirs, apart from the autobiography. He even published two volumes of short stories: they are mainly fables, something in the manner of Voltaire.

Not all these books are of equal merit. For instance, I think it would be generally agreed that Russell's writings on political and social questions do not have the depth of his more academic work. Even so, it would be a mistake to dismiss even the more superficial of these books as mere pot-boilers. They express the moral outlook of a humane and enlightened man and I can testify from my own experience to the stimulating effect that they could have upon the young people to whom they were addressed. If they seem less exciting today, it is because the liberal ideas which they put forward have gained much wider acceptance. Neither are all Russell's books in this field merely popular or propagandist. *The Principles of Social Reconstruction*, which first appeared in 1916, is one of the best defences of an anarchistic form of political theory, and *Freedom and Organisation 1814–1914*, which came out in 1934, is a serious contribution to the history of political ideas. Apart from anything else, these books are worth reading for the beauty of the style in which they are written. Russell, as we shall see, has many points of affinity with David Hume, and he ranks with Hume as a master of English prose.

I shall be concerned only with his philosophy in the narrower, more academic sense. The number of his books which fall into this restricted category is itself impressive. I have already mentioned the four comparatively early works: *An Essay on the Foundations of Geometry*, *A Critical Exposition of the Philosophy of Leibniz*, *The Principles of Mathematics* and the three volumes of *Principia Mathematica*. To continue in chronological order, there is a book of *Philosophical Essays* which appeared in 1910, then *The Problems of Philosophy*, which was published in the Home University Library in 1912 and is still, in my opinion, the best introduction to philosophy that exists in English, then *Our Knowledge of the External World*, a set of Lowell Lectures which came out in 1914, to be followed by *Mysticism and Logic*, a collection of essays appearing in 1918, *Introduction to Mathematical Philosophy* in 1919, *The Analysis of Mind* in 1921 and *The Analysis of Matter* and *An Outline of Philosophy*, both in 1927. There was then an interval before the William James Lectures of 1940 which were published in the same year under the title of *An Inquiry into Meaning and Truth*, to be followed by *The History of Western Philosophy*, a rather more popular work, in 1946, *Human Knowledge: Its Scope and Limits* in 1948, and *My Philosophical Development*, the latest of Russell's philosophical books, in 1959. There was also published in 1956 a volume entitled *Logic and Knowledge* which is a collection of essays and lectures, most of which first appeared between the years 1901 and 1924. Finally, in the Library of Living Philosophers, which is edited by Professor P. A. Schilpp, there is *The Philosophy of Bertrand Russell*, published in 1944, to which Russell contributed a short autobiography and a sixty-page reply to the criticisms which the twenty-one other contributors to the volume had made of his philosophy, in all or very nearly all its multifarious aspects.

Even within the confines of what I have called Russell's academic philosophy, I shall not attempt to cover the whole ground. I shall not discuss his writings on the history of philosophy, and I shall say very little either about his early work on the foundations of mathematics or about his contributions to the philosophy of science. I shall not enter into the technicalities of his work on formal logic, or try to assess his responsibility, as compared, say, with that of Frege, for the extraordinary progress which this subject has made in the course of the present century. On the other hand, I shall have a good deal to say about his philosophy of logic, as exemplified in his Theory of Descriptions, his Logical Atomism, and his conception of meaning and of truth. I shall also engage in a critical examination of his theory of knowledge, to which I shall look for the guiding principles of his whole philosophical approach. Those of his works to which I shall chiefly be referring are: *The Problems of Philosophy*, *Our Knowledge of the External World*, *Introduction to Mathematical Philosophy*, *The Analysis of Mind*, *The Analysis of Matter*, *An Inquiry into Meaning and Truth*, *Human Knowledge: Its Scope and Limits*, and the essays collected in *Mysticism and Logic* and *Logic and Knowledge*.

In comparison with Moore, and indeed with many of the more important representatives of the analytical movement in philosophy, Russell is not a meticulous writer. For all the lucidity of his style, he goes to less trouble to make his meaning absolutely clear. He is often inattentive to points of detail, and can sometimes be caught out in apparent inconsistencies. On the other hand, he has the qualities of these defects. He is incomparably fertile in ideas and uncommonly flexible in his handling of them. So much so, indeed, that the Cambridge philosopher C. D. Broad was able to remark of him that 'he produces a different system of philosophy every few years', in contrast to Moore who 'never produces one at all' and to add that ' "Si Russell savait, si Moore pouvait" seems the only adequate comment on the situation'.[1] This is, of course, unfair to both of them, and perhaps especially so to Russell. It is, indeed, true that he changed his opinions rather frequently, and it is also true that he is a high-spirited philosopher. He is ready to explore a variety of theories to see if they can be made to work. It is this in particular that has led some of those philosophers who advance very few opinions, for fear of being found to be wrong, to suspect or even accuse him of frivolity. They may have been led astray also by his lively manner, mistaking lack of solemnity for lack of seriousness. Even if Russell had developed different philosophical systems in the course of his long career, this would not necessarily have been to his discredit, but the fact is that whatever different conclusions he may have reached at different times, his approach to the problems of philosophy was remarkably consistent. I think it can be shown that basically he always took the same view of the purpose of philosophy and of the methods by which this purpose was to be achieved. Where he changed was in his estimates of the results which these methods could be made to yield.

[1] C. D. Broad, *Contemporary British Philosophy*, 1st Series (1924) p. 79.

B. HIS CONCEPTION OF PHILOSOPHY

For all that contemporary philosophers owe to him, Russell's own conception of philosophy is old-fashioned. He stands much closer to the classical British empiricists, to Locke and Berkeley and Hume and John Stuart Mill, than he does to the followers of Moore or Wittgenstein or Carnap. The main reason for this is that he makes the now unfashionable assumption that every belief that we hold stands in need of philosophical justification. Of course he does not think that any philosophical argument is sufficient to settle such empirical questions as the date of the Battle of Waterloo, or even such formal questions as the validity of Pythagoras's theorem, but he takes it to be necessary. The reason why he takes it to be necessary is that we cannot have reason to believe that the propositions in question are true unless we have reason to believe that certain types of entity exist. There cannot be battles unless there are men who fight them and places and times at which they are fought: unless there are right-angled Euclidean triangles, there cannot be any relation between the squares of their hypotenuses and the squares of their other two sides. But whether we are justified in believing that there are men whose bodies are located in space and time, whether we can rationally believe in the occurrence of events which we situate so far in the past as the Battle of Waterloo, whether and in what sense we are entitled to assume the existence of Euclidean triangles, are all, in Russell's view, questions for philosophy. Not only that, but all the questions which legitimately arise for philosophy are questions of this type or connected with them. Thus we shall see that even Russell's philosophy of logic is linked with his conception of what there is or, rather, of what there can rationally be thought to be.

The central part which this ontological question plays in Russell's treatment of philosophy has not, I think, been at all widely recognised. One reason for this may be that ontology is traditionally associated with speculative metaphysics; and, after his early Hegelian period, Russell's attitude to speculative metaphysics of any kind was predominantly hostile. Another possible reason may be found in the impetus which his work has undoubtedly given to the practice of forms of philosophical analysis in which questions of ontology are at least not explicitly raised. Thus there are many who would agree with the view expressed by Morris Weitz, in his contribution to *The Philosophy of Bertrand Russell*, that the method of analysis, conceived as a method of arriving at real or contextual definitions, is the fundamental element in Russell's philosophy.[1] It is true that Russell himself, in his rather perfunctory reply to his critics, does not demur to this assessment of his work, but I am nevertheless sure that it is mistaken. Russell certainly practised the method of analysis, in the various ways that Weitz records, but I can find no evidence that he ever practised it for its own sake. On the contrary, I think it can be shown that he always used it as a method of justification. We shall find that the motive for his search for definitions is that successful definitions reduce ontological commitments. If it can be shown that one type of entity can be defined in terms of another, then we have only one ontological problem on our hands in place of two: in short, we are giving one less hostage to fortune.

This interpretation of Russell's aims is borne out by his approach to the theory of knowledge, in contrast, say, with Moore's. For Moore, as we shall see, the fact that there are physical objects, of the sort that common sense believes in, is not in question. The function of the theory of knowledge, so far as it relates to our knowledge of the external world, is simply to tell us what we mean by such propositions as that there is a lectern in this room: it has nothing to say with regard to their truth. For Russell, on the other hand, the point of analysing such propositions is to try to find an interpretation of them which will give some of them a fair chance of being true: there is no reason to believe that the interpretation which satisfies this condition will be one that accords with common sense: it can, indeed, be argued that the analysis tells us what we ordinarily mean by talking about physical objects, without knowing it, but Russell is much more inclined to say that it proves the common-sense conception of the physical world to be simply false: finally, even if we are able to formulate a set of propositions of which it can legitimately be said both that they imply the existence of physical objects and that we have good reasons for believing some of them to be true, we are asking too much if we expect these reasons to be conclusive; if we can be said to know for certain only what is not problematic, then we do not know for certain that physical objects exist.

I have said that Russell's conception of philosophy is old-fashioned, but this is not to say that it is misguided. The main objection which is likely to be brought against it is that he brings philosophy into a domain where it has no jurisdiction. There are recognised procedures

[1] M. Weitz, 'Analysis and the Unity of Russell's Philosophy', in *The Philosophy of Bertrand Russell*, pp. 87 ff.

for deciding the existential questions which he raises, and if these procedures are carried out correctly, the questions are settled one way or the other: except in the way of clarification, there is nothing left for philosophy to do. Later on, I shall show that it is an argument of this kind that underlies Moore's defence of common sense; and I believe that a generalisation of Moore's argument occupies a key position in the later philosophy of Wittgenstein. I shall, however, also try to show that the argument is not cogent, either in its generalised or in its more restricted form. For the present, all that I propose is that we suspend judgement. Setting aside, at least for the time being, the question whether there are *a priori* objections to Russell's approach, let us see how he actually conducts it and what are the results which he achieves.

Every philosopher, even a sceptic, starts with certain assumptions. At the very least he must subscribe to some standards of evidence and operate with some criteria of meaning and truth. In Russell's case I think it is possible to distinguish ten main assumptions from which all his characteristic doctrines are derived. In cases where he changed his views, it was nearly always because he put a different construction upon one or other of them.

The assumptions in question are as follows:

(1) There is a special class of propositions which serve as premisses for all the beliefs that we hold concerning empirical matters of fact. Our knowledge of the truth of these propositions is practically, even if not theoretically, certain, in that there are no other premisses from which we could legitimately infer that they were false.

(2) These propositions are atomic both in the sense that they are not compounded out of other propositions and in the sense that any pair of true propositions of this class are logically independent of one another.

(3) The sentences which express atomic propositions are composed of proper names and predicates. A name may be distinguished from a predicate by the fact that it can occur in an atomic sentence of any form, whereas a predicate can occur in an atomic sentence of only one form: for example, a three-termed relational predicate can occur only in an atomic sentence containing three names.

(4) The meaning of a name is to be identified with the object which it denotes. Consequently a name which fails to denote anything is meaningless.

(5) The only things which one is in a position to name are one's own percepts and one's own mental states. These things are said to be known

to us by acquaintance. At one time Russell talked of our being acquainted with sense-data, rather than with percepts, but he gave up this locution when he ceased to believe that there were acts of sensing of which sense-data could be the objects. Like sense-data, percepts are taken by Russell to be private entities. In fact the only way in which percepts appear to differ from sense-data is that they are not correlative to acts of sensing, as sense-data, for Russell, necessarily would be.

When he wrote *The Problems of Philosophy* Russell was also disposed to include one's self among the objects of acquaintance. He gave up this view when he became convinced, by the time that he wrote *The Analysis of Mind*, that the self could be defined in terms of its experiences.

(6) It is also possible to be acquainted with abstract entities of the sort which Russell calls universals. It is not very clear, in Russell's earlier writings, how widely our acquaintance with universals is supposed to extend, but at least in his later work it is made a necessary condition for any universal to be an object of acquaintance that it be exemplified in one's experience. This goes with the principle that a predicate is intelligible only if it stands for a universal which satisfies this condition, or is analysable in terms of predicates which do so stand.

(7) Things which are not known to us by acquaintance may be known to us by description. It is, however, necessary that the descriptions be such as eventually to relate the things in question to things with which one is acquainted. Moreover, the predicates into which the descriptions are resolved must themselves satisfy the rather strong criterion of intelligibility which I have just set out. In fact, it is doubtful if Russell strictly adheres to this second condition. We shall see, for example, that he postulates unobservable objects as causes of our percepts, without showing that a causal relation of this type is capable of being analysed in terms of relations which are exemplified in anyone's experience.

(8) Every description involves a tacit inference: namely, the inference that there is something which bears the requisite relation to the object on which the description is anchored. Such inferences, being inductive, always run the risk of error, but they run a smaller risk if the object to which the inference leads is of the same order as the object from which the inference starts, than if it is of a different order. For instance, on the assumption that physical objects are distinct from percepts, and that point-instants are distinct from physical events, it is safer to infer from a present to a future percept than it is to infer from

the existence of a percept to that of a physical object; it is safer to infer from one physical event to another than it is to infer from the existence of a physical event to the existence of a point-instant. This supplies us with a philosophical motive for trying to 'reduce' physical objects to percepts, or trying to reduce point-instants to physical events. It accounts for Russell's dictum that 'The supreme maxim in scientific philosophising is this: Wherever possible, logical constructions are to be substituted for inferred entities'.[1]

(9) The same maxim holds in the *a priori* domain of logic and pure mathematics. Though Russell eventually took the view that propositions of this sort are analytic, which would imply on the face of it that they gave no hostages to fortune, his work on the philosophy of mathematics always proceeded on the assumption that the existence of the abstract entities to which mathematical propositions ostensibly referred was a legitimate subject for doubt. Thus, as he himself puts it, 'Two equally numerous collections appear to have something in common: this something is supposed to be their cardinal number. But so long as the cardinal number is inferred from the collections, not constructed in terms of them, its existence must remain in doubt, unless in view of a metaphysical postulate *ad hoc*. By defining the cardinal number of a given collection as the class of all equally numerous collections, we avoid the necessity of this metaphysical postulate, and thereby remove a needless doubt from the philosophy of arithmetic.'[2] The same motive may apply within mathematics, as in Russell's definition of an irrational number as a certain class of ratios. And even when mathematics has been reduced to logic, we shall see that queries about the existence of such things as classes and propositions still remain.

(10) To say that we are not to take unnecessary risks is not, however, to say that we are not to take any risks at all. Part of the philosopher's task is to give a general account of what there is, and in giving this account it is reasonable for him to draw on the science of his day. 'Science', says Russell, 'is at no moment quite right, but it is seldom quite wrong, and has, as a rule, a better chance of being right than the theories of the unscientific. It is, therefore, rational to accept it hypothetically.'[3] This does not mean that we have, even provisionally, to

---

[1] 'Sense-data and Physics', in *Mysticism and Logic*, p. 155. See also 'Logical Atomism', in *Logic and Knowledge*, p. 326.
[2] 'Sense-data and Physics', in *Mysticism and Logic*, p. 156.
[3] *My Philosophical Development*, p. 17.

accept the existence of all the types of entity that apparently figure in current scientific theories. We must try to interpret these theories in such a way as to reduce our ontological commitments so far as possible. Even so, there are likely to remain some entities which we shall simply have to postulate, if we are to do justice to the scientific outlook, and at that point we must go ahead and postulate them. Furthermore, the fact that these entities are known, in Russell's usage, only by description does not prevent them from being the primary, or even the solitary, constituents of our picture of the world. Ontological and epistemological priority do not have to go together. Epistemologically, percepts come first. Apart from certain mental occurrences, like images and feelings, they are the only particulars with which one is acquainted. But this does not make them ontologically pre-eminent; it is consistent with their being assigned a very small part in the total scheme of things. In fact, we shall see that Russell identifies them with states of the percipient's brain, and so, with a very limited class of physical events.

C. THE MOTIVES FOR LOGICAL CONSTRUCTION

These, then, are the assumptions on which I believe that Russell's philosophy depends. I call them assumptions because they embody premisses, or distinctions, or procedures which he takes for granted, rather than conclusions at which he arrives by argument. We shall see that he does have an argument to show that universals are not reducible to particulars, and he also advances what we shall find to be questionable reasons for treating percepts as private objects, but he takes it for granted that if universals are not reducible to particulars, they must form a special class of entities, with some members of which one is able to be acquainted, and he takes it for granted that there are immediate data of perception, in a sense which disqualifies physical objects for the role. From this, as we shall see, it automatically follows that his basic propositions are atomic, given the rejection, for which he does give reasons in his early work, of the absurd idealist doctrine that all relations are internal to their terms. The identification of the meaning of a name with the object which the name denotes goes together, in his view, with what seems to him the obvious fact that a sign which fails to denote anything does not function as a name; and it also appears to him to be self-evident that, with respect to any suggested type of entity, whether concrete or abstract, it must, in some sense, be an open factual question whether any entity of that type exists. Finally, the concession to science of the provisional authority for saying what there is may, I think, fairly be described as an act of faith. There are, indeed, pragmatic arguments that can be submitted in its favour, but it is not made clear how merely pragmatic arguments can be used to decide an ontological issue. At least there seems to be no good reason why a thoroughgoing sceptic should yield to them. In fact, Russell's argument against the ordinary run of sceptics is just that they are not thoroughgoing. If they were, he admits that their position could not be logically refuted. His reason for rejecting it is that no one can seriously hold it.

Not all these assumptions would now pass unquestioned. In particular, it has become fashionable to reject the concept of sense-data, on grounds which would also rule out the part that Russell assigns to percepts, and it is also, thanks mainly to the later work of Wittgenstein, now generally thought to be a mistake to identify the meaning of any sign, even a proper name, with the object which it denotes. On the issue of percepts I shall, with a reservation about the question of their privacy, take sides with Russell. I claim to have shown that the arguments, stemming mainly from Austin, Ryle and Wittgenstein, which are believed to discredit any form of sense-datum theory, are not at all cogent.[1] On the other hand, I agree with the Wittgensteinians that it is a mistake to identify the meaning of names with their denotation, and I shall even go further to the point of arguing that there is no good reason why the non-existence of the object which a given sign is understood to denote should necessarily disqualify the sign from being counted as a proper name. Since it was the problem of explaining how expressions which were apparently nominative, but failed to denote anything, could nevertheless be meaningful that led Russell to his famous theory of descriptions, it might be thought that this was a serious point of disagreement. In fact, I believe it to be of very minor importance. I shall try to show that, from a logical point of view, the theory of descriptions is largely independent of the decisions which we take about the assignment of meaning to proper names and the extension which the concept of a proper name is to be allowed to have. We shall see that the question which the theory of

[1] See my *Metaphysics and Common Sense*, pp. 126–48; *The Problem of Knowledge*, pp. 104–25; and *The Concept of a Person*, pp. 39–51.

descriptions poses has little directly to do with any problem that there may be about the relation of names to the objects which they may or may not denote. It is rather the question whether names, as opposed to predicates, have any necessary function to perform at all.

The theory of descriptions is, indeed, one very good starting-point from which to enter into a general examination of Russell's philosophy. We shall, for example, discover that it ties in very neatly with his theory of knowledge and thereby with his Logical Atomism. But before embarking on it, I want first to consider another of his main assumptions which has not been much discussed, perhaps for the reason that it is not at all easy to interpret. This is the assumption which underlies Russell's policy of preferring logical constructions to inferred entities, the assumption that there is always the danger that any inferred entity may not in fact exist. Without going deeply into logical technicalities, I shall begin by discussing this assumption in relation to Russell's philosophy of mathematics.

The first point to note is that Russell was not originally actuated by any suspicion of abstract entities as such. We have seen that he always believed in the existence of universals and in *The Principles of Mathematics*, in which his proposals for reducing mathematics to logic are first set out, he goes a great deal further. The key passage is one to which he himself refers in his introduction to the second edition of the book as representing a view of language which by 1937, when the second edition was published, he had long since come to think mistaken. It runs in part: 'Whatever may be an object of thought, or may occur in any true or false proposition, or can be counted as *one*, I call a term. . . . Every term has being, i.e. *is* in some sense. A man, a movement, a number, a class, a relation, a chimaera, or anything else that can be mentioned, is sure to be a term: and to deny that such and such a thing is a term must always be false.'[1] To this Russell added that every term is a logical subject and also, most surprisingly, that every term is 'immutable and indestructible'. 'What a term is,' he says, 'it is, and no change can be conceived in it which would not destroy its identity and make it another term.'[2] I think that what he must have had in mind here was his assumption that every sign had what Frege would call a determinate sense, but this would not justify what he actually says. The trouble is that in the case of proper names he makes it quite clear that the term which is indicated by a name is not the

---

[1] *The Principles of Mathematics*, 2nd ed., p. 43. See also Introduction, p. 8.
[2] Ibid., p. 44.

sense of the name but the thing for which the name stands. But even if we accept the very dubious assumption that a proper name like 'Socrates' can have an immutable and indestructible sense, it is unhappily just false to speak of Socrates himself as being either immutable or indestructible. Curiously enough, these epithets do in a manner apply to the concrete particulars which came to occupy the fundamental position in Russell's ontology. For, as we shall see, he came to think of the world as being composed of physical events, and events themselves do not change nor are they destructible except in the sense that one gives way to another. Still I do not suppose that Russell envisaged anything of this sort when he wrote *The Principles of Mathematics*.

It is not, however, my present purpose to criticise the details of Russell's former Platonism. The question in which I am interested is why, even at this stage, he was concerned to exhibit mathematical objects as logical constructions. As is well known, his procedure, in which he was anticipated by Frege, was to conceive of numbers as being essentially applicable to classes, and to give a purely logical account of what it is for a given class to have a given number. Thus, to say of a class K that it has the number 0 is to say that there is no object x such that x is a member of K, to say that it has the number 1 is to say that there is an object x such that x is a member of K and in the case of any object y, if y is a member of K, y is identical with x, to say that K has the number 2 is to say that there are objects x and y such that x is not identical with y, x is a member of K and y is a member of K and in the case of any object z, if z is a member of K either z is identical with x or z is identical with y; and so forth. In this way, the number of a class is determined by whichever of this series of definitions the class in question satisfies, and the number itself is identified with the class of all those classes that are alike in this respect. So, for example, the number 1 just is the class of classes of each of which it is true that there is some object x which is a member of it and that in the case of any object y, if y is a member of it, y is identical with x. By these means we can define any given cardinal number without circularity, since the number of whatever class is in question will itself have been defined without reference to numbers. On the other hand, unless we suppose ourselves capable of conjoining an infinite number of propositions, we cannot use this method to arrive at a definition of numbers in general.[1]

---

[1] I have to thank Professor Burton Drebben for pointing this out to me.

To obtain a general definition Russell employs a different method. In *The Principles of Mathematics*, and in *The Introduction to Mathematical Philosophy*, he defines the number of a class as a class of classes which are similar to a given class, where the similarity of two classes consists in the co-ordination of their members by a one–one relation, and a one–one relation is defined as one which is such that if x has it to y, no other term than x has it to y, and x has it to no other term than y. Then a number can be defined as anything which is the number of some class. It has, here, to be admitted that in many cases the one–one relation in question will be a merely notional and not, as one might wish, an actually existent relation; but this is unavoidable if the requisite generality is to be achieved.

What this definition gives us, when the corresponding procedures have been introduced for handling arithmetical operations, is a set of rules for transforming propositions about natural numbers into propositions about classes: and what is meant by saying that numbers are reducible to classes, or that they are logical constructions out of classes, is that this transformation can be carried out. Then, if Russell is right in saying that 'All traditional pure mathematics, including analytical geometry, may be regarded as consisting wholly of propositions about the natural numbers',[1] the first essential step in the reduction of mathematics to logic has been taken.

But now I want to return to the question why, in the context of *The Principles of Mathematics*, Russell should have attached so much importance to its being taken. If the fact that we can think of numbers, the fact that numbers are terms, in Russell's sense of the word, is sufficient to ensure that they have being, why not leave it at that? Even if we can effect a reduction, what purpose will it serve?

The answer is, I believe, that Russell did not really adhere to the assumption, which I earlier attributed to him, that every sign has a determinate sense. Or, if he did adhere to it, he did not think that the fact that a sign was in customary use entailed that its sense was known. In the case of numerical signs, he thought that they needed to be given a clear sense, though he may also have thought that the sense which he was giving to them was the sense which they already implicitly had. The child who is told to think of a number is unlikely to know that he is thinking of a class of classes; very probably he will go through life without knowing it. Later on, if he is asked what a number is, he may not know how to reply except by giving examples.

[1] *Introduction to Mathematical Philosophy*, p. 4.

This is not at all a bad reply, but if there is a mystery about numbers, the examples share it. Russell's aim is to dispel the mystery. On the assumption that classes are not in the same degree mysterious – an assumption which I shall discuss in a moment – he provides us with a more down-to-earth substitute which does all the work that numbers do. The question whether numbers are *really* something different, whether God when he thinks of a number thinks of something other than a class of classes, is, indeed, allowed by Russell to be meaningful, though we shall see that it is not at all clear what meaning it can have: but even if it is meaningful, it is of no interest to us. So long as all our actual mathematics is preserved, we have what we want.

Looking at the matter more generally, I think we may distinguish three different reasons why a given type of entity may be thought to stand in need of existential reduction. It may be, as in the case of numbers, that the entities are just thought to be mysterious. Another example, with which Russell also deals, is that of points and instants. Yet another example would be that of the waves and particles of modern physics. A second reason, which is not exclusive of the first, is that the entity, as it stands, is logically disreputable. This applies obviously to contradictory entities, like Meinong's round square; it applies, in Russell's view, to the infinitesimals which used to be invoked to explain continuity: and in the view of some philosophers, though not of Russell, it applies to all merely possible objects, in so far as they are not provided with definite criteria of identity. The third reason is epistemological. Entities which are not regarded as being logically defective or mysterious in themselves may still be thought to invite reduction because there are felt to be difficulties in the way of knowing that they exist. Some philosophers, including Russell at one period, have put physical objects into this category, and it is often thought to apply to the mental states of persons other than oneself.

D. CLASSES AND THE THEORY OF TYPES

In the case where the reason for undertaking a reduction is that the type of entity on which it is practised is felt to be mysterious, it would seem to be essential that the type of entity which is substituted for it should not be mysterious to the same degree. In the present instance, we must therefore ask whether the concept of a class is in a better position than the concept of a number. In the sense in which even people who practise mathematics may be said not fully to understand what they mean by numbers, do we understand any better what we mean by classes?

At first sight, it might appear obvious that we do. I suppose that the most natural way to conceive of classes is to view them extensionally as collections of objects, which we could in principle enumerate. Then, provided that we have the means of identifying the objects concerned, all that we need to understand is the notion of conjunction, the logical operation which is signified by the most common use of the English word 'and'. We shall need also to be able to think of classes of classes, but the idea of a collection which is obtained by conjoining elements which are themselves collections does not seem to present any special difficulty.

There are, however, reasons for thinking that this way of conceiving classes is not adequate for Russell's purpose. For one thing, if mathematical propositions are to be transformed into propositions about classes, we shall have to deal with classes which have an infinite number of members: but the idea of an infinite conjunction is of doubtful validity: if the conjunction is formed according to a rule, like the rule of addition which yields the infinite series of natural numbers, it may, indeed, follow that we could enumerate any element of it (though in claiming even so much as this we have to ignore such practical difficulties as that presented by a number which has more digits than anyone could write down in a lifetime), but it is not clear that this entitles us to say that we could enumerate them all. In the next place, it is hard to see how the null-class, the class with no members, can be a collection, and there is also a difficulty about unit-classes. For logical reasons, we need to distinguish a unit-class from its only member, but to distinguish a collection of one from the one thing collected does not appear significant. More generally, indeed, it is doubtful if it is ever significant to think of a collection as something existing alongside of the items which compose it, so that when you buy a pair of shoes you are buying not two but three things, the right shoe, the left shoe, and the pair. If it were legitimate to form assemblages of this sort, it would seem that one could significantly speak of the totality of the things that there are, a totality which need not of course be finite. But then, as Russell points out, one would fall into contradiction. For it is mathematically demonstrable that, given any set of n objects, one can make 2^n different selections from them: and Cantor has proved that, even where n is infinite, 2^n must always be greater than n. But that means that if all possible collections of things are themselves to be reckoned in the totality of the things that there are, we obtain the self-contradictory result that the number of things that there are is greater than their totality. We have, therefore, as Russell puts it, 'a precise arithmetical proof that there are *fewer* things in heaven and earth than are dreamt of in *our* philosophy'.[1]

Another way to conceive of classes, which is not open to all these objections, is to view a class intensionally as the set of objects which fall under a given concept or, as Russell mainly prefers to put it, a set of objects which satisfy a given propositional function. This procedure is intensional, in the sense that classes are defined in terms of concepts, rather than by the enumeration of their members: it does not present classes themselves intensionally as abstract objects. On the contrary, its tendency is to eliminate classes in favour of propositional functions. For instance, instead of saying that the class of Christ's apostles has twelve members, we are to say that the propositional function 'x is an apostle' is satisfied by just twelve values of x, or rather, for a reason which I shall go into when I come to talk about Russell's logical atomism, we are to say that some function which is formally equivalent to the function 'x is an apostle' is satisfied by just twelve values of x, where what is meant by saying that two functions are formally equivalent is that the same values of the variable satisfy them both. Again, instead of saying that the class of apostles is included in the class of Jews, we are to say that anything which satisfies any function which is formally equivalent to the function 'x is an apostle' also satisfies any function which is formally equivalent to the function 'x is a Jew', and so forth. Were it not for the complication about formal equivalence, we should not in these examples even have to mention propositional functions. We could say more straightforwardly: 'for all x, if x is an apostle, x is a Jew', or: 'for some x^1, . . . , x^{12}, x^1 is an apostle, x^2 is an apostle, . . . , x^{12} is an apostle, and for all y, if y is an apostle, y is identical with x^1 or y is identical with x^2, . . . , or y is identical with x^{12}.' To the extent that we do still have to mention propositional functions, we have not wholly freed ourselves from mystery. Propositional functions are abstracts of propositions, and we have yet to learn what propositions are. We shall see that Russell moves from regarding them as genuine abstract entities, whatever that may imply, to a position where he seeks to identify them with

[1] *Logic and Knowledge*, p. 260.

linguistic expressions, and so eventually with series of inscriptions or noises. It remains, however, to be shown that this treatment of propositions is consistent with the demands that we make upon them. But the status of propositions is a question which arises not only within the philosophy of mathematics; so that if we really are able to make classes do all the work of numbers, and propositional functions do all the work of classes, we may surely be said to be making progress in our understanding of arithmetic.

Unfortunately, the position is not quite so simple. It is natural to suppose that every propositional function determines a class, even if it be only the null-class, and in some cases what a given function will determine will be a class of classes, though here we must assume that when the functions which range over classes are fully analysed, they will be shown to be replaceable by functions which range over individuals. But now, unless we place some restriction on the nature of the functions which range over classes, we shall again fall into contradiction. The notorious example is that of predicating of a class that it is or is not a member of itself. For instance, it seems reasonable to say on the one hand that the class of things which can be counted is itself something that can be counted and, on the other, that the class of men is not itself a man. In this way we seem to obtain two classes of classes: the class of classes which are members of themselves and the class of classes which are not members of themselves. But now if we ask with regard to this second class of classes whether or not it is a member of itself, we get the contradictory answer that if it is, it is not, and if it is not, it is.

It was Russell's discovery of this contradiction that led him to his celebrated Theory of Types. This theory has had an influence outside formal logic, in that it has given currency to the view, which was taken up enthusiastically by the Logical Positivists in their onslaught on metaphysics, that sentences to which there is no obvious objection on the score of grammar or vocabulary may nevertheless be meaningless. Russell believed that it offered the means of escape from other well-known antinomies, including that of Epimenides the Cretan who said that all Cretans were liars. I shall here give only such an account of the theory as is relevant to my general theme of Russell's ontology.

In its simplest form, the theory of types lays down the principle that a propositional function presupposes the totality of its possible arguments, which is to say that its meaning is not specified until we specify the range of objects which are candidates for satisfying it. It follows that these candidates cannot meaningfully include anything which is defined in terms of the function itself. So the solution of Russell's class paradox is that to say of the class of classes which are not members of themselves that it either is or is not a member of itself is neither true nor false but meaningless. What we have then is a system in which propositional functions, and consequently propositions, are arranged in a hierarchy. At the bottom of the pyramid are functions which can have only individuals for their arguments, at the next stage functions which have for their arguments functions of the first order, at the third stage functions which have for their arguments functions of the second order, and so forth. Objects which are candidates for satisfying functions at a given level are said to constitute a type, and the guiding principle of the construction is that what can be said, truly or falsely, about objects of one type cannot meaningfully be said about objects of a different type. This is put in realistic language, but it is easy to see that the principle can be rephrased in the form of a rule as to what combinations of symbols are to be regarded as significant. Since there will be an order of propositions, corresponding to the order of propositional functions, it follows, among other things, that we cannot significantly attribute any property to propositions in general, but only at best to propositions of such and such an order. So Epimenides the Cretan could not meaningfully have said that all propositions asserted by Cretans were false but only, at best, that all propositions of order n which were asserted by Cretans were false: and since this would itself be a proposition of order $n + 1$, no paradox arises.

This result is very satisfactory, but it is arguable that the means by which it is reached are not. It is certainly not obvious that references to objects of different types can never significantly be fitted into the same propositional pattern. An apparent counter-example is to be found in the very sort of question with which I have argued that Russell is principally concerned, the question whether entities of different kinds exist. He clearly attaches meaning to the proposition that there are concrete particulars, which he thinks true, and to the proposition that there are classes, which he thinks false, so that it would seem that the expression 'there are' can after all be significantly conjoined with designations of objects of different types. Russell's answer to this is that expressions like 'there are', in these usages, are, as he puts it, 'systematically ambiguous'. They have to be differently interpreted according to the order of the propositions which they help to express. We shall in fact see that Russell's own analysis of existential propositions brings this out quite clearly. For, according to this analysis, what is meant by saying that there are particulars is that some first-order functions are satisfied, and what is meant by saying that that there are classes, of which the only members are particulars (it would of course be an offence against the theory of types to speak of there being classes in general), is that some second-order functions are satisfied: and evidently these are themselves propositions of different orders. It is, however, also obvious that this way of analysing existential propositions does not represent what Russell has in mind when he raises such ontological questions as whether there are classes. For he certainly does not intend his conclusion that there are not classes, that classes are 'logical fictions', to imply that no function of an order higher than the first is ever satisfied. He would not, for example, want to deny that there are values of n for which the function 'n is a prime number' is true. We have, indeed, yet to find a clear meaning for such statements as that there are universals, or that there are not numbers, as made by philosophers when they are dealing in ontology, but in our search for such a meaning I do not think that we want to be limited by the assumption that the attribution or denial of existence, in the sense in question, to different sorts of entity is bound to be ambiguous.

It is easy to find other examples in which the theory of types obliges us to attribute systematic ambiguity to expressions which, on the face of it, are not ambiguous at all. One obvious class of cases is that in which we are speaking of people's beliefs, or other propositional attitudes. For instance, since Bradley, in common with other Hegelians, believed that only the Absolute really existed, I suppose that it can truly be said of him both that he did not believe that there were particulars, and that he did not believe that there were first-order functions. On the face of it, this would seem to entail that one and the same predicate, that of not being believed by Bradley to exist, was attributable to particulars and to first-order functions, and indeed to anything whatsoever except the Absolute. But, if the theory of types is true, there is no such predicate: the expression 'Bradley did not believe' has a different meaning in these different contexts. I admit that I am not sure how statements about propositional attitudes are to be analysed, but, whatever their correct analysis may be, I do not find this conclusion plausible.

These objections are damaging to the theory of types, but perhaps not fatal to it. A defence to them might be found in the position, to which we shall see that Russell came on other grounds, that expressions like 'there are' have no meaning in isolation. The systematic ambiguity

of words like 'believe' might be held to amount to no more than a
decision not to *say* that they preserved a constant meaning in different
sorts of company, even though they admittedly made the same sort of
contribution to the meaning of the different sentences in which they
occurred. There are, however, also logical grounds for thinking that
the original theory of types was too strong. It appears that if one were
seriously to outlaw all impredicative definitions, that is to say, definitions of an object by reference to a totality which includes itself or
objects definable only in terms of itself, one would not only have to
sacrifice a great deal of accepted mathematics but would also be
jeopardising the complete programme of deriving mathematics from
logic. By what alterations to, or emendations of, the theory these
unfortunate consequences can be avoided is a question of technical
logic into which I shall not enter. There is, however, one suggestion
on which I wish to make a brief remark, because of its relevance to my
general theme.

   This is the suggestion made by Gödel,[1] in his contribution to *The
Philosophy of Bertrand Russell*, that the difficulty arises only for those
who make a constructivist approach to logic and not for those who
make a realistic approach. Impredicative definitions are forbidden to
constructivists, because there is an obvious logical fallacy in the enterprise of *constructing* an entity out of materials in which it is already
included. On the other hand, Gödel maintains, the position is quite
different if it is only a matter of our having to *describe* an entity which
we think of as objectively existing. There is no inconsistency in the
idea of there *being* a concept which we have not found any means of
describing except by reference to a totality which includes itself.
There would be an inconsistency only if it were held that the concept
owed its existence to the description.

   My interest in this suggestion is not in its technical adequacy, but
in the clue that it gives to the interpretation of ontological statements.
On the face of it, the fight between Platonists and their adversaries is
only a piece of shadow-boxing. What conceivable means is there of
deciding whether or not there is a world of abstract entities, and if,
for the sake of argument, we admit that there is such a world, how
can we possibly make an inventory of its contents? When viewed in
this literal way, questions of this kind appear completely pointless,
if not nonsensical. To give them the meaning and interest that they

---

[1] See Kurt Gödel, 'Russell's Mathematical Logic', in *The Philosophy of Bertrand Russell*,
pp. 131 ff.

nevertheless seem to have, I believe that they should be construed as questions about our powers of construction. The position of the realist, as I see it, is essentially a negative one: he is convinced that the constructivist cannot deliver what he promises. This being so, he is content to postulate the entities which will do the work that both sides agree to be necessary. Russell characteristically remarked that postulation has the 'advantages of theft over honest toil',[1] and certainly we should toil as hard as we can. The realist is open, if not to the charge of dishonesty, at least to that of laziness. Nevertheless it may be that there are things, like the love-charm in one of Kipling's stories, that only work for those who steal them. The problem then will be to distinguish between the venial and the culpable sorts of theft.

How far Russell himself is driven to theft will become clear only when we have gone more deeply into his theories of meaning, truth and knowledge. As I have indicated, the bridge between his work in logic and these other aspects of his philosophy is to be found in his theory of descriptions, and it is to this that I now turn.

[1] *Introduction to Mathematical Philosophy*, p. 71.

2 The Theory of Descriptions

A. ON DENOTATION

I have said that one of Russell's basic assumptions is that the meaning of a name is to be identified with the object which the name denotes. This makes it a necessary, though not a sufficient condition for anything to be named that it be capable of being denoted. At the time that he wrote *The Principles of Mathematics*, Russell interpreted this condition very liberally. Anything that could be mentioned was said to be a term; any term could be the logical subject of a proposition; and anything that could be the logical subject of a proposition could be named. It followed that one could in principle use names to refer not only to any particular thing that existed at any place and time, but to abstract entities of all sorts, to non-existent things like the present Tsar of Russia, to mythological entities like the Cyclops, even to logically impossible entities like the greatest prime number. Not only that, but Russell also held that expressions like 'all men', 'every man', 'any man', 'a man', 'some man', all denoted separate objects. 'All men' was supposed to denote the members of the class of men, taken collectively, 'every man' the members of the same class, taken severally, 'any man' a variable member of the class, and so forth. Neither any man, a man, or some man was identical with any particular man, and none of the objects denoted by any of these expressions was identical with the abstract object which was denoted by the word 'humanity'.[1]

Very soon afterwards, however, Russell came to think that this picture of the world was intolerably overcrowded. Even before he was persuaded that classes were logical fictions, he ceased to find it credible that to speak of the members of a class collectively and to speak of them all severally was to speak of different single objects, or that any man could be an object distinct from any man in particular. He also found himself unable any longer to believe in the being of logically impossible entities or even in that of possible things which

[1] See *The Principles of Mathematics*, pp. 55–62.

were known not to exist. His comment on his earlier theory was that it showed 'a failure of that feeling for reality which ought to be preserved even in the most abstract studies'. 'Logic', he continued, 'must no more admit a unicorn than zoology can; for logic is concerned with the real world just as truly as zoology, though with its more abstract and general features.'[1] Curiously enough, the last half of this sentence is quoted by Gödel as a reversion on Russell's part to logical realism,[2] though I should have thought it clear in the context that its implications were intended to be nominalistic. On either interpretation, the fact remains that Russell denied any place in the real world to such entities as unicorns, or the golden mountain, or the round square; and he also denied that there were any worlds, other than the real world, in which they could be thought to abide.

It was, however, not only the growth in his feeling for reality that led Russell to look for a different account of denotation. He found that the position which he had adopted in *The Principles of Mathematics* raised problems to which it could not supply an answer. Some of these problems are set out in an article 'On Denoting' which first appeared in *Mind* in 1905 and is reprinted in *Logic and Knowledge*. For example, if 'the author of *Waverley*' is a denoting phrase, it has, on Russell's original theory, to function as a name. But on the assumption, to which Russell still adheres, that the meaning of a name is identical with the object which the name denotes, it would follow that what was meant by saying that Scott was the author of *Waverley* was simply that Scott was Scott. Yet it is surely obvious, as Russell remarks, that when George IV wished to know whether Scott was the author of *Waverley*, he was not expressing an interest in the law of identity. Again, if the phrase 'the present King of France' denotes a term, and if the law of excluded middle holds, one or other of the two propositions 'The present King of France is bald' and 'The present King of France is not bald' must be true. Yet if one were to enumerate all the things that are bald and all the things that are not bald, one would not find the present King of France on either list. Russell remarks characteristically that 'Hegelians, who love a synthesis, will probably conclude that he wears a wig'.[3] Indeed, we run into trouble even in saying that the present King of France does not exist. We are required to attribute being to the term as a condition of denying its existence. The same difficulty can arise even in the case of abstract entities. If *A* and *B* differ,

[1] *Introduction to Mathematical Philosophy*, p. 169.   [2] Kurt Gödel, op. cit., p. 127.
[3] *Logic and Knowledge*, p. 48.

it can be said, rather pedantically, that the difference between *A* and *B* subsists. If *A* and *B* do not differ, this difference does not subsist. But if the difference does not subsist, how can we significantly speak about it? 'How can a non-entity be the subject of a proposition?'[1]

Russell does not think that any of these difficulties can be met by having recourse to Frege's well-known distinction between sense and reference. On this view, when we say that Scott was the author of *Waverley*, we are, indeed, saying no more than that Scott was Scott, but the way in which we express this trivial statement implicitly conveys the non-trivial semantic information that the senses of the two names 'Scott' and 'the author of *Waverley*' have the same reference. It might be thought that we should do better to construe the utterance as explicitly making the implied statement which gives it its point, but this would not yield the desired result, because in saying only that the senses of 'Scott' and 'the author of *Waverley*' had the same reference, we should not be saying what reference they had. This difficulty could, indeed, be met by adopting the construe: 'The sense of "the author of *Waverley*" refers to Scott', but then we are exposed to the objection that in saying that Scott is the author of *Waverley*, we are surely not talking about the English words 'the author of *Waverley*', as indeed becomes obvious if we translate our statement into French. There is also the more fundamental difficulty that we do not know what senses are, or how they, as opposed to the expressions which have them, can be said to refer. Another odd feature of the theory is that whereas, according to it, the question which George IV actually asked, in saying 'Is Scott the author of *Waverley*?', was whether Scott was Scott, the question which we report him as having asked, when we say 'George IV wanted to know whether Scott was the author of *Waverley*', is the quite different question whether the senses of 'Scott' and 'the author of *Waverley*' had the same reference. This follows from Frege's assumption that when an expression occurs in *oratio recta* it refers to its denotation, but when it occurs in *oratio obliqua* it refers to its sense. It is to be observed that neither of these questions is equivalent to the question whether Scott wrote *Waverley*, which is, after all, what George IV wanted to know.

Russell's own argument against this theory is not very easy to follow. Translating Frege's *Sinn* and *Bedeutung* by 'meaning' and 'denotation' respectively, rather than 'sense' and 'reference', he sets himself to show that the distinction is not tenable, or at least that it is not properly made

[1] Ibid.

out. As an example of a denoting phrase, which is supposed to have both meaning and denotation, he takes the expression 'the first line of Gray's *Elegy*'. Now if we speak of the meaning and denotation of the first line of Gray's *Elegy*, without putting this denoting phrase in quotation marks, what we shall be speaking of will be the meaning and denotation of 'The curfew tolls the knell of parting day', which is not what we want. So let us put in the quotation marks. Then the denotation of 'the first line of Gray's *Elegy*' will be 'The curfew tolls the knell of parting day', which is correct, but what will its meaning be? If we say that its meaning is the first line of Gray's *Elegy*, we shall be equating its meaning with its denotation, which is obviously wrong, since even if 'The curfew tolls the knell of parting day' were not the first line of Gray's *Elegy*, the meaning of the expression 'the first line of Gray's *Elegy*' would remain the same. We therefore have to introduce a new denoting phrase, distinct from 'the first line of Gray's *Elegy*', which is to denote not what 'the first line of Gray's *Elegy*' denotes but what 'the first line of Gray's *Elegy*' means, and is to mean not what 'the first line of Gray's *Elegy*' means but what 'the meaning of "the first line of Gray's *Elegy*" ' means. No doubt this can be done, but it still does not give us what we want. What we want is that 'the first line of Gray's *Elegy*' and 'the meaning of "the first line of Gray's *Elegy*" ' should have different meanings but the same denotation, since the denotation of an expression is supposed to depend upon its meaning, but what we have given these expressions is both different meanings and different denotations. It might be thought that we could escape this conclusion by using 'the meaning of "the first line of Gray's *Elegy*" ' as a denoting phrase without quotation marks, and then saying that 'the first line of Gray's *Elegy*' and the meaning of 'the first line of Gray's *Elegy*' have different meanings but the same denotation. But, in the first place, if we speak of the meaning of 'the first line of Gray's *Elegy*', without enclosing the whole phrase in quotation marks, we shall be speaking not of a denoting phrase but of an object, and it is hard to understand how an object, which is not a denoting phrase, can be said to have either meaning or denotation. And secondly, if we are asked what *is* the meaning of 'the first line of Gray's *Elegy*', the natural answer is that it is whatever line in Gray's *Elegy* precedes all the other lines in Gray's *Elegy*. But this is in fact 'The curfew tolls the knell of parting day', and what this denotes is not what 'the first line of Gray's *Elegy*' denotes but what, if anything, 'The curfew tolls the knell of parting day' denotes, which is obviously not the same. The only solution for

Frege would be to conceive of the meaning of 'the first line of Gray's *Elegy*' as an object distinct from whatever line in Gray's *Elegy* precedes all the other lines. But then it is left wholly mysterious what this object is and how it is related to the first line of Gray's *Elegy*. So the upshot of Russell's argument, which I believe to be valid, is that if one assumes with Frege that every denoting phrase has both a sense and a reference, and if one treats the sense as an object, the requisite connection between sense and reference cannot be established.

Another objection which Russell brings against Frege's theory is that it has no satisfactory means of dealing with the cases where a referential expression misses its intended mark. For instance, if we speak of Mr Smith's only son, and the fact is either that Mr Smith has more than one son, or that he has no son at all, what our words denote, according to Frege, is the class of Mr Smith's sons, which, in the case where he has no son, will be the null-class. Russell observes, I think reasonably, that 'This procedure, though it may not lead to actual logical errors, is plainly artificial, and does not give an exact analysis of the matter.'[1] A fact which is not often remarked is that if we do take expressions like 'the present King of France' as denoting the null-class, the proposition 'The present King of France is bald' and 'The present King of France is not bald' both turn out to be true, since the null-class is included in all classes. As I shall be saying later on, I do not find this particularly objectionable, but it makes it seem odd that Frege's approach should have been preferred to Russell's by philosophers who profess respect for ordinary usage.

B. RUSSELL'S ANALYSIS OF DESCRIPTIONS

It appears, then, that the main source of the difficulties which Russell has brought to light is the assumption that all the expressions which he earlier classified as denoting phrases have the properties which he attributed to names. This being so, there are two courses that he could take: he could look for a different theory of the use of names, or he could drop the troublesome assumption. It is the second course that he chooses. His theory of descriptions is designed to show that expressions like 'every man', 'some man', 'an English author', 'the author of *Waverley*', 'the present King of France', that is, expressions classifiable

[1] Ibid., p. 47.

either as indefinite or as definite descriptions, are not used as names, in as much as it is not necessary for them to denote anything in order to have a meaning. Or rather, since he concludes that expressions of this kind have no meaning in isolation, we should say that it is not necessary for them to denote anything in order that they should contribute in the way that they do to the meaning of the sentences into which they enter. Such expressions are said by Russell to be 'incomplete symbols', and what he means by saying of an expression that it is an incomplete symbol, apart from its not needing to have a denotation, is that the meaning of any sentence in which it occurs can be spelled out in such a way that the resulting sentence no longer contains the expression or any synonym for it. Accordingly, what is required of the theory of descriptions is that it should provide the machinery for handling descriptions in such a way that they are shown to be incomplete symbols in this sense.

In the earliest version of the theory, which is set out in the article 'On Denoting', and repeated, anachronistically, in the *Introduction to Mathematical Philosophy*, this machinery is rather complicated. Russell takes as primitive the concept of a propositional function's being always true, that it to say, its being true for all the values of the variable. Let us suppose that the function has the form ϕx. Then the sentence 'everything has the property ϕ' is taken to mean just that ϕx is always true, 'nothing has ϕ' is taken to mean that 'ϕx is false' is always true, and 'something has ϕ' is taken to mean that it is false that 'ϕx is false' is always true, a definition for which 'ϕx is sometimes true' can be used as an abbreviation. Having got so far, we can clearly see how to deal with indefinite descriptions. To say, for example, that some man has walked on the moon is to say that the propositional function 'x is human and has walked on the moon' is sometimes true, or in other words, true for at least one value of x. When it comes to definite descriptions, there is the further complication that we have to stipulate that the function is true for only one value of the variable. This is achieved by adding the rider that it is always true of any object y that if y satisfies the function in question y is identical with x. So the translation of 'Scott is the author of *Waverley*' is 'It is sometimes true of x that x wrote *Waverley*, that it is always true of y that if y wrote *Waverley* y is identical with x, and that x is identical with Scott'.

In *Principia Mathematica*, this whole procedure is very much simplified by the use of quantifiers. Instead of 'ϕx is always true' we can say 'for all x, ϕx': instead of ' "ϕx is false" is always true' we can say 'for all x, not ϕx' and instead of 'ϕx is sometimes true' we can say 'for some x, ϕx' or 'There is an x such that ϕx'. Then 'Some man has walked on the moon' becomes 'There is an x such that x is human and has walked on the moon', and 'The author of *Waverley* was Scott' becomes 'There is an x such that x wrote *Waverley*, such that for all y, if y wrote *Waverley*, y is identical with x, and such that x is identical with Scott'. The use of quantifiers not only simplifies the translation, but also avoids the undesirable implication of Russell's earlier formulae that whenever we use a descriptive phrase we are speaking in metalinguistic fashion *about* propositional functions and the extent to which they are satisfied.

With the introduction of quantifiers, it also becomes clear that the theory itself is very simple. It rests on the premiss that in all cases in which a predicate is attributed to a subject, or two or more subjects are said to stand in some relation, that is to say, in all cases except those in which the existence of a subject is simply asserted or denied, the use of a description carries the covert assertion that there exists an object which answers to it. The procedure then is simply to make this covert assertion explicit. The elimination of descriptive phrases, their representation as incomplete symbols, is achieved by expanding them into existential statements and construing these existential statements as asserting that some thing, or in the case of definite descriptive phrases, just one thing, has the property which is contained in the description. So 'The present King of France exists' explicitly asserts that just one thing has the property of being King of France at the present time; 'The present King of France does not exist' explicitly asserts that no one thing has this property; 'The present King of France is bald' covertly asserts that just one thing has this property and explicitly asserts that whatever has this property also has the property of being bald. The case of 'The present King of France is not bald' is slightly more complicated, because the sentence can be interpreted in two ways, according as we assign a wider or narrower scope to the word 'not'. If we take it as only negating the adjoining predicate, so that what is being asserted is that there is a present King of France and that he is not bald, the proposition will again be false: if we take it as negating the whole sentence, so that what is being asserted is that it is not the case that the present King of France is bald, the proposition will be true. On the first interpretation, the descriptive phrase 'the present King of France' is said by Russell to have primary occurrence: on the second interpretation, it is said to have secondary occurrence. This distinction comes out more clearly in symbolic notation, a descriptive phrase having primary occurrence if and only if the quantifier which governs the existential statement into which it is expanded also governs the whole statement in which this statement occurs. It is a distinction which is mainly important in the interpretation of indirect discourse. Suppose, for example, that I say that it is not known whether Stalin was Lenin's murderer. If the expression 'Lenin's murderer' is construed as having primary occurrence, I shall be understood to be committing myself to the assertion that Lenin was murdered, but leaving it undecided whether Stalin was responsible: if it is construed as having secondary occurrence, I shall be understood to be admitting the possibility not only that Stalin was innocent of the murder but that Lenin was not murdered at all.

C. THE MEANING OF EXISTENCE

A point in which Russell can be said to agree with Frege is in his treatment of existence as a property of concepts. This is not, of course, to say that they attribute existence *to* concepts, let alone exclusively to concepts, but rather that they take the attribution of existence to anything to consist in the attribution to a concept of the property of having application, or, as Russell would put it, in the attribution to a propositional function of the property of being satisfied. It follows that the kinds of objects that are said to exist will depend upon the kinds of propositional functions that are said to be satisfied, and this is the source of Professor Quine's celebrated dictum that to be is to be the value of a variable. Although I think that this analysis of existential statements gives an illuminating and correct account of one way, perhaps the most common way, in which they are employed, we have seen that it does not cover their use in philosophical ontology. I have, however, already put forward a theory about the way in which existential statements of this particular sort are to be construed, and I shall not pursue the matter here, though I shall be returning to it at a later stage.

An interesting consequence of Russell's analysis is that existence cannot significantly be attributed to anything which is designated by what he would take to be a proper name. The assumption, which we have seen that Russell makes, that a name has meaning only on the condition of there being something which it denotes, already implies that to couple a name with an ascription of existence would be pleonastic and that to couple a name with a denial of existence would be in a manner contradictory, since we should in the one case be repeating and in the other denying what the use of the name presupposed; but Russell goes further because of his theory of types. If existence is only a property of propositional functions, it follows not only, as we have seen, that expressions like 'there is' are systematically ambiguous, since they can go with expressions which designate functions of different orders, but also that what is denoted by a name, which cannot, like a description, be expanded into a propositional function, cannot meaningfully be said either to be or not to be. If we want to say that a named object exists, we shall have to use such a device as that of saying that it has some property or other, or that it is identical with itself.

This conclusion of Russell's has, however, been disputed by Moore in an article in which Moore was discussing the question whether existence is a predicate.[1] Assuming, correctly, that the demonstrative 'this' was an instance of what Russell would take to be a proper name, Moore argued that one could significantly say of the object to which the name was being used to refer that this might not have existed. But to say that this might not have existed is to say, or at least to imply, that the proposition 'This does not exist' might have been true; from which it follows that the sentence 'This does not exist' must be significant. But if the sentence 'This does not exist' is significant, it expresses a false proposition. Consequently, 'This exists' is a true proposition, and from this it follows that the sentence 'This exists' is also significant.

I see no answer to this argument and am, therefore, inclined to say that Russell was mistaken in thinking that the result of coupling what he regards as a name with an ascription or denial of existence will always be nonsensical. I do not, however, regard this as a refutation of his theory, but rather as a further proof that words like 'exist' can be legitimately used in senses other than the one that Russell analyses. This particular usage is, indeed, degenerate, in that the utterance of the sentence 'This exists' would be pleonastic and the utterance of 'This does not exist' pragmatically contradictory. But there are many sentences, like the sentence 'I never speak English', the utterance of which is pragmatically contradictory, without their being either formally contradictory or meaningless. If this is a legitimate use of the word 'exist', it is different both from what I have called the ontological use, and from that which Russell has analysed, and no doubt there are other uses which are different from any of them. For instance, I think

[1] G. E. Moore, 'Is Existence a Predicate?' in *Supplementary Proceedings of the Aristotelian Society*, xv (1936). Reprinted in *Philosophical Papers*.

that to say that the owner of Bleak House did not exist is not normally to say that the function '*x* alone owned Bleak House' is false for all values of *x*, but rather that, since Bleak House is avowedly fictional, the function is not a candidate for truth or falsehood, unless it occurs in a context where the question at issue is what Dickens actually wrote. The proof of this is that if it were discovered that a man answering to the appellation and description which Dickens gives of Mr Jarndyce did at the relevant time own a house answering to the appellation and description which Dickens gives of Bleak House, we should not say that Dickens had asserted a true proposition, but only that he had taken his materials from life. I should, however, add that while this is the interpretation of avowedly fictional statements which I believe to be most closely in accord with ordinary usage, I do not regard this consideration as being of overriding importance; so that if anyone found it more convenient to analyse statements of this sort in a Russellian manner, which would make them false, rather than sacrifice the law of excluded middle, I should not feel obliged to say that he was wrong. This is another point to which I shall have occasion to recur.

A further consequence of Russell's theory about the meaning of existential statements is that what are ordinarily counted as proper names are not proper names at all, in his sense of the word. This is shown by the fact that it clearly makes sense, in a way that is not self-refuting, to couple an ordinary proper name with a denial of existence. We can legitimately claim to know that Sir Walter Scott did exist, but anyone who asserted that Scott did not exist would be making a historical, not a logical mistake; his statement would be false, but not nonsensical. I do not say that names of this sort are never used as demonstratives, but ordinarily they are not, as is proved by the fact that they commonly have the same significance, whether they are used in the presence or absence of the objects to which they are intended to refer.

It follows that ordinary proper names function as descriptions. Russell admits this consequence, though in his untechnical exposition of his theory, he tends to write as if appellations like 'Scott' really were names, and, in his examples, to contrast them with rather than assimilate them to expressions like 'the author of *Waverley*'. When he remembers, he says that such names are descriptions, which is misleading to the extent that it might be thought to imply that standard descriptions were substitutable for them. Russell does not go into this question in detail, but his view appears to be that a proper name of this sort is a substitute for whatever description of its intended reference the speaker has in mind when he uses the name, or the hearer when he understands its use. Since these descriptions are likely to vary from speaker to hearer, and even to differ for the same speaker, or the same hearer, on different occasions of the use of the name, it cannot therefore be assumed that any two sentences which contain a name of this sort will express the same proposition, even though the name is intended in each case to refer to the same object and the same property is attributed to it. This is, however, only part of a more general problem for Russell, since his assumptions that all descriptions are ultimately linked to objects of acquaintance, that the only objects of acquaintance other than universals are one's own percepts, and that percepts are momentary private entities, together entail, not indeed that no two persons can express the same empirical proposition, since they can couple the same set of predicates with the same quantified variables, but at least that they cannot definitely refer to the same particulars, and that it is only to the limited extent that remembered percepts remain objects of acquaintance that the same person can definitely refer to the same particular on different occasions. How serious a problem this is and how one might try to deal with it are questions into which I shall enter later on.

The conclusion that only sense-data can be named is often thought to be a burden which is foisted on Russell's theory of descriptions by his dubious theory of knowledge. Such, for example, is the view taken by David Pears in his book on *Bertrand Russell and the British Tradition in Philosophy*.[1] I shall, on the contrary, now try to show that the opinions which Russell holds about names could not consistently have led him to any other result.

D. RUSSELL'S THEORY OF NAMES

We have seen that for anything to be a name, in Russell's usage, it is necessary first that it denote an existent object, and secondly that the object which it denotes be one with which the user of the name is acquainted. A third condition, about which I have so far said nothing, is that the name be a simple symbol, from which it is taken to follow that it denotes a simple object, or at any rate one that has not yet been

[1] Published in the Fontana Library, 1967.

discovered to be complex. In his lectures on 'The Philosophy of Logical Atomism', which were delivered in 1918, Russell defines a simple object as one that it is impossible to symbolise otherwise than by simple symbols, and he defines a simple symbol as a symbol whose parts are not symbols.[1] Unfortunately, both definitions are inadequate for his purpose. If the word 'symbolise' is used here as a synonym for 'name', it will be true of all objects that they cannot be symbolised otherwise than by simple symbols, since in Russell's view an object which cannot be named by a simple symbol cannot be named at all: on the other hand, if the word 'symbolise' is being used to mean 'name or describe', there will be no objects that satisfy the definition, since descriptions are not simple symbols, and however simple an object may be it can always be described as bearing some relation to some other object. In fact, all that Russell requires to say on this score is that a simple object is one that *can* be symbolised by a simple symbol, since the distinction which he needs to draw is that between simple objects which alone can be named, and complex objects which can only be described.

The onus, therefore, is thrown on the definition of a simple symbol. Here again what Russell actually says is not acceptable. Taken literally, it would prevent the word 'this' from being a simple symbol, since it contains the letters 'h', 'i', 's', in that order, which also form an English word. One might try saying that a symbol is simple if and only if it contains no part the use of which as a symbol contributes to the meaning of the symbol as a whole, in the way in which the word 'say' contributes to the meaning of the word 'saying' but not to the meaning of the word 'essay', but it is obvious that by this criterion a great many objects, which Russell would certainly wish to regard as complex, would turn out to be symbolised by simple symbols: indeed, by resorting to an artificial language, we could make their number as large as we pleased. We must, however, remember that when Russell put his definition forward he was speaking about atomic propositions, and this, I think, gives us the clue to what he must, or at any rate should, have had in mind. I suggest that what he must mean by a simple symbol is one that remains intact, with no parts that are symbols in the sense that I have just defined, when the proposition which it helps to express has been fully analysed, or at least as fully analysed as we are capable of analysing it. In short, a simple symbol is one that resists reduction A predicate is simple if it cannot be represented as a conjunction or disjunction of other predicates. A name is simple if it carries no descriptive load.

There will clearly be difficulties in the way of applying this definition to predicates. In their case, unless we impose restrictions on the kind of conjunctions and disjunctions that are to constitute complexity, it is never going to be satisfied, since any allegedly simple predicate f can always be represented as a conjunction of the predicates g and not-h. where g is equivalent to f or h, and as a disjunction of the predicates j and k, where j is equivalent to f and h, and k is equivalent to f and not-h. On the other hand, the application of the definition to names is quite straightforward. Any connotation that a nominative sign carries is taken from it and turned into a propositional function; when an object is found which satisfies the function, the same treatment is applied, so that the original function is augmented by another predicate: and so the process continues until we get to the point where the owner of all these predicates is named by a sign which has no connotation at all. This is the whole technique of the theory of descriptions. Applying it is like feeding an insect, which absorbs all the nourishment into its body. The body swells and swells and the head remains vestigial. All that one can say about it is that it is something to which the body is attached.

It follows that it is misleading for Russell to speak of there being both simple and complex objects. If he is to be consistent, he must hold that the distinction between the simple and the complex applies only to predicates. It cannot apply to objects, since Russell is committed to the view that all genuine objects are simple, as is indeed implied by his speaking of all objects which are designated by complex symbols, and consequently of all objects which are designated by descriptions, as logical fictions. This is incorrect, as it stands, since we have seen that an object which can be named can *also* be described, but it does apply, on Russell's principle, to all those objects which can *only* be described. Accordingly, when in the course of the short discussion which is reproduced at the end of the second of his published lectures on *The Philosophy of Logical Atomism*, Russell admitted that 'It is perfectly possible to suppose that complex things are capable of analysis *ad infinitum*, and that you never reach the simple',[1] what he should be taken to have meant, as indeed the context would suggest, is that it is possible to suppose that one never reaches the bedrock of atomic fact. But if there is room for doubt on the point, it can only be because one is not sure whether the predicates at which one has arrived are not

[1] Ibid., p. 202.

capable of further analysis. This doubt could arise in two ways. One might wonder whether the predicates which one was taking to be simple were not susceptible of expansion at the same logical level: or one might wonder whether the function which one was supposing to range over individuals did not really range over classes, in which case one would have to reduce the classes to functions of a lower order and hope that the same mistake was not being repeated. These possibilities are of course not mutually exclusive. In either case, the position with regard to the subjects of the predicates will be quite clear-cut. Either one has arrived at simple objects, or one has not yet arrived at any genuine objects at all. If one has arrived at genuine objects, they will be what Russell calls 'bare particulars', owing their simplicity to their nakedness and functioning exactly like Lockean substances, at least in Berkeley's rendering of Locke. How Russell is eventually able to dispense with these substances, and so in a way with objects altogether, without doing any serious damage to the theory of descriptions, is a question to which I shall come a little later on.

A point which emerges from what I have just been saying is that the question whether a nominative sign is really a name is partly dependent on the question whether some other sign is a simple predicate. If one were mistaken about the logical status of some predicate, one might believe that one was naming the subject of the predication, although the sign which one took to be a name was in fact a concealed description. So far as I can see, this is the only sense in which Russell's theory allows it to be said that a sign which is not a name can be used as a name; and even then one would not really be using it as a name. It has, however, been maintained by David Pears that Russell allows the possibility of our using ordinary proper names as if they were genuine names, even when we know that we are not using them to denote simple objects. The reason which he attributes to Russell for admitting this possibility is that sometimes when a person uses an ordinary proper name 'he will be thinking of its actual denotation directly without the intervention of any descriptions: in his thought the denotation will not be split up into its elements'.[1] The textual evidence on which Pears relies is the sixth of the Logical Atomism lectures, in which Russell several times speaks of 'Scott' as a name, at one point saying that ' "Scott" taken as a name has a meaning all by itself',[2] and in particular says that 'If you substitute another name in place of

---

[1] D. F. Pears, *Bertrand Russell and the British Tradition in Philosophy*, p. 49.
[2] *Logic and Knowledge*, p. 253.

"Scott" which is also a name of the same individual, say, "Scott is Sir Walter", then "Scott" and "Sir Walter" are being used as names and not as descriptions, [and] your proposition is strictly a tautology'.[1] I admit that, taken literally, these passages do support Pears's view, but I find it rather slender evidence on which to base a conclusion which runs so strongly counter to almost everything that Russell says about names. For one thing, it would mean that he was quietly abandoning his principle that one can name only objects with which one is acquainted, since even if he were willing, in the context, not to insist upon the point that one is acquainted with sense-data and not with persons, he can hardly have supposed that any of his audience had actually set eyes on Sir Walter Scott. A more plausible explanation, it seems to me, is that here, as on some other occasions when he is giving a popular exposition of his theory, Russell is *pretending* that 'Scott' is a genuine name. The reason for the pretence would be that it yielded him a simple example, and one that would make his point clearer to his audience than if he had formulated a proposition about sense-data. It was remiss of him not to enter his usual caveat that ordinary proper names like 'Scott' are really descriptions, but it has to be remembered that these were popular lectures, not revised for publication, and that Russell was concerned with making the *distinction* between names and descriptions clear to his audience, rather than expounding to them his special theory about names.

The decisive argument, in my view, against Pears's interpretation is that Russell cannot have thought it possible to think of the actual denotation of a name like 'Scott' without the intervention of any descriptions. He cannot have thought this possible, because he held, in my view rightly, that one cannot think of an object of any kind except as something which has such and such properties. And his reason for holding this is that we cannot observe an object as distinct from its properties. As he puts it in the chapter on 'Proper Names' in his *Inquiry into Meaning and Truth*, 'We experience qualities, but not the subject in which they are supposed to inhere'.[2] But if we never experience the subject, it must follow, on Russell's principles, that we never think of it either, except by description as the subject which is the owner of such and such qualities or a term in such and such relations. It is true that we can use an ordinary proper name, to refer even to an absent object, without having any particular description of the object explicitly in mind. But if the name is to have any significance for us, if our use of it is to entail that there is some particular object of which we are thinking, then it must, as it were, be holding a place for a description which we could furnish on demand; at the very least we must be disposed to acknowledge some set of properties as being properties of just that object which we intend to denote by the name: if we merely associate the name with an image, we are implicitly describing the object as the one and only object which the image represents.

But does not this argument prove too much? If names are the names of bare particulars and we never experience bare particulars or are able to think of them except by description as the owners of their properties, how can Russell consistently say that names denote objects with which we are acquainted? Is he not forced to conclude that all our knowledge of objects is knowledge by description, and that our acquaintance extends only to qualities and relations? It would then follow that we had no use at all for names. All that we should need would be predicates and the apparatus of quantification.

The answer to this is that Russell thinks that there are two ways in which we can refer to an object. We can say of it that it is the one and only object which has such and such properties, or we can simply *point* to it by the use of a demonstrative symbol. In the first case, the object is identified by description, in the second case by name. It is true that even in the second case what we are pointing to, strictly speaking, is still a set of properties, but our being actually confronted with the complex of properties is held to constitute acquaintance with the object which has them. In short, naming for Russell in the end simply consists in a process of demonstrative identification; and the only objects which can be demonstratively identified are those which are directly presented to us through our observation of their properties. Genuine names, therefore, are pure demonstratives, from which all connotation has been taken away. Everything that we are capable of saying is built into propositional functions and then the names do not describe but indicate the particular objects by which the functions are satisfied.

It can now be seen why this theory of names, when its implications are fully developed, requires that the objects which are denoted by names should be of the order of sense-data. It is not enough, for anything to be a name, that it should in fact refer to an existent object, since this can also be achieved by a description. The name has to guarantee the existence of its object, in the sense that the failure of the object to exist deprives the name of any significant use. But this entails that the object which a name denotes cannot be physical, since, on any tenable theory of perception, it is at least conceivable that the physical object which we suppose our demonstrative symbol to be indicating should not exist. If the use of the demonstrative is to guarantee the existence of its object, it must be a sufficient condition for the object to exist that it make its appearance on just this occasion; what happens at other times or what appears to other observers must be irrelevant. But this condition is satisfied only by what Russell calls sense-data or, at a later stage, percepts, and indeed only by present percepts. If at one period Russell allowed the possibility of our being acquainted with, and so being able to name, past sense-data, it was because he held the view that, in the most favourable conditions, remembering could be assimilated to sensing. In memory, we had, or could have, direct acquaintance with the past, so that an object which figured in our act of memory could be ostensively symbolised in the same way as a present sense-datum. When, in *The Analysis of Mind*, Russell discards the conception of such mental acts, he also, very properly, gives up this view of memory. The knowledge obtained through memory now becomes indirect, being based on the content of present experience. Russell does not himself relate this change of view to the theory of descriptions but the consequence clearly is that any percept which lies outside the confines of the specious present cannot be named but only described.

It appears, then, that the part played by names in Russell's system is extremely limited: so much so that one again begins to wonder whether he needs them at all. A point which he does not bring out clearly, and perhaps only saw much later when, as we shall find, he revised his theory of names, is that while he permits names to work only very short hours, he overworks them while they are working. They are made to perform a double duty. They refer to the substances in which the sensory properties that we perceive inhere, and they also do the work of orientation: in the second capacity the demonstrative shows us where to look for what is being talked about. But the task of referring to substances, whatever their properties may be taken to be, is perfectly well performed, in the case of anything but present percepts, by the signs for quantified variables, and even in the case of present percepts the names achieve nothing more: they do not extract the substances from their covering of properties; they have no penetrative power that signs for quantified variables lack. If names are essential, it must therefore be for the work of orientation. But here we see at once that they are not needed either. It is obvious that demonstrative signs can do the work of indicating the area in which we are to look for the fulfilment of a description, without our having to suppose that there are objects which they infallibly denote. In fact, on Russell's principles, the assumption that demonstrative signs are names makes it very much more difficult for them to do the work of orientation. After all, the main use of demonstratives is to make it easier for other people to take up one's references, and there is going at least to be a difficulty in explaining how they achieve this, if we start with the assumption that each of us uses them to name objects which are not perceptible to anyone else. If we cease to conceive of them as names, we are no longer obliged to relate them to percepts: we can give an account of their employment which would be neutral with respect to theories of perception; so far as this goes, our only ontological commitment will be to the existence of some sorts of context in which they are produced. This is not to say that the question how communication is possible will not still present a problem, or that we are entitled to leave percepts altogether out of account: on the contrary, I have no doubt that Russell was quite right in taking them to be epistemologically primitive. The point that I am now making is that he would have done better not to bring them into his account of reference. Thus, while I think that I have succeeded in showing that the conclusion that names denote percepts does follow logically from Russell's ideas about names, I agree with his critics that it is an excrescence on the theory of descriptions, not because it represents an intrusion into the philosophy of logic of Russell's theory of knowledge, but rather because we improve the theory of descriptions by detaching it from this particular theory of names.

An interesting fact is that Russell himself came to think that this part of the function which I have shown that he assigned to names was not really called for. In *An Inquiry into Meaning and Truth*, he argues that it is possible, at least at the lowest logical level, to dispense with substances. Sensory properties do not need a *substratum* to support them, and the work of holding them together can be done, he now thinks, by a relation of compresence. Unfortunately, instead of drawing the conclusion that names become otiose, he chooses to drop the assumption that they denote simple objects, and now thinks of them as denoting the complexes of properties which he supposes that we perceive. Since this gives names a connotation, there is no longer any difficulty in holding that they can refer to past as well as to present percepts. The complexes of qualities which names denote include spatial and temporal qualia, conceived as constituents of private sense-fields. This is an interesting and difficult view about which I shall have more to say in another context. Russell also speaks of names as designating continuous portions of space-time, where what appears to be meant is physical space-time, rather than the sensory spaces and times which he believes to enter into our experiences.[1] It also apppears, however, that he is here thinking of ordinary proper names, which he still regards as eliminable in favour of descriptions.

But now if the particulars which names denote are to be no more than complexes of qualities, then, so far as their denotation is concerned, there is no longer any reason to distinguish names from descriptions. It can no longer be maintained that the use of the name guarantees the existence of its object, since it is clearly conceivable that the qualities of which the complex in question is meant to be composed should not in fact be found in that combination; consequently, the name will retain its meaning even though the object which it purports to denote does not exist: and from this it will also follow that, just like a description, a name can be significantly coupled with an assertion or denial of existence. It may be objected that the possibility of the name's failing to denote anything is still excluded by the fact that it can refer only to an object with which one is acquainted. But the point is that this is now an arbitrary stipulation: it is not logically connected with the meaning of the name, which would remain the same even if we were mistaken in thinking that we had been acquainted with the object which we took it to denote. We can, of course, decide to use the *word* 'name' only for those descriptive signs that denote existent objects with which we are acquainted, but this division of descriptive signs would not correspond to any semantic differences between them. It follows that we can dispense with names altogether in this employment.

But if we can dispense with names in this employment, then Russell would himself agree that we do not need them at all. For, in *An Inquiry into Meaning and Truth*, he divides names into two classes, those that designate spatio-temporal and other perceptible qualities, and those that have, as he puts it, 'an egocentric definition'.[2] This second class consists of demonstrative signs like 'I', 'you', 'this', and 'that'. And while he still speaks of such demonstratives as names which denote what he calls egocentric particulars, the account which he gives of them reveals that he really no longer thinks of them as names, in any

---

[1] See, e.g., *An Inquiry into Meaning and Truth*, p. 96.   [2] Ibid.

sense which he had previously given to the term. He shows that they can all be defined in terms of the one demonstrative 'this', and then explains the meaning of this demonstrative in terms of the causal conditions of its use rather than in terms of the objects which it may denote. In particular, he now represents the word 'this' as 'having, in some sense, a constant meaning',[1] whereas if he were still treating it as a proper name, he would have to say that it had a different meaning on every occasion on which it denoted a different object.

This completes my argument that the logical development of Russell's theory of descriptions leads to the elimination of proper names. We are left with descriptive signs, which stand for properties or groups of properties at various logical levels; with demonstrative signs, which are neither names nor predicates but signals, which simply do the work of orientation; and of course with connectives which may or may not be limited to the logical constants of *Principia Mathematica*. Whether these logical constants are bound to include the signs for quantified variables is a matter for debate. We have seen that quantified variables do the work of substances, so that if Russell is right in thinking that substances can be eliminated at the experiential level in favour of complexes of qualities, and if the same result can be achieved at all other levels, and if we can devise other operators for the work of generalisation and the assertion of existence, we can conclude that they are theoretically dispensable. This is, in fact the conclusion at which Professor Quine arrives in his paper 'Variables Explained Away'.[2] The question, though technical, is of more than technical interest, since if Quine's method works we at last have a proof of Berkeley's contention that things are bundles of qualities, and with it the solution of an old philosophical problem.

I have included demonstrative signs in the list of materials with which the theory of descriptions leaves us because Russell has never thought that one could do without them. It can, however, be argued that they too are dispensable. I shall return to this question a little later on.

E. EVALUATION OF THE THEORY

Historically, as we have seen, Russell's theory of descriptions is rooted in his assumption that the meaning of names is to be identified with

---

[1] Ibid., p. 109. [2] W. V. Quine, *Selected Logical Papers*.

the objects which they denote. We have, however, also seen that the theory, when logically developed, leads to the elimination of names, so that it is not in the end affected by the truth or falsehood of the assumption from which it originated. In fact, I have no doubt that this assumption is mistaken. In the case of ordinary proper names, the decisive objection to it is that the name makes the same contribution to the meaning of the sentences in which it occurs, whether the object which it purports to denote exists or not. In the case of the purely demonstrative signs which Russell called logically proper names, the main argument against his original assumption is that it prevents them from having any constant meaning. We have seen that Russell eventually yielded to this argument, though I think it would be better to explain the meaning of such signs in terms of the functions they perform, rather than, as he proposes, in terms of the causal conditions of their use. There is no serious objection, so far as I can see, to identifying the meaning of predicative signs with the properties they stand for, so long as one does not suppose that one is thereby contributing anything to the analysis of meaning. But these signs are not commonly regarded as names, and we have seen that there is no good reason to follow Russell in speaking of certain groups of properties as being denoted by proper names, even if we think of these groups as constituting particulars. If we are interested in pinning down the distinction which may be said to obtain in ordinary usage between descriptions and proper names, I think that the best course would be to represent it as a distinction between referential expressions which have a fixed connotation, and those that have a variable connotation. The fact that descriptions often incorporate proper names creates a complication but not, I think, any difficulty of principle. In the case of neither class of expressions does the analysis of their meaning need to be burdened with the question whether or not there is anything that actually possesses the connoted properties. Consequently, there is no justification for making it a necessary condition for anything to be a genuine name, let alone a genuine description, that it be successful in its intended reference. It is not a semantic but a historical or geographical question whether any such reference succeeds.

None of this enters into the theory of descriptions, because the theory is not concerned with giving an account of ordinary usage. Its purpose is to elaborate a different way of speaking, what Wittgenstein would call a different grammar, which brings out distinctions that our ordinary way of speaking is thought to obscure. In so far as it can be said that the facts remain the same, however we describe them, Russell would claim that by following out the theory of descriptions we arrive at a truer representation of the structure of the facts. There are, however, difficulties about this way of putting it which I shall go into when I come to talk about Russell's Logical Atomism.

The point that the theory of descriptions is, in this sense, revisionary has commonly been missed both by its champions and its critics. Thus, Moore, in the long essay on 'Russell's "Theory of Descriptions"' which he contributed to *The Philosophy of Bertrand Russell*, interprets the theory as offering an account of what is ordinarily meant by a certain class of sentences, and consequently by the propositions which these sentences express. He defines the class of sentences in question by reference to Russell's example 'the author of *Waverley* was Scotch' and attributes to Russell the proposition that the meaning of this sentence can be correctly defined by saying that it means neither more nor less than the conjunction of the three sentences 'At least one person wrote *Waverley*', 'At most one person wrote *Waverley*' and 'There never was a person who wrote *Waverley* but was not Scotch'.[1] Moore, in fact, maintains that this particular proposition is false, on the ground that if Scott had merely excogitated *Waverley* without actually writing it, he could still correctly be said to have been its author (a pedantic objection, certainly, but if one is concerned with identity of meaning, one has to be strict), but he believes that 'an enormous number' of similar propositions are true, and he regards the fact that so many of them are true, together with the fact that when a definite descriptive phrase figures in the expression of a true proposition of this sort, it is only the sentence in which it occurs that can be defined and not the phrase by itself, as being sufficient to justify F. P. Ramsey's description of the theory as 'a paradigm of philosophy'.[2]

It was excusable in Moore to give this account of what Russell was doing, since Russell himself claims in the *Introduction to Mathematical Philosophy* that the propositions expressed by the first two of Moore's *Waverley* sentences together with the proposition 'Whoever wrote *Waverley* was Scotch', which for lexicological reasons Moore thinks ought to be replaced by the proposition expressed by his third sentence, 'may be taken as defining what is meant by the proposition "the author of *Waverley* was Scotch"'.[3] Nevertheless, I am sure that it is a mis-

---

[1] *The Philosophy of Bertrand Russell*, p. 187.
[2] See F. P. Ramsey, *The Foundation of Mathematics*, p. 263 n.
[3] *Introduction to Mathematical Philosophy*, p. 177.

taken account, or at least that it misrepresents the import of the theory. What Moore and, in this passage, Russell have overlooked is that the idea that Russell's analyses preserve identity of meaning owes its plausibility to the fact that the definite descriptive phrases, which occur in his favourite examples, establish the uniqueness of their reference by incorporating proper names. If we carried the analyses a stage further, so that instead of talking about '*Waverley*' and 'France', we made some such assertion as that there was at least and at most one book which contained such and such words in such and such an order, or that there was at least and at most one country that had such and such a shape and area, or such and such events in its history, we should be much less tempted to say that the sentences with which we ended had collectively the same meaning as that with which we began.

Another relevant fact, to which Professor Strawson has called attention in his article 'On Referring',[1] is that on most occasions on which we use a definite descriptive phrase our words do not themselves carry the claim that the description is uniquely satisfied. We speak of the policeman on the corner of the street, or the book at the end of the shelf, without intending or being understood to imply that there are no other street corners or shelves to be found. The uniqueness of reference is determined by the context. It might be thought that this point could be dealt with by bringing in demonstratives, on the ground that a phrase like 'the book at the end of the shelf' can be expanded, without any alteration of the meaning which it contributes to the sentence in which it occurs, into the sentence 'There is at least and at most one book which is at *that* end of *that* shelf'. But, as I think I have shown, it is foreign to the logic of the theory of descriptions to rely on a demonstrative to convey information which could be given descriptively: and if, in every instance of this kind, we are going to replace the reference to the street, or the shelf, or whatever it may be, with an identifying description and then expand these descriptions into existential statements, it will soon become clear that what we are giving is not a translation of the original sentence but a paraphrase. If we were to leave out any information which the original sentence conveyed, the paraphrase would be incorrect. On the other hand, once it is understood that we are not aiming to preserve identity of meaning, there is no reason to object to the fact that the paraphrase conveys more information than the original sentence; as indeed, it nearly always would.

[1] P. F. Strawson, 'On Referring', in *Mind* (1950).

The way of speaking which develops out of the theory of descriptions is not only a more prolix but also a stricter way of speaking than that which we normally employ. In the ordinary way, we are prepared to allow even a false description of an object to count as a successful reference to it, so long as the direction of the intended reference can be determined by other means. Suppose, for example, that someone who accepted the claims of Anastasia to be a Russian Grand Duchess habitually referred to her as the daughter of the Tsar, and suppose that it were proved that her claim was fraudulent, or simply mistaken. We should not want to say that everything that this man had ever said about Anastasia was false. On the other hand, if we analyse his statements in accordance with the theory of descriptions, we are bound to conclude that they are all false, just because a conjunction is falsified by the falsity of one of its conjuncts. If every one of the man's statements is construed as a statement to the effect that there is one and only one person who both answers to the description of being the one and only living person at such and such a date who is the daughter of such and such an absolute ruler of such and such a country and also possesses such and such other properties, then either the fact that no one person answers to this description, or the fact that the one and only person who does answer to it does not possess the other properties in question, will be enough to render all the statements false. More generally, the theory of descriptions does not distinguish between a failure of reference and a false statement about an object to which a definite reference has been established. Everything is reduced to the question whether or not there is just one object which has a listed set of properties. Nevertheless, if it were thought important, we could preserve this distinction by taking the predicates to which the uniqueness clause was attached as specifying the reference, and we could also adopt a pragmatic rule which would permit us, in certain circumstances, not to count the falsity of the initial conjunct as falsifying the whole conjunction.

The fact that we do not automatically rule a statement to be false when its subject is identified by a false description, whereas there would be no question of its not being false if the description were predicated of a subject which had been otherwise identified, seems to me to be a good argument in favour of the view that when we use a denotative expression we normally presuppose rather than assert the existence of the object to which it purports to refer, with the result that if the object does not exist our statement is not false, but lacking in truth-value.

Nevertheless, if we are taking the position that the theory of descriptions is a revisionary theory, I think it should rather be counted as a point in its favour that it does allow statements of this sort to have a truth-value. For one thing, as Mr Dummett has pointed out,[1] if we deprive them of truth-value, we place a strain on what seems to be the obvious equivalence between '*p*' and 'It is true that *p*', since if '*p*' has no truth-value, it is at least very tempting to infer that 'It is true that *p*' is false. If we are assigning a truth-value to propositions like 'The present King of France is bald', then it is clearly most natural to call them false. Indeed, it is not obvious that in so doing we are seriously violating ordinary usage; it is open to question whether most English speakers would think it more correct to say that, since France is no longer a monarchy, the question of truth or falsehood did not in this case arise. It would be a serious violation of ordinary usage to call such a statement true, but, as I said earlier, this also would be possible, even within the general framework of the theory of descriptions. We could not, within this framework, transmute the present King of France into the null-class, but we could achieve the same result by construing particular statements, in the way that Russell construes universal statements, as statements of material implication. Instead of transforming 'The thing that has ϕ has ψ' into 'There is just one thing that has ϕ and it also has ψ', we should transform it into 'If there is just one thing that has ϕ, it also has ψ'; and then, by the rules of material implication, our statement would be true if its antecedent was not satisfied. This would have the advantage that we could assign the same truth-value, namely truth, to 'Pegasus is mettlesome' and 'All winged horses are mettlesome', whereas, on the official theory, we get the slightly anomalous result that while 'Pegasus is mettlesome' is false, 'All winged horses are mettlesome' is true. It would, however, have the disadvantage of making the symbolic expression of particular descriptive statements considerably more complicated; and since we can also avoid the anomaly by construing universal statements as carrying the additional clause that something satisfies their antecedents, I think that Russell's interpretation is to be preferred.

The great merit of the theory of descriptions, in my view, is that it thoroughly disentangles the descriptive from the demonstrative forms of expression, rightly giving primary importance to the descriptive forms, to the point, indeed, where it becomes doubtful whether the demonstrative forms are needed at all. I think that the main objection

---

[1] Michael Dummett, 'Truth', *Proceedings of the Aristotelian Society*, LIX (1958–9).

to doing without demonstratives, though Russell actually regards it as an advantage,[1] is that it commits us to the identity of indiscernibles, which has not yet been shown to be a necessary truth.[2] Apart from this, as I have shown elsewhere,[3] the programme of eliminating demonstratives can easily be carried through. All that we need for the work of orientation is to find uniquely describable landmarks to serve as points of origin for our spatio-temporal co-ordinates. If we are disturbed by the possibility that our descriptions of the landmarks will turn out not to describe them uniquely, we can simply postulate our points of origin, as is in fact done in our dating system. It is true that the depersonalised language with which we are left is not so well fitted for the expression of our feelings. To express pleasure at the timeless fact that one uniquely described event precedes another has not quite the emotive force of saying 'Thank goodness, that's over'. Nevertheless the more detached form of expression does not comport any loss of information. It is also true that the use of demonstrative signals is incomparably more convenient: but that again is not what is in question.

If this is correct, the main problem with which the theory of descriptions leaves us is that of the possibility of eliminating substances. I shall discuss this further in connection with Russell's Logical Atomism.

[1] See, e.g., *An Inquiry into Meaning and Truth*, p. 102.
[2] Cf. my article on 'The Identity of Indiscernibles', in *Philosophical Essays*.
[3] In an article on 'Names and Descriptions', in *The Concept of a Person*.

3 Logical Atomism – Part 1: The Primary Objects

A. CRITERION OF SIMPLICITY

The philosophical system to which Russell gave the name of Logical Atomism is in many ways the direct outcome of the theory of descriptions. He first set it out in 1918 in the series of lectures on 'The Philosophy of Logical Atomism', which I have already described as being rather popular in tone, and he gave a somewhat different version of it in the essay, called 'Logical Atomism', which he contributed to the first volume of *Contemporary British Philosophy* in 1924. This too is reprinted in the collection *Logic and Knowledge*. In its earlier form at least, the system incorporated the neutral monism which Russell had already expounded in *Our Knowledge of the External World* and in two of the essays collected in *Mysticism and Logic*. It does not, however, take this neutral monism so far as Russell subsequently took it in the *Analysis of Mind*, which came out in 1921. The theory of truth which goes with the system was not expounded in the lectures but is to be found in an article 'On Propositions: What they are and how they mean', which was written in 1919 and is also reprinted in *Logic and Knowledge*. In the preface which he wrote for the lectures, when they were first published in the *Monist*, Russell acknowledges a debt to his 'friend and former pupil' Ludwig Wittgenstein, and indeed his system of logical atomism is very close in many ways to Wittgenstein's *Tractatus Logico-Philosophicus*. Russell had not, however, read the *Tractatus* when he delivered the lectures, and indeed remarked in the preface, as he did also in his *Introduction to Mathematical Philosophy*, that he did not then even know whether Wittgenstein was alive or dead.

The basic thesis of logical atomism is that the world consists of simple particulars, which have only simple qualities, in the sense that any complex qualities which they may have are analysable into simple ones, and which stand in simple relations to one another. It is left open whether the number of these particulars is finite or infinite. Both qualities and relations are external to their subjects, in the sense that no single one of them, and not even any conjunction of them, is essential to the subjects' identity: in principle, it could have a wholly different set of properties and still be the same particular. Nevertheless, it is only through the properties which it happens to have at a given time that any particular is identifiable. There is no inconsistency here, since it is plain that an object can be identified by any feature which distinguishes it from other objects, for instance its spatio-temporal position, without our having to infer that its possession of this feature is essential to its being the object that it is.

Since we have already seen that Russell's own definition of a simple object, as one that is denoted by a simple symbol, is not satisfactory, we might think of improving on it by saying that a simple object is one that has only external properties. But the trouble is that, on the view which Russell took of substance, this would apply to all objects, so that it would not mark any distinction between simple and complex objects; or rather, since Russell in fact holds that all genuine objects are simple, I should say that it would not mark any distinction between simple objects and logical fictions. I therefore prefer my earlier suggestion that simple, or genuine, objects be defined as those that resist reduction, in the way I explained. This in any case entails that they have only external properties, since if we were to try to attribute any internal properties to them, we could only succeed in issuing descriptions: and then, by the theory of descriptions, the object which we thereby appeared to be describing would be transmuted into a set of predicates which could stand only for external properties of anything that satisfied the resultant propositional function.

It follows, as I said earlier, that since reduction operates on predicates, and since it is true also of predicates that they are simple only if they are irreducible, the criterion for the simplicity of an object lies in the simplicity of the properties which are attributable to it. We have already seen that a difficulty arises here from the fact that, with a little ingenuity, we can represent any property as a conjunction or disjunction of other properties. I do not know how this is to be met except by simply listing the predicates which we are going to count as primitive. To answer Russell's requirements, these predicates must be so chosen that the properties for which they stand are absolutely specific, homogeneous, and directly exemplified within our experience. If we construe direct acquaintance in such a way that it cannot incorporate memory of the recent past, we must add the condition that the properties must be wholly exemplified in some specious present. This will have the consequence that the only relations which we can allow to be designated by primitive predicates are those that obtain between present percepts. There will, however, be no objection to our extending their range beyond the specious present, once their basis in experience has been secured.

The fact that his simple properties were properties of percepts, or, as he then put it, sense-data, led Russell, in the second of his Logical Atomism lectures, to draw the startling conclusion that no two people ever mean the same by their words. He took this to follow from his assumption that no two people can sense the same sense-datum. But surely this is an invalid inference. It does, indeed, follow that no two people can name the same object, and consequently that they cannot express the same atomic proposition, if the sentences which express atomic propositions have to contain names. On the other hand, it does not follow that they cannot make use of the same predicates. This would be the case if predicates had to be defined extensionally, or even by reference to one particular object, but this is clearly not necessary, and indeed open to serious objections, as I shall show later on. If simple predicates are defined ostensively, in such a way that any occasion on which the corresponding property is exemplified will serve as well as any other for illustrating what the predicate means, then there is no reason why different people should not mean the same by them. The fact that my sense-data are numerically different from yours in no way entails that they cannot have the same qualities or stand in the same relations to one another. Of course it can still be argued that it can never be known that they have the same qualities, on the ground that no one can be in a position to compare them, but if this is to be the criterion, it can equally well be said that we can never know that we mean the same by the predicates which we attribute to physical objects, since even the most naïve realist can hardly suppose that our perceptions of physical objects can be compared. Consequently, the argument does not show that Russell's attribution of his simple properties to sense-data creates any special difficulty about the possibility of communication. This point is important since it means that when Russell comes to identify sensory particulars with complexes of qualities, he will, in effect, be starting with neutral and not, as he still supposes, with private data.

B. THE WORLD OF SENSIBILIA

So far, we have not gone beyond the theory of descriptions. Russell now takes a step beyond it by relaxing the rule that simple objects must be objects with which one is actually acquainted. He still makes it necessary for anything to be a simple object that it have only simple properties, in the sense which I have just explained, but it need not any longer manifest itself to any given person, or indeed to any person at all. One's own sense-data then become a sub-class of a set of objects to which Russell gives the name of 'sensibilia'. These will include the sense-data which are sensed by persons other than oneself and also objects of 'the same metaphysical and physical status as sense-data'[1] which are not sensed by anyone. The existence of the sense-data of other persons, or of sensibilia which are not known to be sense-data, is, of course, a matter of inference, but it is what one may call a horizontal rather than a vertical inference. That is to say, it is an inference to entities of the same type as those from which the inference proceeds, and not to entities of a higher type. If we are to be strictly accurate, this applies only to unsensed sensibilia, or at any rate to sensibilia not known to be sensed. To speak of a sense-datum as being sensed by another person is to imply the existence of that person, and therefore to make a vertical inference. The same applies, indeed, to speaking of a sense-datum as sensed by oneself, if one conceives of oneself as an embodied person and not as a pure ego. The correct distinction, therefore, at this stage, is that between sense-data and unsensed sensibilia. The sense-data are in fact one's own but must not, and indeed at this stage cannot, be defined as being so. The sense-data are objects of acquaintance: the existence of the sensibilia is inferred. It is true that if the programme of reduction is fully carried out, all inferences end by being horizontal. Even so, there will still be a difference between postulating objects of the same type as those which are already known or assumed to exist, and postulating the elaborate relations between these objects which are required to construct objects of a higher type. So long as we are engaged on a programme of this kind, what we must not do is postulate objects of a higher type before we have constructed them.

Unfortunately, this is just what Russell appears to do when he explains what he means by sense-data and by sensibilia. Writing at a time when he still believed in the existence of mental acts, he says, in

[1] *Mysticism and Logic*, p. 148.

an essay on 'Sense-data and Physics', which is reprinted in his *Mysticism and Logic*, that sense-data are physical, on the ground that they are not the constituents but the objects of mental acts. From this he infers that it is not logically impossible that sense-data should be both public and persistent. If he nevertheless thinks of them as being private and momentary, it is because he takes them to be causally dependent upon the condition and the location of the observer's body. The reason for taking sense-data to be private will then presumably be that, even supposing that two different persons can at the same time be in exactly the same physiological state, they cannot simultaneously occupy exactly the same position, and the reason for taking them to be momentary is that even if one is able to remain in exactly the same position and attitude for some length of time, it is improbable that during that time there will be no relevant change in the environment or in one's physiological condition. These considerations would not, however, apply to unsensed sensibilia, as Russell seems to have recognised. Thus, in the lecture which lends its title to *Our Knowledge of the External World*, he says: 'If two men are sitting in a room, two somewhat similar worlds are perceived by them; if a third man enters and sits between them, a third world, intermediate between the two previous worlds, begins to be perceived. It is true that we cannot reasonably suppose just this world to have existed before, because it is conditioned by the sense-organs, nerves, and brain of the newly arrived man: but we can reasonably suppose that *some* aspect of the universe existed from that point of view, though no one was perceiving it.'[1] This clearly implies that the set of sensibilia which constitute what Russell here calls the intermediate world are not momentary, since they existed in some guise before the third man turned them into sense-data, and it also implies that they are not private, in as much as it is open to anyone to come and sense them. On the other hand, they become private as soon as anyone does sense them, and having turned into sense-data they will go out of existence as soon as the person who senses them ceases to do so.

All this seems to me unnecessarily complicated, not to say confused. It is true that Russell does not bring higher-order entities into his actual definition of a sense-datum, which is simply that it is any such part of the whole which is given to sense at any one time as might be singled out by attention.[2] This does not, however, justify the assignment to sense-data of properties which are defined in terms of their

[1] *Our Knowledge of the External World*, pp. 87-8.   [2] *Mysticism and Logic*, p. 147.

relation to physical objects, at a stage when physical objects have not yet been constructed, or any basis established for inferring to them. Moreover, the distinction which Russell draws, in respect of their properties, between sense-data and sensibilia is inconsistent. If the causal dependence of sense-data upon sentient bodies is to be sufficient to make them private and momentary, it must be an existential and not merely a qualitative dependence. But if sense-data are existentially dependent on the presence of observers, they cannot exist, in the absence of observers, as unsensed sensibilia. And if they could exist as unsensed sensibilia, there is no good reason why they should not exist subsequently as well as previously to being sensed. It might be thought that one could restore order by equating the existence of a sensibile with the permanent possibility of obtaining a sense-datum of the kind in question under the appropriate conditions, but this will not do for Russell, since he needs sensibilia as primitive objects. They would not be available for his atomic propositions, if references to them had to be expanded into hypothetical propositions about sense-data.

Russell's assumption that sense-data are private also leads to difficulties in his account of space. In an essay on 'The Ultimate Constituents of Matter', which was first published in 1915 and is reprinted in *Mysticism and Logic*, he argues that if it is not the case that 'two men ever both perceive at the same time any one sensible object' and 'if, as is generally assumed, position in space is purely relative, it follows that the space of one man's objects and the space of another man's objects have no place in common, that they are in fact different spaces, and not merely different parts of one space'. 'I mean by this,' he continues, 'that such immediate spatial relations as are perceived to hold between the different parts of the sensible space perceived by one man, do not hold between parts of sensible spaces perceived by different men. There are therefore a multitude of three-dimensional spaces in the world: there are all those perceived by observers, and presumably also those which are not perceived, merely because no observer is suitably situated for perceiving them.'[1]

Russell speaks of any two particulars which occur simultaneously in the same private space as belonging to the same perspective, and he appears to assume, here and elsewhere, that particulars of the same sense-modality which are not simultaneous, and therefore belong to different perspectives, will still be located in the same space if they are sensed by the same observer. The assumption is, in short, that each

[1] Ibid., pp. 138-9.

observer is presented throughout his life with a single space of sight and a single space of touch, which he fuses to obtain a single private space. But if sense-data are momentary, then, by the argument that spatial relations can hold only between objects which are perceived together, it would seem to follow that each of one's sense-fields constitutes a space of its own. We could, perhaps, avoid this conclusion, at least in the case of visual data, by relying on the fact that successive sense-fields overlap, but even so it would still seem to follow that whenever one shuts one's eyes and opens them again, one is opening them to a different private visual space. Moreover, if private spaces are to be more than momentary, there will again be a difficulty about sensibilia. For what is to be the private space in which a given sensibile is permanently situated? It is fairly clear that Russell thinks of this space as being constituted by the series of perspectives which would be presented to an ever-vigilant observer who permanently had the appropriate point of view; but apart from the objection that the character of a perspective is supposed to depend not only on the location but also on the physical condition of the observer, and that there is no reason to assume that all hypothetical observers would be in the same physical condition, it is not easy to see how the point of view of the hypothetical observer can be specified except in terms of the physical space which Russell looks to his perspectives to construct.

The actual process of the construction brings further difficulties. Russell's ingenious theory is that each perspective can be made to function as a point in what he calls 'perspective-space', which being a three-dimensional arrangement of three-dimensional perspectives, is itself a space of six dimensions. He illustrates the way in which this is brought about by giving an example in which it is assumed that the same physical object appears in an indefinite number of different perspectives, the physical object being itself identified with the class of all its actual and possible appearances. 'Suppose', he says, 'that a certain penny appears in a number of different perspectives: in some it looks larger and in some smaller, in some it looks circular, in others it presents the appearance of an ellipse of varying eccentricity. We may collect together all those perspectives in which the appearance of the penny is circular. These we will place on one straight line, ordering them in a series by the variations in the apparent size of the penny. Those perspectives in which the penny appears as a straight line of a certain thickness will similarly be placed upon a plane (though in this case there will be many different perspectives in which the penny is of the same size: when one arrangement is completed these will form a circle concentric with the penny) and ordered as before by the apparent size of the penny. By such means, all those perspectives in which the penny presents a visual appearance can be arranged in a three-dimensional spatial order.[1] Russell then goes on to say that in each of these series a limit will be reached at the point 'where (as we say) the penny is so near the eye that if it were any nearer it could not be seen'.[2] If we now imagine each of them prolonged, so as to form a line of perspectives continuing 'beyond' the penny, the perspective in which all the lines meet can be defined as 'the place where the penny is'.[3]

Each sensibile, then, is associated with the place where the thing is of which it is a member. This is the place *at* which the sensibile appears. There is also the place *from* which the sensibile appears, which is the perspective to which the sensibile belongs. Russell says that 'We may define "here" as the place in perspective space, which is occupied by our private world' and adds that this makes it possible to understand 'what is meant by saying that our private world is inside our head'; for the place in perspective space which our private world occupies 'may be part of the place where our head is'.[4] The distinction between the place at which a sensibile appears and the place from which it appears also enables us to distinguish the various distances from which a thing may be perceived. Russell speaks rather confusingly of the various appearances of a thing as being nearer to or further from it, forgetting that the place *at* which they all are at a given time will be the same. The places *from* which they are, on the other hand, will be nearer to the thing if they are perspectives which are nearer to 'the place where the thing is'. This in turn makes it possible to distinguish changes in the object from changes in the environment or in the state of the observer. 'We may say,' says Russell, 'as a matter of definition, that a thing changes when, however near to the thing an appearance of it may be, there are changes in appearances as near as, or still nearer to, the thing. On the other hand, we shall say that the change is in some other thing if all appearances of the thing which are at not more than a certain distance from the thing remain unchanged, while only comparatively distant appearances of the thing are altered.'[5] This rests on the assumption that the hypothetical observers who are massed in the immediate neighbourhood of the object are not themselves undergoing any significant change.

[1] *Mysticism and Logic*, p. 161.   [2] Ibid., p. 162.   [3] Ibid.
[4] *Our Knowledge of the External World*, p. 92.   [5] *Mysticism and Logic*, p. 164.

So far, in spite of the mention of change, the construction of space has proceeded without reference to time. The basis for the construction of 'the one all-embracing time' is taken by Russell, in my view correctly, to be 'the direct time relation of before and after' which obtains between two perspectives which belong to the same person's experience. Overlooking the fact that persons are not continuously conscious, he then defines a 'biography' as 'everything that is (directly) earlier or later than, or simultaneous with, a given "sensibile" ' and says that 'by this means, the history of the world is divided into a number of mutually exclusive biographies'.[1] How biographies are to be assigned to hypothetical persons is not explained. The correlation of the times in different biographies is achieved by starting with the principle that 'the appearances of a given (momentary) thing in two different biographies are to be taken as simultaneous',[2] and then emending it in such a way as to take account of the velocities of light and sound.

Since Russell is giving only the sketch of a theory, he does not attempt to deal in any detail with the problem which is presented by the existence of illusions and dreams. His main idea, which I again believe to be correct, is that what we come to classify as illusory sense-data, including those that occur when one is asleep, are not intrinsically distinguishable from those that we take to be veridical. Initially, all perspectives have the same status. If some are set aside, at a later stage, as being 'merely subjective', it is because they do not fit into the general scheme. Since the world is constituted by the mass of coherent sensibilia, which are patterned on sense-data, it is a necessary fact that most sense-data are veridical.

This whole theory, as I have said, is very ingenious, but it is open to serious objections on the ground of circularity. How, for example, are the perspectives which converge on the penny to be selected? Evidently, we cannot use the penny itself to collect the appearances which going to constitute it and define its position. If Russell does this, it can only be for convenience of exposition. The appearances have to be associated on the basis of their qualities. But since different pennies look very much alike, the only way in which we can hope to avoid mixing up sensibilia which belong to different things is by bringing in the other constituents of the perspectives in which they occur. It is, however, obvious that even in an unchanging world this will not be sufficient. If two pennies are placed separately on different pieces of cloth, of the same shade of colour, under conditions in which

[1] Ibid., p. 167.   [2] Ibid., p. 168.

the piece of cloth occupies one's whole field of vision, there will be nothing to show that the two perspectives do not belong to the same set. To put them into different sets, we should have to refer to adjacent perspectives. But how are we to determine what are adjacent perspectives? The obvious course would be to define adjacency in terms of minimal overlap and to say that two perspectives overlap if and only if they contain common constituents. But how are we then to determine, in the case of unperceived perspectives, whether or not they have constituents in common?

Even if this difficulty could be overcome, there is the further objection that the rule which Russell gives for the spatial ordering of perspectives which contain appearances of the same thing is not adequate for the purpose. He assumes that the apparent size of an object varies continuously with the distance, and its apparent shape with the angle, from which the object is viewed. But in the first place, this is contrary to the facts, unless apparent sizes and shapes are to be determined physiologically, which would mean that we were again making use of physical objects before we had constructed them; in the second place, more venially, it takes no account of the complexities which are introduced by the use of magnifying instruments; and in the third place, the size of an appearance, if it is not determined physiologically, can be measured only by the ratio of its extent to that of the perspective in which it occurs; it can, therefore, be increased by narrowing the angle of vision, even though the distance between the observer and the relevant object remains the same.

In the much more summary account which Russell gives of the construction of time, the circularity is obvious. To say that appearances in different biographies are to be taken as simultaneous if they belong to a given momentary thing is only another way of saying that they are to be taken as simultaneous if they belong to the same momentary state of a given thing; and this is to say no more than that they are simultaneous if they occur at the same moment. In fairness to Russell, it should, however, be added that if he really had succeeded in building up his system of objects in physical space, in such a way that different states of the system could be qualitatively distinguished, he could identify the momentary state of a thing with a given state of the system: he could then arrange the different states of the system in a temporal order according to the order of their partial representation in a given perspective; and then by taking account of the differences in the order in which these states, or the relevant parts of them, were

represented in different perspectives, and correlating these differences
with differences in the spatial position of the perspectives themselves,
he could without circularity arrive at an objective temporal order.
The trouble is that the spatial construction which would permit such
a development has not been achieved.

In face of all these difficulties, which beset the basis of the theory as
well as its superstructure, I believe that the right course is to try a
different line of approach. The trouble mainly arises, in my view,
through the introduction at the primitive level of questions which do
not there arise. We should take advantage of the assumption, on which
Russell himself relies in his later writings, that epistemological and
ontological priority need not go together. When we have developed
our physical theory out of its sensory material, whether by construction
or by postulation or by a mixture of the two, we can reinterpret our
primary set of objects in terms of the theory which is founded on
them. Unsensed sensibilia will give way to the physical objects with
which the theory replaces them, and sense-data, or percepts, if they
are not simply identified, as Russell proposes, with certain physiological
states, will remain, not as objects, but as constituents of a certain class
of mental processes, which will be predicated of those physical objects
to which consciousness can be attributed. Since these mental processes
will not be shared by different objects, there will *then* be a sense in which
percepts can be said to be private. On the other hand, so long as we
are concerned, as we now are, with the primary system, they cannot
be held to be either private or public: the question, as I said, does not
arise. This is true independently of the fact that percepts can be conceived as complexes of qualities: even if we retain particulars to support
the qualities, the existence of the particulars will still be established by
the fact that the qualities are manifested on a given occasion. Thus, in
speaking of percepts at this level, we commit ourselves to no more than
the fact that certain sensory qualities are presented. We are not committed to any view about the status of the objects, if any, in which the
qualities inhere: it is not implied that the qualities are presented *to*
anyone, and nothing whatsoever is implied about any relation in
which they may stand, or fail to stand, to physical objects. Since there
is no rule for the identification of these qualities, other than their being
simply recognised, a follower of Wittgenstein might, indeed, maintain that, in spite of all these disclaimers, we are still employing what
he would call a private language; but since, as I have shown elsewhere,[1]

[1] See my essay on 'Can There Be a Private Language?' in *The Concept of a Person.*

it is true of any but a purely formal language that the understanding of it depends in the last resort on just such processes of recognition, this objection need not worry us.

To obtain the equivalent of sensibilia, on the basis of our primitive percepts, all that is needed, I believe, is the projection of spatial and temporal relations beyond the sense-fields in which they are originally given. This is justified inductively, by our finding that qualitatively similar series of percepts appear sometimes in the same order as a given series, sometimes in the reverse order, very often with the counterparts to members of different sense-fields appearing in the same sense-field together. By a natural process, which I have described elsewhere,[1] we come to think of a percept of a given sort as being permanently obtainable at the end of one or other of a set of predominantly stable sensory routes, where these sensory routes consist in the prolongation of a current sense-field in one direction or another. These standardised percepts are not yet conceived as being the appearances of physical objects. For them to do the work which Russell initially requires of sensibilia, it is enough that they have fixed positions in the space which we construct by the general application of the process of spatial projection which I have outlined. The main reason why the construction can proceed in this relatively simple fashion, rather than by the highly complex ordering of a multitude of perspectives, is that we are not burdened with private spaces. There are, indeed, no perspectives to be correlated. What I have called a standardised percept is a type of sensory quality, or rather of a set of sensory qualities, of which it is open to anyone to perceive a specimen.

Having secured these landmarks, we then, by a further inductive inference, locate sensibilia in positions which we have not actually traversed. Finally, the great majority of actual percepts, or sense-data, are identified with the sensibilia of which they are now regarded as temporary phases. Thus, with some further adjustments, such as the fusion of visual and tactile space, the correlation with visual and tactile data of the data of the other senses, the disregarding of percepts which cannot be made to fit into the main pattern – percepts which in the light of the developed theory will be characterised as illusionary – and the introduction of temporal order in the way that I described, we arrive at the universe of sensibilia which I shall henceforward take to be Russell's primary system.

[1] See *The Origins of Pragmatism*, pp. 239–41, 322–3.

C. THE REQUIREMENT OF ATOMICITY

If this rewriting of Russell is acceptable, the position from which he must be held to start is not quite epistemologically primitive. The atomic propositions of the primary system are verified by the occurrence of percepts which they do more than simply monitor. They are the outcome of a process of interpretation which is capable of going astray; not every sense-datum is suitable for identification with a sensibile, and it may take us time to discover that such and such a one does not fit into the general pattern. Conversely, we are postulating many sensibilia that are not actually sensed. It therefore has to be admitted that the practical certainty which Russell attributes to atomic propositions does not belong to the propositions which we are now regarding as atomic but only to the more primitive propositions which monitor actual percepts. On the other hand, we shall see that Russell thinks of the totality of true atomic propositions as yielding a complete picture of the world, and this could hardly be thought to apply to a set of propositions which simply monitor percepts as they occur, without subjecting them to any more interpretation than is involved in listing their given properties, and without attempting to combine them into any sort of system. In favour of the system which I have assigned to Russell as a starting-point, I think it can be said both that it is broadly in accordance with his own approach and that it is the most primitive system that has any chance of being able to do the work that he requires.

The objects of this primary system are like the physical objects of common sense in that they have perceptible properties like shape and colour and a location in an 'objective' space and time. They are, however, unlike the physical objects of common sense in that they do not have dispositional or causal properties. Causality is a concept of the secondary, theoretical, system whose relation to the primary system has yet to be determined. It might be argued that I was mistaken in saying that our primary objects do not have dispositional properties, on the ground that the properties of colour and shape which we are attributing to them are themselves dispositional. To say that a thing is red and round is not to say that it looks red or that it looks round on any actual occasion, but rather that it would look red and round to a normal observer under normal conditions: in the case of the objects's shape there may be thought to be a tacit reference to the hypothetical results of certain processes of measurement; even in the case of its colour there could be thought to be a reference to the possible experiments which would determine the wave-length of the light which it reflected. But the answer to this is that these properties are not dispositional as they are represented in the system. In the first place, they are purely phenomenal properties; whatever may or may not be implied in the ordinary usage of words like 'red' and 'round', they are to be understood here, not in any sophisticated sense, but simply as standing for characteristic ways in which things look, and, it may be, feel. And secondly, though such properties may be dispositional with respect to the infrastructure of properties which merely monitor percepts, they are occurrent at our primary level: their assignment to a particular object at a particular time carries no implication with regard to its actual or hypothetical state at any other time, or with regard to the actual or hypothetical properties of any other object. It does allow for some variation in the character of the percepts by which the object's possession of the property is, or would be, discovered, but these variations, which will at a later stage be put down to some special characteristic of the observer or the environment, have already been discounted in the process of turning sense-data into sensibilia. It was this that I had in mind when I spoke of sensibilia as *standardised* percepts. Accordingly, if words like 'red' do not figure in the list of our primitive predicates, it will not be because the properties for which they stand are dispositional, but because they are not sufficiently specific.

The qualities of the primary objects have to be specific, in order that the objects should be simple. For what makes these objects simple, as we have seen, is not that they are denoted by logically proper names, but just that they have simple qualities. From the simplicity of their qualities, and the simplicity of the relations in which they stand to one another, it follows also that the propositions in which the objects figure must be atomic. What makes the propositions atomic is not just that they are expressed by sentences which contain no logical constants, but rather that when they are true they state logically independent facts. A consequence of this will be that from the fact that an object has a given quality it cannot be inferred that it bears any relation to any other object, and that from the fact that two objects stand in a given relation to one another it cannot be inferred that they stand or fail to stand in any relation to a third object. If we conceive of qualities as monadic relations and so enable ourselves to represent all atomic propositions as being relational, we can generalise this conclusion by saying that from the atomic fact that a given relation holds among n objects, it in no case follows that an $n+1$th object exists.

But now a difficulty arises with respect to the identification of these objects, since it seems obvious that one cannot predicate anything of an object unless it has been previously identified. Even if we allow demonstrative identification, it can serve only for a relatively small number of objects; the great majority of them will be identified only by description, either as uniquely possessing a certain combination of qualities, or as bearing a unique relation to some object or set of objects which have already been identified whether by their qualities or demonstratively. The use of relational descriptions for this purpose would, however, appear to be inconsistent with the requirement of atomicity, since at least one of the terms in any atomic proposition would have to be identified by means of its relation to some other object than those to which the proposition in question represented it as being related; otherwise the condition of previous identification would not be met. We have, therefore, to rely upon identification by quality. But now it must be remembered that the objects with which we are dealing are standardised percepts; and while, if we accept the identity of indiscernibles, we can, indeed, be sure with regard to different objects of this kind that there will be some differences of quality among the objects to which they are severally related, we have not only no logical but not even any empirical justification for supposing that they can always be differentiated by their intrinsic qualities alone.

It may be argued that this difficulty can be met by Russell so long as he retains the concept of substance. It will still be true that we have to identify most objects by description, in the sense that it is only by the descriptions which we give of them that we can make it intelligible, even to ourselves, what objects we are talking about, and it will still be true that some of these descriptions will have to be relational. It can, however, now be claimed that the use of relational descriptions for this purpose is not inconsistent with the requirement of atomicity, on the ground that the object's identity does not consist in its standing in any such relation to other objects, but only in its being the substance that it is. But the objection to this is that it meets the requirement of atomicity at the cost of robbing it of all its interest. That objects are mutually independent will now simply follow from the assumption that all their properties are external to them, an assumption which is itself grounded in the decision to postulate substance as something which merely supports a set of properties. It is misleading even to speak of a substance, in this sense, as 'something we know not what',[1] since this suggests, what Locke appears to have held, that it has a nature which we are unable to discover, whereas in truth, since whatever properties we did discover it to have would still be external to it, it would be more accurate to say that it had no nature at all. This is, indeed, the reason for trying to dispense with it, rather than subscribe to a criterion of identity of which we can never hope to make any practical use. In any case, whether or not we retain the concept of substance, we shall have to admit that it is only by their properties that any two objects can be descriptively distinguished, and it is therefore only if it is interpreted as bearing on the properties of objects that the thesis of their logical independence is worth discussing. I shall return to it after I have given an account of Russell's own attempt to eliminate substance, and I shall discuss this in the context of his general treatment of the problem of particulars and universals.

D. PARTICULARS AND UNIVERSALS

Until he published *An Inquiry into Meaning and Truth*, in 1940, Russell had always maintained that there was, as he put it, an ultimate dualism between universals and particulars. What he meant by this was that both particulars and universals were in some sense real, and that neither was reducible to the other. The considerations which led him to this view are set out most fully in an essay 'On the Relations of Universals and Particulars', which was his presidential address to the Aristotelian Society in the year 1911–12. It is reprinted in *Logic and Knowledge*.

The first problem to which Russell addresses himself in this essay is that of trying to make clear what the distinction between particulars and universals is. After remarking that one might seek to equate it with the distinction between percepts and concepts, or with that between things which exist in time and things which do not, or with that between things which are in only one place at one time and those that are either in many places at one time or not in any place at all, he argues that while all these distinctions may indeed reasonably be thought to obtain between what we commonly take to be particulars and what we take to be universals, they are subordinate to a more fundamental distinction which is that between 'terms which can only

---

[1] Cf. John Locke. *An Essay Concerning Human Understanding*, bk ii, chap. 23.

be subjects and terms which may be either subjects or predicates',
the terms which can only be subjects being particulars, and the others
universals. Consequently, the question whether there is an ultimate
dualism between universals and particulars turns on the question
'whether there is an ultimate simple asymmetrical relation which may
be called predication, or whether all apparent subject–predicate propositions are to be analysed into propositions of other forms, which do
not require a radical difference of nature between the apparent subject
and the apparent predicate'.[1] This still leaves it unclear when we are
to say that two terms differ radically in their nature, but we may hope
that it will become clear as the discussion proceeds.

   Some clue to what Russell has in mind may be found in his treatment
of what he describes as 'the theory which admits only particulars, and
dispenses altogether with universals': that is, 'the theory advocated by
Berkeley and Hume in their polemic against "abstract ideas" '.[2] That
he speaks of this theory as one which dispenses with universals already
shows that his distinction between subject and predicate is not just the
grammatical distinction, since he does not debit Berkeley and Hume
with the absurd suggestion that a significant sentence need never
consist in anything more than a string of substantives without any
verb. What he does represent them as holding is that expressions which
stand for perceptible qualities can be replaced by expressions which
stand for relations of resemblance, so that instead of saying of some
particular patch of colour that it is, for example, white, we are to say
that it is exactly similar in colour to some other patch, which itself
serves as the standard of whiteness. Russell allows that this would lead
to the elimination of universals, at least in this class of cases, if we were
able to suppose that ' "Exact likeness" is a simple relation, not analysable into community of predicates',[3] but objects that this supposition
leads to an infinite regress: for in order to avoid being a universal,
this relation of likeness will have to be likened to some standard relation
of likeness, and then the likeness between these relations will itself
have to be likened to some further model, and so *ad infinitum*. From
this he infers that the relation of likeness, at least, will have to be admitted as a universal, and he argues that if we are going to admit one
universal, there is no good reason not to admit more.

   It appears, then, that we can dispense with universals only if we can
avoid using any expression which stands for some repeatable feature of

---

[1] 'On the Relations of Universals and Particulars', in *Logic and Knowledge*, p. 109
[2] Ibid., p. 111.   [3] Ibid.

our experience, and clearly this is not going to be possible if we are to achieve anything more in the way of communication than making demonstrative gestures; indeed, even a demonstrative gesture, if it has a constant use, requires that there be some recurrent element, of danger or whatever, in the situations to which it refers. There is no question, therefore, but that Russell is right in saying that universals are, in this sense, indispensable. In fact, I think that he concedes too much to the nominalists when he says that it is possible, though point-less, to replace universal qualities by relations of exact resemblance between particulars. If the replacement is supposed to preserve identity of meaning, the move is not merely pointless but incorrect. A proof that to say of something A that it is white is not equivalent to saying that A exactly resembles in colour some other thing B, is that from the proposition that A is white it does not follow that B exists. Though this point is obvious, it is often missed because of the fact that, if B is white, one will not be applying the word 'white' to A correctly unless there is a resemblance in colour between A and B. But from the fact that one will not in these circumstances be using the word 'white' correctly unless A does resemble B, it by no means follows that when we do use it correctly we are asserting that A resembles B. There is a difference between formulating a rule of usage and actually using a word in accordance with the rule. To predicate a quality of an object is not to say anything at all about the semantic conditions which have to be satisfied for the choice of the predicate to be correct.

I may remark that the same objection holds against the theory that a proposition like 'A is white' can be transformed into 'A belongs to the class of white things', if this is understood to imply that the class con-tains other members besides A. This theory is also open to the more obvious objection that if its purpose is to be achieved, such classes will have to be defined by enumeration; from which it will follow that all true propositions of this kind are truths of logic, since to say that A is white will be equivalent to saying that A is identical with either A or B or C or . . . , where A, B, C, etc., are a list of white things. It will also follow that the meaning of a predicate varies with its extension, so that when I whitewash a green fence I change the meanings of the words 'green' and 'white', and that when I say that 'A is not white' I am implicitly mentioning every white thing in the universe, and deny-ing that A is identical with any of them. These objections do not, of course, apply if the class of white things is defined intensionally, but in that case the universal will not have been eliminated.

There is no doubt, then, that there are universals, both in the form of qualities and relations, if this is taken to mean no more than that we cannot dispense with expressions which pick out recurrent features of the world. Probably, most of those who have insisted on the reality of universals have meant something more than this, but what more they have meant has not been made clear. Russell himself, in *The Problems of Philosophy*, maintains that universals 'appear to have a being which is in some way different from that of physical objects, and also different from that of minds and that of sense-data', but he does not explain what he takes this being to be, beyond saying that it is not merely mental. His ground for saying that it is not merely mental is that if we consider such a true proposition as the proposition that Edinburgh is north of London, we are bound to admit that this spatial relation holds between these two places, independently of anybody's thinking that it does. This is, indeed, true, but it does not imply anything more than we have already acknowledged in saying that relational expressions pick out recurrent features of the world. It would appear, therefore, that if we want the question whether there are universals to be of any further interest, we must find a new interpretation for it. One possibility would be to interpret it, in accordance with Professor Quine's view of ontological commitment,[1] as the question whether we can avoid quantifying over properties. Another possibility would be to interpret it as the question whether we can give any more illuminating account of the meaning of general signs than by simply saying that they stand for abstract entities. As usual, when it comes to ontology, it is the negative answer to these questions that carries the affirmation of existence, and the positive answer its denial. We are to say that there are universals only if we *cannot* avoid quantifying over predicates or if we *cannot* give a more informative explanation of the meaning of general signs. I shall not enter into these questions here beyond remarking that the negative answer to them is not at all implied by there being universals, in the sense that we have found it necessary to admit. In particular, the fact that the theory which Russell attributes to Berkeley and Hume is false in the form in which he states it still leaves it open for it to provide at least a partial explanation of the way in which general signs function. Once again we have to distinguish between a statement in which a predicate is used to characterise an object, and a statement in which the conditions which govern the use of the predicate are described: and it is to statements of the second and not of the first class that the nominalist theory applies.

The problem with which Russell is mainly concerned in his Aristotelian Society paper is not, however, whether there are universals but whether there are particulars. It being established that we cannot manage without predicates, the question arises whether we can manage without subjects, or rather, whether we can construct our subjects wholly out of predicates. Russell goes into this question at some length and comes to the conclusion that particulars too are indispensable. His main argument rests on the premiss that 'It is logically possible for precisely similar things to co-exist in two different places'.[1] Then, the argument continues, either the places themselves, which cannot be supposed to differ in quality, must be counted as particulars or, if we are taking a relational view of space, we must distinguish the two places by a difference in the things which occupy them. But since, *ex hypothesi*, these things need not differ in quality, they must differ simply as particulars. It might be suggested that things which did not themselves differ in quality could be distinguished by a difference in the qualities of the things to which they severally stood in some spatial relation, but Russell's answer to this is that it depends on the proposition that one and the same thing cannot occur at the same time in different spatial contexts, and that this proposition already presupposes that the objects which it may be used to distinguish are numerically diverse.

Russell thinks that very much the same argument applies to minds. Having remarked that different particular beliefs may be distinguished only by the diversity of the subjects who hold them, he maintains that 'these subjects cannot be mere bundles of general qualities', on the ground that whatever qualities we ascribe to one of the subjects, it will remain logically possible that the others should have them as well. 'The subjects, therefore, must be regarded as particulars, and as radically different from any collection of those general qualities which may be predicated of them.'[2]

It seems to me that Russell's argument, in both its applications, simply comes down to a denial of the identity of indiscernibles. He is, I think, mistaken in saying that the proposition that two things must be different if they differ in their spatial contexts already presupposes that the things in question are numerically diverse. It does, indeed, appear to carry this presupposition, when it is expressed in this way, but in

[1] *Logic and Knowledge*, p. 113.   [2] Ibid., p. 120.

expressing it in this way Russell has forgotten his own theory of descriptions. We can say that there is an x such that x has the set of qualities q_{1-n} and stands in the relation R to y, which has such and such qualities, and also that there is an x which has the qualities q_{1-n} and does not stand in the relation R to y, and we can then infer from these propositions that there are at least two objects that have the properties q_{1-n}. The question is whether in a case where we cannot draw this inference, a case where the expression which follows the introductory phrase 'There is an x, such that' is exactly the same in the two assertions, and where it is understood that it would remain the same however long it were continued, it still makes sense to speak of there being two objects which have the properties concerned. If the principle of the identity of indiscernibles is false it does make sense, and if it is true it does not. In the same way, it is only if the principle of the identity of indiscernibles is false that it can make sense to talk of there being two persons who have all their properties in common, in the sense that 'everything concerning one of the subjects and otherwise only concerning universals'[1] is also true of the other.

As I said earlier, I do not know whether the principle of the identity of indiscernibles is true or false. My reason for thinking that it may be false is that fantasies like that of there being another universe which mirrors this one, or the Nietzschean idea of an infinite repetition of the world's history, do not strike me as being obviously self-contradictory or unintelligible. On the other hand, the fact that such hypotheses could not conceivably be verified still makes me doubt whether they really are significant, and I am also not sure that I find it intelligible that things should differ only in substance. On the other hand, I think that I can make sense of the idea that things which cannot be distinguished descriptively may be distinguished demonstratively. Accordingly, if I were persuaded that the principle of the identity of indiscernibles was false, I should not regard this as a sufficient ground for retaining the concept of substance, but rather for admitting purely demonstrative as well as descriptive identification.

In a postscript to the Aristotelian Society paper, which he added forty-three years after the paper was first published, Russell, who in the meantime had come to believe in the identity of indiscernibles, rejected his previous argument, at least in its application to things in space, on the ground that he had also come to think it false that there were 'any spatial or temporal relations which always and necessarily

[1] Ibid.

imply diversity'.¹ The theory from which he derives this conclusion is first set out in *An Inquiry into Meaning and Truth* and developed in greater detail in *Human Knowledge: Its Scope and Limits*. The position which it seeks to establish is that sensory particulars are after all dispensable: they can be replaced by complexes of qualities. For this purpose, Russell introduces the undefined relation of 'compresence' which holds between qualities which occur at the same time in the same total experience. So, Russell implies, if at one and the same time I am seeing something and hearing something else, remembering what happened yesterday and anticipating what will happen tomorrow, my visual and auditory percepts and whatever feelings or images form the psychological content of my remembering and anticipating are all mutually compresent. A 'complete complex of compresence' is then defined as one that satisfies the following two conditions: first, that all the members of the group are compresent and, secondly, that nothing outside the group is compresent with every member of it'.²

It is by reference to the complete complexes of compresence into which they enter that groups of qualities are individuated. In our construction of space, we have to reckon with the occurrence of the same quality, or even the same group of qualities, at different places at the same time, but if the group in question belongs to two different complete complexes, the principle that the same 'thing' cannot occupy two different places at the same time can still be maintained. It will, however, no longer be a necessary principle. It is not logically impossible that exactly the same complete complex should recur, so that it might be the case that a particular thing existed at a spatial or temporal distance from itself. It is for this reason that Russell now denies that spatial and temporal relations necessarily imply the diversity of their terms. Nevertheless, mainly on the ground of their containing memory experiences, he thinks it very improbable that complete complexes of compresence ever do recur, and therefore concludes that such empirical propositions as that the same thing is not to be found in two places at once, or that if *A* wholly precedes *B*, *A* and *B* are not identical, are sufficiently likely to be true for us to be justified in assuming them.

In view of the crucial part that the notion of a complete complex of compresence plays in this theory, let us look once again at the way in which it is defined. Though Russell intends that his relation of compresence should hold between qualities which are found together on a

¹ Ibid., p. 124.
² *Human Knowledge: Its Scope and Limits*, p. 294.

given occasion, he cannot stipulate that this be so, since his qualities do not have any instances. The occasions on which a quality might be said to be manifested have themselves to be created out of the uniqueness of the complexes in which the qualities participate. This means that the relation of compresence has to have the logical property of not being subject to composition. That is to say, if a quality q_1 is compresent with another quality q_2 and also compresent with a quality q_3, we are not permitted to infer that q_1 is compresent with q_2 *and* q_3. The reason for this is that if composition were allowed, Russell's criteria could not be counted on to yield the groups that he requires: for it might very well happen that a quality which he would want to exclude from the group as not being a property at the relevant time of the 'thing' which the group was meant to constitute was nevertheless compresent with every member of the group on some occasion or other: the ground for excluding it would be that it was not compresent with them all at once. However, if it seems too unnatural to say that a quality which is compresent with each member of a group may not be compresent with them all, we can obtain the desired result by introducing a new relation of joint compresence, which will require not fewer than three terms. This relation will be understood, though not of course defined, as holding between three or more qualities just when they are compresent on a given occasion. It will be stronger than the relation of compresence in that, while from the fact that three or more qualities are jointly compresent, it will follow that they are severally compresent, the converse will not necessarily obtain.

But even if we make this emendation, and even if we assume that no complete complex of compresence is ever exactly repeated, Russell's theory still will not give us quite what we want. The difficulty is that the uniqueness which he attributes to complete complexes, in their capacity as total momentary experiences, cannot plausibly be claimed for the combinations of qualities which characterise the neutral objects of our primary system. Russell himself extends his analysis to physical objects, or rather, to physical events, saying, somewhat cavalierly, that the relation of compresence which appears in psychology as 'simultaneity in one experience' appears in physics as 'overlapping in space-time'. He adds that if, as he maintains, one's thoughts are in one's head, 'it is obvious that these are different aspects of one relation', but claims that 'this identification' is not essential to his argument.[1] Whether or not it is essential, it is certainly not sufficient, since what he

[1] Ibid., p. 296.

would have to show, in order to obtain a high probability of uniqueness for his spatial complexes, would be not that simultaneity in one experience was a special case of overlapping in space-time, but that overlapping in space-time was a special case of simultaneity in one experience: and evidently he cannot show this, if only for the reason that most of the physical events which he postulates will not actually figure in anyone's experience: they will be, or be constructed out of, sensibilia, rather than sense-data, and their qualities will not be jointly compresent with any other qualities than those that make up the groups which determine the kinds of occurrences that they are. But then, as we have seen, there will be no justification for supposing that these groups are not duplicated.

So the problem of individuation remains. This does not mean that we cannot eliminate particulars. In this respect I see no good reason why a theory, along the lines of Russell's, should not be found to work. What it does mean is that having resolved our primary objects into complexes of qualities, we have still to find a way of distinguishing one object from another. At this point there are, I think, three courses that we could follow.

The first of these courses would be to expand each of our atomic propositions into a set of indefinite existentials. We should say that there was such and such a group of qualities and such and such another group and such and such another group, which were spatio-temporally related to each other in such and such ways, and we should continue the story to the point where we felt reasonably safe in assuming that the whole complex of complexes was not repeated. As our language would contain no referential expressions of any kind, it might be found necessary to have some pragmatic rules to do the work which I described earlier, when I was talking about names and demonstratives, as that of orientation. Atomicity would be preserved, in the sense that each existential proposition would be logically independent of all the rest. The objects themselves would have internal properties, to the extent that if a complex were defined by enumeration, its constituent qualities would be analytically contained in it, but the fact that such qualities were jointly compresent would, of course, always be contingent. Indeed, objects would be introduced only as a measure of economy. Any mention that was made of them could be expanded into a statement about simple qualities and their purely external groupings. The objections which might be taken to this procedure are that it assumes the identity of indiscernibles, and that it gives us no security of identification. Even if we do not demand logical security, we shall be uncertain in practice how far we have to go in order to reach the point where the threat of reduplication can be safely discounted.

A second course, which would meet these objections, would be to rely on demonstrative identification. Every primitive proposition would pick out the objects, that is to say, the complexes of qualities, to which it was intended to refer, by stating their spatio-temporal relations to something that was demonstratively indicated. As we have already seen, this would violate the condition of atomicity, if our primitive propositions had to attribute predicates to objects which had already been identified. We could, however, avoid this consequence by making indefinite existential statements and then adding the information that just one object, which satisfied the description that we had given, stood in such and such relations to whatever we indicated by our demonstrative sign. The loss of atomicity would then consist only in our acceptance of the rule that this information had always to be provided, and this might well be thought to be a price worth paying for obtaining uniqueness of reference. What makes the price excessive, in my view, is that our primary system becomes egocentric. Not only will this have the consequence that the same sequence of words, when uttered by different speakers, or even by the same speaker at different times, will seldom express the same proposition, since it is not very probable that the same objects will be indicated by the demonstrative signs, but the situation in which the speaker happened to be would always have to figure in the description of things to which it might not have any relevance. Having gone to so much trouble to secure the neutrality of our primary objects, we should, I think, take the further step of freeing our references to them from any dependence upon a particular point of view.

The third course, for which I have already expressed a preference, is to set up a spatio-temporal system in which identification is achieved by landmarks. If we want to run no risk of finding our points of reference reduplicated, we can have recourse, as I have said, to the device of choosing fictitious landmarks and postulating their uniqueness. Here again, there will be a small sacrifice of atomicity, if we are to follow Russell in casting our primitive propositions into the subject–predicate or relational forms. I regard this, however, as unimportant, first because it would be open to us, as in the case of demonstrative identification, to preserve at least the form of atomicity by resorting to indefinite existentials: secondly, because the relations of the objects to the landmarks will in all cases be contingent; and thirdly, because the choice of our landmarks, whether real or fictitious, will be arbitrary, in the sense that it will be dictated only by convenience; so that even if our propositions are so framed that in referring to an object we always imply the existence of something else, there will be no two objects of which it has to be true that referring to either implies the existence of the other. For these reasons, I do not think that the decision to dispense both with particulars, conceived as substances, and with demonstratives, subjects our primary objects to any serious loss of logical independence.

4 Logical Atomism – Part 2: Russell's Theories of Judgement and of Truth

A. PROPOSITIONS AND FACTS

So far, I have spoken only about the objects which figure, or may be taken to figure, in Russell's system of logical atomism, and about the atomic propositions of which they are sometimes said to be constituents. We have now to see what he makes out of these atomic propositions and how he supposes them to be related to the world which they depict.

In the first of his Logical Atomism lectures Russell draws the attention of his audience to what he describes as 'truisms so obvious that it is almost laughable to mention them'. These truisms are 'that the world contains *facts*, which are what they are whatever we may choose to think about them, and that there are also *beliefs*, which have reference to facts, and by reference to facts are either true or false'.[1] Although, in this passage, Russell speaks of beliefs as being true or false, he more commonly predicates truth and falsehood of propositions, and indeed immediately goes on to say that what he means by a fact is 'the kind of thing that makes a proposition true or false', remarking that he intends this to be an explanation, not a definition. This discrepancy is not important, since it is clear that if we are able to define truth either as an attribute of propositions, or as an attribute of beliefs, we can easily extend this definition to cover the other usage. A true belief can be defined as a belief in a true proposition; or, alternatively, a true proposition can be defined as one that is the object, or expression, of a true belief. Whichever way we put it, we shall have the problem of deciding what propositions are, and exactly how they are related to beliefs, and there will also be the question how belief itself is to be analysed.

In the lecture from which I have just quoted, Russell says that a proposition is just a complex symbol. This is, indeed, a legitimate, if nowadays not very common, use of the word 'proposition', and one

[1] *Logic and Knowledge*, p. 182.

that Russell quite often says that he adopts; but in fact he seldom adheres to it. For the most part, he actually uses the word in the sense now generally current, in which a proposition is equated not with an indicative sentence, but with what an indicative sentence may be used to mean: that is to say, not with a symbol but with something that is symbolised. If he really took propositions to be complex symbols, it would not be possible for him to say, as he frequently does, that a proposition like 'Socrates is wise' contains Socrates as a constituent: for he does not confuse Socrates with his name. It is true that he sometimes also denies that Socrates is a constituent of a proposition like 'Socrates is wise', but the explanation of this is not that he has changed his usage of the word 'proposition', but that he is identifying the proposition 'Socrates is wise' with the proposition which it would become when it had been fully analysed; and this proposition will contain only genuine objects as constituents, and not the logical fictions for which, as we have seen, Russell takes ordinary proper names to stand.

It may seem strange in any case that Russell should think of propositions, which are abstract entities, as literally containing concrete objects; but this is, in fact, a logical consequence of his assumption that the meaning of a name is the object which the name denotes. For clearly, if a proposition is to be identified with the meaning of an indicative sentence, and the sentence contains a name, the proposition must contain the meaning of the name; and from this, on Russell's assumption, the conclusion that the proposition contains an actual object follows. Since Russell also holds, as we have seen, that the universals for which predicates stand are in some sense real, he might easily think himself committed to believing in the reality of propositions as well.

This conclusion was, in fact, accepted by Russell in the period of his Platonic realism. It comes out most strongly in the series of three articles on 'Meinong's Theory of Complexes and Assumptions' which he published in *Mind* in 1904. He there takes the view that different mental attitudes, including even perception, as well as assumption and judgement, are all directed upon propositions, which subsist independently of anyone's having any attitude towards them. For a proposition to be perceived it is, in general, necessary that it be 'an existential proposition concerning a time which is very nearly the present',[1] but any proposition can be assumed or queried or judged to be true or false. Russell does have some hesitation about admitting the reality of false

[1] 'Meinong's Theory of Complexes and Assumptions', in *Mind*, XIII (1904) 216.

propositions, but decides in favour of it on the ground that false propositions can be the premisses of valid inferences and that he finds it impossible to maintain that a true negative proposition is an objective entity, if the corresponding affirmative proposition is not.[1] But on what grounds can truth or falsehood be ascribed to these objective entities? Russell declares that this presents no problem. He is content to say that the view which he believes to be correct is 'that some propositions are true and some false, just as some roses are red and some white', adding 'that belief is a certain attitude towards propositions which is called knowledge when they are true, error when they are false'.[2] He admits that this makes it rather difficult to explain why knowledge should be thought preferable to error – for why should one not have a greater affection for false propositions just as one may have a greater affection for white roses? – and decides that it is because of an ethical principle: 'It is good to believe true propositions and bad to believe false ones',[3] for which no further reason can be given.

This is a courageous example of the willingness to follow an argument wherever it leads, but the result was not one with which it could be expected that Russell would continue to be satisfied. Not only did the postulation of objective falsehoods offend against his growing 'feeling for reality', but as he points out in an essay 'On the Nature of Truth' which he contributed to the *Proceedings of the Aristotelian Society* for 1906–7, and reprinted, with some revisions, in his *Philosophical Essays* in 1910, his earlier theory 'has the further drawback that it leaves the difference between truth and falsehood quite inexplicable'.[4] 'We feel', he continues, 'that when we judge truly some entity "corresponding" to our judgement is to be found outside our judgement, while when we judge falsely there is no such "corresponding" entity'.[5] In other words, propositions, or at any rate empirical propositions, are made true or false by what actually goes on in the world, and the fatal objection to regarding truth and falsehood as intrinsic attributes of propositions, conceived as real entities, is that it leaves this entirely out of account.

But now, once Russell has admitted that false propositions are not real entities, he has to conclude that true propositions are not real entities either, since it cannot be supposed to make any difference to the status of a proposition, as an entity, what its truth-value happens to be. He is still able to hold that both true and false propositions have

---

[1] Ibid., pp. 516–23.   [2] Ibid., p. 523.   [3] Ibid., p. 524.
[4] *Philosophical Essays*, p. 52.   [5] Ibid.

real constituents, and also that there are real entities, as distinct from their constituents, which make them true or false. These entities are facts, in which the constituents of true propositions, or at any rate of true atomic propositions, are arranged in the way that the propositions represent them to be. Being a real entity, a fact is not identical with a true proposition. It is not, Russell argues, even what the proposition means, since the proposition must have the same meaning whether it be true or false, and in the case where it is false, there will be no fact to be its meaning. But if the fact and the true proposition have the same constituents, arranged in the same manner, how can they fail to be identical? How can it be supposed that exactly the same combination of elements yields two different entities, one real and the other not?

An obvious way out of this difficulty, if one is to continue to conceive of a proposition as the meaning of a sentence, would be to drop the assumption that the meaning of a word is the concrete or abstract object that it stands for. Russell does not quite take this course: what he does is to maintain the assumption, but render it innocuous. He is still prepared to say, for example, that the meaning of the English word 'red' is identical with the colour red, but no longer regards this as a sufficient account of the meaning of the word. It tells us what the word means, but not what is meant by saying that this is what it means. In the same way, to say that such and such a sentence means such and such a proposition is one way of giving the meaning of the sentence, but it contributes nothing to the analysis of the fact that it has this meaning. When Russell tries to give such an analysis in his later writings, propositions, in the sense of which we have been speaking, play no part in it at all. He continues to use the word 'proposition', occasionally still making it stand for a set of verbal or pictorial symbols; but when he does not identify propositions with symbols, he treats them as psychological or behavioural accompaniments of the use of sentences, rather than as entities which stand between sentences and facts. I will go into this more fully when I come to Russell's analysis of belief which is closely linked, as we shall see, with his later theories of meaning and of truth.

Propositions, then, do not 'belong to the objective world', but facts do. Once more it is difficult to interpret this existential statement. Russell also speaks, at various times, of the objective world as consisting of events and it is not clear whether he thinks that there are facts as well as events, in the sense that a complete inventory of the world would have to include them both, or whether, what would

appear more sensible, he would regard speaking in terms of events and
speaking in terms of facts as alternative ways of telling what is in effect
the same story. This point is not decided by the arguments which he
gives in favour of there being facts, which are, first, that a true description of the world, or any part of it, cannot consist simply in a list of
objects and, secondly, that something's being the case is not, in general,
dependent on anyone's believing it to be so. It may be, indeed, that
in saying that facts belong to the objective world, he means no more
than that both these arguments are valid; and in that case his claim
that he was only putting forward a truism would be justified.

Facts can be asserted, or denied, or doubted, or willed, or wished,
but they cannot, in Russell's view, be named. One might, he thinks,
be tempted to regard propositions, or the sentences which express
propositions, as names for facts, but the objection to this, which
Russell says was pointed out to him by Wittgenstein, would be that
there are two propositions corresponding to each fact. To illustrate this,
he supposes it to be a fact that Socrates is dead. We shall see that,
strictly speaking, this is not a fact for Russell but rather an assemblage
of facts: but it will do for an example. Then, corresponding to this
fact there will be the proposition that Socrates is dead and the proposition that Socrates is not dead, the one being true to the fact and
the other false to it. What Russell takes these relations of being true
or false to a fact to consist in, we shall see when we come to his theory
of truth.

It may not be immediately obvious that the doctrine that a fact
has two propositions corresponding to it entails that facts cannot be
named. Why should we not say that the sentence which expresses
the true proposition of the pair names the fact to which they both
correspond? The answer is that such a sentence could not be a logically
proper name, because it would still have a sense, and indeed the same
sense, even though the corresponding fact did not exist. In short, what
prevents a sentence from being a name is that the proposition which it
expresses may be either true or false and, as Russell puts it, that 'there
is nothing in the nature of the symbol'[1] to show us which it is. A point
which he overlooks here is that this would not apply to sentences
which express necessary propositions: for in their case, presumably, it
does depend only on the sense of the sentence whether or not the proposition which it expresses is true to the corresponding fact. On the
other hand, if it is a mark of a logically proper name that it has to have

[1] *Logic and Knowledge*, p. 187.

a denotation in order to have any meaning, even sentences which state necessary facts will not qualify as names, unless we are going to hold that sentences which express necessarily false propositions are meaningless: and while this view has been held, it does not appear to have anything much to recommend it.

From his conclusion that facts cannot be named, Russell seems to draw the inference that nothing can be predicated of them. At least he says that 'You can never put the sort of thing that makes a proposition to be true or false in the position of a logical subject'.[1] He has not, however, given any reason why facts cannot be described: and if a fact has been described, there seems to be no good reason why one should not go on to predicate something of it. His point, therefore, may be only that if we expand any reference to a fact, in accordance with the theory of descriptions, the denoting phrase, by which the reference is made, will not, as we have seen, remain as a subject-expression but will be transformed into a predicate. At the same time it has not yet been shown that we can dispense with quantification over propositions, so that even if facts cannot be named, they could still be logical subjects in the sense of being the things that satisfied a special set of propositional functions. They could not, indeed, be the logical subjects of atomic propositions, though even this does not follow merely from their not being denoted by logically proper names, since we have seen that this is true also of the 'sensibilia' which Russell requires for his primary system. It does, however, follow from the theory of types.

Having said something, though perhaps not enough, about the status of facts, Russell goes on to say that there are a great many different kinds of them. We shall see, in a moment, that this is an exaggeration. Russell does not make provision for there being a great many different kinds of facts, though he does allow for negative as well as positive facts and for general as well as particular ones. What he does not hold is that there is a fact corresponding to every pair of propositions, in the sense that if we take two propositions which are not logically equivalent, there will necessarily be different facts to which they and their negations are respectively true or false. For example, we do not have to admit conjunctive facts. There may be the fact that p and the fact that q, but there need not be, in addition to them, the fact that p and q. Neither does Russell believe that there are disjunctive facts. If 'p or q' is a true proposition, it may be true in virtue of the fact that

[1] Ibid., p. 188.

p, or the fact that q, or possibly both the fact that p and the fact that q, but we have no ground for supposing that there is a distinct fact that p or q. Here, indeed, Russell does not go further than saying that 'It does not look plausible that in the actual objective world there are facts going about which you could describe as "p or q"',[1] with the proviso that it is not always safe to rely on what looks plausible. This leaves us with the difficulty of seeing how we could possibly determine whether there really were such facts or not – a difficulty which Russell does nothing to resolve. He simply follows his usual policy of dispensing with extra entities if he finds that he can manage without them, as in this instance he obviously can. It is in the same spirit that he refrains from asserting the existence of facts straightforwardly corresponding to propositions like 'Socrates is dead' which refer to what he calls 'logical fictions', that is to say, to entities which undergo reduction when the propositions into which they enter are further analysed. The only sense in which these propositions and their negations can be said to correspond to facts is that there will be a set of facts corresponding to the atomic propositions into which they are finally resolved.

Since Russell's policy is always to diminish his ontological commitments so far as possible, it may appear strange that he admits negative facts. Again he will not say positively that there are such things, and again he does not tell us how the issue could be settled one way or the other, but he does say that he thinks it likely that there are. The reason why he thinks it likely is that he does not see what else but a negative fact can be supposed to make an atomic proposition false. The obvious answer to this is that we can suppose an atomic proposition p to be made false by the positive fact which verifies some other atomic proposition q with which p is incompatible. Russell considers this answer and objects first, that the fact that p and q are incompatible might itself be considered negative, and secondly, that since incompatibility is a relation between propositions, inasmuch as all facts must be mutually consistent, you get rid of negative facts, if you do get rid of them, only at the much greater cost of assuming the reality of propositions: for 'It is quite clear', he now says, 'that propositions are not what you might call "real". If you were making an inventory of the world, propositions would not come in.'[2] But these objections are unsound. If incompatibility is a relation between propositions, as indeed it is, and if facts must have real constituents, and if propositions are not real, then what follows is not that the incompatibility of two propositions

[1] Ibid., p. 209.   [2] Ibid., p. 214.

is a negative fact, or that it is a fact implying the reality of propositions, but that it is not a fact at all. This would, indeed, be a very awkward conclusion if it implied that propositions of the form 'p is incompatible with q' could never be true, but unless the word 'fact' is taken as being simply equivalent to 'true proposition', which is not Russell's usage, there is no need for it to imply this. All that it need imply is that there must be some other way of accounting for the truth of propositions of this sort than by there being facts to which they truly correspond; they must be among those propositions which depend on other propositions for their truth. But then, since all that is required for the elimination of negative facts at the atomic level is that these propositions about incompatibility be true, not that there be facts corresponding to them, and since Russell holds, as we shall see, that the truth of all other propositions depends upon the truth of atomic propositions, it would appear that he can after all dispense with negative facts.

It should be added that Russell himself arrived at this conclusion in his book on *Human Knowledge: Its Scope and Limits*, though not by the same line of argument. His suggestion there is that a judgement of perception like 'This is not red' can be interpreted as expressing disbelief in 'This is red', 'disbelief being a state just as positive as belief'. Then 'A sufficient (not necessary) condition for the truth of disbelief in "This is red" is that the disbelief should be caused by a "this" having to red the relation of positive dissimilarity.'[1] But the objection to this is that we could equally well interpret the judgement that this is red as expressing disbelief in 'This is not red'. If our concern is only to eliminate the sign 'not', there are various ways of achieving it, including the adoption of Ramsey's proposal to negate sentences by writing them upside-down; but if there is a problem about the analysis of negative statements, these devices do not go to the root of it.

It may also be noted that if there is a problem about incompatibility, the admission of negative facts does not solve it; for whatever view we take about negative facts, the difficulty that a proposition like 'p is incompatible with q' appears to have propositions rather than facts for its constituents will still remain. This is, indeed, only a special case of a difficulty which applies to all necessary propositions. They cannot have facts for their constituents, if only because their truth does not require that the propositions which enter into them be true: in the case

[1] *Human Knowledge; Its Scope and Limits*, p. 125.

where they relate propositional functions, it again is not necessary for their validity that the functions be satisfied. But from this it will follow, on Russell's principles, that, in any straightforward sense, there are no necessary facts. It will also follow, since the disqualification of propositions presumably extends to propositional functions, that the question what the constituents of necessary propositions are becomes difficult to answer. In the fifth of his Logical Atomism lectures, Russell admits that 'It seems as though all the propositions of logic were entirely devoid of constituents',[1] but then goes on to say that he does not think this can be quite true. Instead he tentatively adopts the view that they have forms as their constituents, not indeed their own forms, since he holds that the form of a proposition is never a constituent of it, but the forms of other propositions, or perhaps of propositions in general. He does not develop this any further, nor does he explain how the forms of propositions can be real, when propositions themselves are not.

What Russell has overlooked here is that if he is not going to hold that propositions are genuine entities, he is no longer under any obligation to supply them with real constituents. He is then left only with the problem of accounting for the truth of necessary propositions in some other way than by saying that they correspond to necessary facts. He does not discuss this question in his later writings, beyond saying, in the introduction to the second edition of *The Principles of Mathematics*, that the propositions of mathematics, and by implication the propositions of logic, must have the property which Wittgenstein calls 'tautological' and Carnap 'analytic'. Though he goes on to say that 'it is by no means easy to get an exact definition of this characteristic',[2] the reference to Wittgenstein, and a similar reference in *The Analysis of Matter*, suggest that he agrees with Wittgenstein's characterisation of a tautology, as a proposition which is compatible with every possible distribution of truth and falsehood among atomic propositions. We shall, indeed, see in a moment that this is the view which naturally results from his logical atomism.

Even if this definition of a tautology is acceptable, it does not dispose of the problem, since it applies only to those necessary propositions that owe their necessity to the operations of logical constants. How Russell would deal with necessary propositions which do not fall into this category is never made clear, but there is no doubt that he accepts the analytic–synthetic distinction, and some evidence that he would be content with the characterisation of an analytic proposition

---

[1] *Logic and Knowledge*, p. 239.   [2] *The Principles of Mathematics*, 2nd ed., p. ix.

as one the truth of which depends only on the meaning of the words by which it is expressed. If the meaning of logical constants is defined in terms of the truth-possibilities which they leave open, this characterisation would also cover tautologies, in Wittgenstein's sense. But even if this approach were itself free from difficulty, which it notoriously is not, it would not be enough for Russell, since, in his later works at any rate, he takes the view that not all necessary propositions are analytic. The example which he gives in *An Inquiry into Meaning and Truth* is the proposition: 'At a given time and in a given visual field, if the colour A is at the place θ, ϕ, no other colour B is at this place.'[1] He is sure that this is not an empirical generalisation, and equally sure that it is not logically true. 'Red and blue', he says, 'are no more *logically* incompatible than red and round.'[2] He does not actually draw the conclusion that such propositions are synthetic *a priori*, perhaps because he realises that to say this is to say nothing positive at all, but he does not have anything else to offer. In this, it must be said, he is not alone. I have, indeed, tried elsewhere to account for such incompatibilities in a way that shows them to be, if not logical, at any rate semantic,[3] and although I am not entirely satisfied with my explanation, I am not able to improve upon it.

In arguing that the incompatibility of atomic propositions, whatever explanation may be given of it, allows us to dispense with negative facts, I am not implying that we can dispense with negative propositions, in the sense of being able to reduce them to affirmatives. In the article in which I wrote about incompatibility I also tried to show that the question what is to be counted as a negative proposition is not so straightforward as it might appear, but in any account of negation which is at all intuitively acceptable, we shall find, what indeed seems obvious, that a sentence which expresses a negative proposition cannot be replaced by a sentence which expresses an affirmative proposition without alteration of meaning. For instance, if, as I suggested in my essay, the distinction between what are ordinarily counted as affirmative and what are ordinarily counted as negative propositions predominantly coincides with the distinction between propositions which are more or less specific, it is evident that propositions which have different degrees of specificity cannot be equivalent. There are, indeed, those who believe that the elimination of negative propositions can be accomplished by turning them into disjunctions, but even if

---

[1] *An Inquiry into Meaning and Truth*, p. 82.   [2] Ibid.
[3] See my article on 'Negation', in my *Philosophical Essays*, pp. 54–9.

there were anything to be gained by this manœuvre, which there clearly is not if there are not to be disjunctive facts, it would not preserve equivalence. To begin with, it is very implausible to suggest that in saying, for example, that something is not red, one is implicitly mentioning every other colour: and secondly, as Russell points out, even if such a disjunction were finite, we should need the additional statement that there were no other alternatives.

There are some indications that Russell regarded the impossibility of any such elimination of negative propositions as a further argument in favour of the admission of negative facts, but if this was his view, he was mistaken. There is no more difficulty in allowing that a negative proposition is made true by an affirmative proposition, which entails it but is not entailed by it, than there is in allowing that a disjunctive proposition is made true by a simple proposition which entails it but is not entailed by it; and since the falsehood of any such proposition always implies the truth of some other, particular facts are needed by Russell only for the work of making atomic propositions true. He will still be able to maintain his principle that every fact has two propositions directly corresponding to it, one of them atomic, and the other, its negation, not. What he will not be able to maintain will be the converse principle that every atomic proposition is a member of such a pair; for when the atomic proposition is false, neither it nor its negation will directly correspond to a fact; they will correspond, only indirectly, in their different ways, to some fact to which another atomic proposition, and its negation, directly correspond.

The same considerations apply to the admission of general facts, for which Russell also argues. It is clear that universal propositions are not equivalent to conjunctions of singular propositions – to say that all men are mortal is not to say what men there are – and it is also clear that indefinite existential propositions, propositions which assert merely that there are things of such and such a kind without spatio-temporally locating them, are not equivalent to disjunctions of atomic propositions. Nevertheless, it is only on the truth of atomic propositions that the truth of general propositions, of either of these forms, depends; so that, here again, the only facts that are asserted are facts that have atomic propositions directly corresponding to them. Russell's argument in favour of there being 'general facts as distinct from and over and above particular facts' is, in effect, that no list of singular propositions entails a universal proposition, without the additional premiss that the list is exhaustive. Just as the proposition 'All men are mortal' does not follow from 'Socrates is mortal', 'Plato is mortal', and so on, without the premiss that the men enumerated are all the men that there are, so, Russell says that 'When you have enumerated all the atomic facts in the world, it is a further fact about the world that those are all the atomic facts there are about the world, and that is just as much an objective fact about the world as any of them are'.[1] But the answer to this is that if you have said of each man that he is mortal, you have made a set of assertions which, when analysed out, will cover all the facts that make 'All men are mortal' true. All that you have not done is express the second-order proposition that these are all the facts in question. And similarly, if you were able to list every atomic fact, you would have given a complete description of the world. What you would have failed to do would be to say that your description was complete, but the description would not cease to be complete through not being said to be so.

We see, then, that within the framework of Russell's logical atomism there is no call to burden the universe with even the three kinds of facts for which he explicitly argues, let alone the many different kinds that he begins by saying that there are: there is need only for one. Moreover, facts of this simple kind will have the same character, however we choose to formulate our atomic propositions. Whether we bring in demonstratives, or rely on spatio-temporal landmarks, or try to make do without any form of definite linguistic reference, our propositions will be made true or false by facts to the effect that such and such groups of qualities are jointly compresent at such and such places and times. These are the only facts that there are, and it is in their totality that the world is held to consist.

B. THE THESIS OF EXTENSIONALITY

It may be objected to what I have just said that even if Russell is mistaken in thinking that he has to admit facts which would be stated by the negation or generalisation of atomic propositions, and even if it be granted that all propositions which refer to what he calls logical fictions can be reduced to propositions about his primary objects, it still will not follow that there are only atomic facts. Why, even within the sphere of primary objects, should there not be facts which are

[1] *Logic and Knowledge*, p. 236.

non-atomic, in the sense that our atomic propositions do not suffice to state them? This objection is justified in that the conclusion that there are only atomic facts depends on a further premiss which I have not yet made explicit. This premiss is that all the logical operations which can legitimately be performed on atomic propositions are truth-functional. What Russell calls molecular propositions are obtained from atomic propositions either by quantification, or by the operations of negation, conjunction or disjunction, all of which can be defined in terms of the single function 'p/q' which can be interpreted either as having the force of 'neither p nor q', or, yielding formally different but equivalent definitions, as having the force of 'not both p and q'. Russell himself takes the second option, characterising 'not both p and q' as 'p is incompatible with q'.[1] This is misleading in that it is intended to mean no more than that p and q are not in fact both true, not that it is logically impossible that they should both be true: but throughout his Logical Atomism lectures, Russell is careless in his use of modal terms, as when he speaks of propositional functions as being necessary, possible and impossible, when all that he means is that they are respectively satisfied by all, or some, or no values of the variable.[2] There may, however, be a suggestion here that Russell has no use for modal concepts, in any stronger sense than this, and it is, indeed, true that as ordinarily conceived they play no part in his system. On the other hand, they would appear to come in when one speaks about the system, as when it is said that different primary qualities are logically incompatible. But for the present all that concerns us is that they are not needed for the representation of any empirical matter of fact.

Since the truth or falsehood of any proposition which is constructed by means of the 'p/q' operator, on either of its interpretations, depends only on the truth or falsehood of the propositions on which it operates, and since we have seen that the same applies to the propositions which result from quantification, we are able to conclude that the truth-value of every molecular proposition is entirely determined by the truth-values of the atomic propositions out of which it is generated. This is, indeed, what is meant by saying that molecular propositions are all truth-functional. There is here a very close parallel between Russell's system and that which Wittgenstein sets out in his *Tractatus Logico-Philosophicus*, the main difference being that Wittgenstein conceives not only of atomic facts but also of atomic propositions as being logically independent, with the result that, unless an intolerable

---

[1] Ibid., p. 210.   [2] Ibid., p. 231.

restriction is to be placed on the choice of primitive predicates, his atomic propositions must be cast in a form in which they do not carry any definite reference. In both cases, the effect of making all molecular propositions truth-functional will be that to assert a molecular proposition becomes equivalent to asserting that such and such a distribution of truth-values obtains among the relevant atomic propositions. It was for this reason that I said earlier that the acceptance of Wittgenstein's characterisation of a tautology would be in line with Russell's logical atomism. For in a system of this sort it is natural to take tautology and contradiction as limiting cases, a tautology being a proposition which is true for every possible distribution of truth-values among atomic propositions, and a contradiction one which is false.

A system is said to be extensional when the replacement in any sentence of a nominative expression by another which has the same reference, or a predicative expression by another which is satisfied by the same objects, or the expression of a proposition by that of another which has the same truth-value, always leaves the truth-values of its propositions unchanged. It may be inferred from what we have already seen of it that Russell's system is intended to be a system of this kind. The thesis of extensionality, to which Russell hesitantly subscribes, is that such a system is adequate for the conveyance of all significant information.

Notoriously, this thesis is exposed to very serious objections. A great deal, indeed almost the whole, of our ordinary discourse appears to run counter to it. Consider, for example, the dispositional concepts which normally enter into the definition of the physical objects of common sense. It is natural to analyse them in terms of open conditionals; to say that an object is soluble is to say that if at any time it is immersed in water it dissolves. But our system admits only the material conditional: 'if p then q' is to be read as 'not-p or q', which is true in all circumstances except when p is true and q is false. But are we prepared to say that a proposition like 'This table is soluble' is true, just because the table never is immersed in water? The same difficulty extends, indeed, to all unfulfilled conditionals. Since Hannibal did not march on Rome after the battle of Cannae, any sentence beginning 'If Hannibal had marched on Rome' will express a true proposition, whatever we put for the apodosis. Yet the proposition 'If Hannibal had marched on Rome after the battle of Cannae, the Romans would have escaped on winged horses' would not ordinarily be taken to be true. Another set of apparent counter-examples is to be found in

propositions involving modal concepts. For instance, it is true that my
son is necessarily male, because being male is part of what is meant by
being someone's son, but it is not true that the last person who spoke
to me is necessarily male, even though as a matter of fact my son was
the last person who spoke to me. Finally, the thesis appears to be
violated on every count by propositions which describe mental
attitudes. To take only the most obvious example, the true proposition
that A believes p, where p is itself true, is clearly not going to have the
same truth-value, no matter what other true propositions are substituted for p. I am sure that I believe many true propositions, but there
are certainly many that I do not believe. I do not claim to be omniscient.

From this it is clear that if it is to satisfy the requirement of extensionality, our ordinary discourse will have, to use Quine's useful phase,
to be severely regimented.[1] There are various ways in which this
might be attempted. The procedure which I should favour would to be
concentrate the difficulties into a single area. I think that the problems
set by modal as well as dispositional concepts can be resolved into the
problem of the interpretation of conditionals, and that this problem
can be resolved, in its turn, into that of the analysis of propositions
about mental attitudes. The way in which modal concepts are connected with conditionals is through the concept of a law or a rule. We
speak of something as a possibility when we do not know of any law
with which it would be incompatible. This account has the advantage
of bringing logical and physical possibility under the same general
heading. What is logically possible is what is compatible with the laws
of logic, or, more generally, with the rules of our language: what is
physically possible is what is compatible with the laws of nature. Then,
logical necessity can be represented as depending on our inability to
conceive of counter-examples, and physical necessity on the hypothesis
that none of the logically possible counter-examples would in fact occur.
Now it is characteristic of every true proposition that there are in fact
no counter-examples to it; what distinguishes a generalisation of law
from a mere generalisation of fact is that it is conceived as holding
good for hypothetical instances: it is construed as entailing unfulfilled
conditionals, in a way that the generalisation of fact does not. But a
difference which relates only to hypothetical instances is not a difference
with regard to anything that actually happens. Consequently, the
question whether a given proposition is a generalisation of fact or a
generalisation of law has no bearing on its factual content. What it

[1] See W. V. Quine, *Word and Object*, chap. v.

bears on, as I have tried to show elsewhere,[1] is our attitude towards the proposition. To treat a proposition as a generalisation of law is to conceive of it as still being true in an altered world, in which we should not expect it to be true, if we were treating it merely as a generalisation of fact. A generalisation of law, in the strongest sense of the term, may therefore be said to be a universal proposition towards which our attitude is such that we conceive of it as remaining true under any imaginable alteration to the world which is logically compatible with it. I repeat, however, that the counter-factual validity which we attribute to such a proposition adds nothing to its factual content. No matter what we may imagine as happening in merely hypothetical circumstances, what makes it true, if it is true, is just that it holds in every actual instance.

Similarly, I want to say that the factual content of an unfulfilled conditional does not go beyond that of the corresponding material conditional. If we were to insist on treating propositions about what would have happened if Hannibal had marched on Rome as statements of fact, we should have to count them all as true, just for the reason that Hannibal did not march on Rome; and the same would apply to the proposition that this table is soluble, in the event that it is never immersed in water. The reason why, in many cases, we find it more natural to call them false than true is that we judge them by a different standard. We treat them not as statements of fact, but as the expression of conditional beliefs, and we call them false because we find these beliefs unacceptable. What makes these beliefs unacceptable is that they do not accord with our general conception of the way the world works. We have, as Peirce put it,[2] a system for the arrangement of facts, in terms of which we can pronounce on hypothetical as well as actual cases. But to speak of our having a system for the arrangement of facts is to speak of our holding a set of conditional beliefs. This is not, indeed, to say that unfulfilled conditionals can be translated into propositions about people's beliefs, but the force of such conditionals, the part that they play in our language, is to be explained in terms of what is involved in believing them, and the reasons for which such beliefs are held to be or not to be acceptable. The result, if this line of approach is correct, is that we can explain away intensional concepts if we can show that they do not have to enter into the analysis of mental attitudes, and, most importantly, into that of belief.

[1] See my essay on 'What is a Law of Nature?', in *The Concept of a Person*, pp. 209–35.
[2] See C. S. Peirce, *Collected Papers*, x 403.

It might be said that Russell tacitly accepted this conclusion, since the only example which he actually gives of an apparent violation of the thesis of extensionality is that of propositions like '*A* believes that *p*'. It would, however, probably be more accurate to say that he ignored the other problems with which I have just been trying to deal. The only question which seems to have troubled him in this connection, apart from the analysis of belief, was that of ensuring the parallelism between statements about propositional functions and statements about classes. For this it is required that statements about propositional functions should be extensional, since if there were a case in which the replacement of one propositional function by another, which was satisfied by the same objects, changed the truth-value of the proposition in which the replacement was made, the assumption that in talking about these propositional functions one was talking about the class with which they were both associated would lead to the contradictory conclusion that one and the same predicate both did and did not apply to this class. Admitting that on the face of it not all statements about propositional functions are extensional, Russell meets this difficulty by supposing that 'If you have any statement about a function which is not extensional, you can always derive from it a somewhat similar statement which is extensional',[1] and then ruling that it is this derived extensional statement that is to be regarded as being about the associated class. What is stated by the derived statement is that there is a function of which it is true both that it is formally equivalent to the intensional function, in the sense that it is satisfied by the same arguments, and that what is predicated of the intensional function also holds of it.

How this is meant to work is illustrated by Russell in his *Introduction to Mathematical Philosophy*.[2] He takes as an example the proposition 'I believe that all men are mortal', regarded as a function of '*x* is human'. This is not itself an extensional function, since one may believe that all men are mortal without, for example, believing that all rational animals are mortal if one happens not to believe that men are coextensive with rational animals. We can, however, derive an extensional function by replacing our original statement with the statement 'There is a function formally equivalent to "*x* is human" and such that I believe that whatever satisfies it is mortal'. Evidently, if it is in fact the case that men are coextensive with rational animals, this statement will have the same truth-value as that which is obtained from it by substituting '*x* is a rational animal' for '*x* is human'. The method of

---

[1] *Logic and Knowledge*, p. 266.   [2] *Introduction to Mathematical Philosophy*, p. 187.

this derivation is just to transfer a function which has secondary occurrence into a position where it has primary occurrence.

There is no doubt that this device preserves extensionality, but only at the cost of altering the original statement rather more considerably than Russell seems to acknowledge. How great the difference is may be brought out more clearly by another example. Consider the proposition 'Smith knows that Dickens wrote *David Copperfield*'. This is intensional, since Smith may very well know that Dickens wrote *David Copperfield* without knowing, with regard to each of the other works of Dickens, that Dickens wrote it. The corresponding extensional proposition is: 'There is a function formally equivalent to "*x* wrote *David Copperfield*" and such that Smith knows that Dickens satisfies it.' This proposition will be true if the original proposition is true, since the function '*x* wrote *David Copperfield*' is formally equivalent to itself, and it will have the same truth-value as any proposition which is obtained from it by substituting for *David Copperfield* the name of any other book by Dickens, let us say *Our Mutual Friend*, since even if Smith does not know that Dickens wrote *Our Mutual Friend*, there will be some function formally equivalent to the function '*x* wrote *Our Mutual Friend*' which he must know that Dickens satisfies if there is any single book by Dickens that he knows him to have written. On the other hand, although the derived proposition is entailed by the original proposition, it obviously does not provide the same information, and indeed may not even have the same truth-value. All that it states with regards to Smith is that there is one book which he knows that Dickens wrote: it does not state which book this is. Consequently, it may be true even when the original proposition 'Smith knows that Dickens wrote *David Copperfield*' is false, since the fact that Smith did not know that Dickens wrote *David Copperfield* would not preclude there being some other book by Dickens which he did know him to have written.

This is not an objection to Russell's procedure, since he does not claim that his derived propositions are adequate paraphrases of their originals, let alone translations. All that he is concerned with is to preserve the association of propositional functions with classes: and this he achieves. Nevertheless, it is clear that he needs to do a great deal more if he is to uphold the general thesis of extensionality. His derivation of extensional from intensional function is no substitute for an extensional analysis of belief.

C. RUSSELL'S THEORIES OF JUDGEMENT

The question of the analysis of belief, or, as he has sometimes preferred to put it, the analysis of judgement, is indeed one to which Russell gave a good deal of attention; and he offered different answers to it at different stages in his philosophical career. He began, as we have seen, with the notion that different mental attitudes, including that of belief, were directed upon the alleged objective entities to which he gave the name of propositions. When, for the reasons which I have given, he ceased to think that there were any such entities, he concluded that it was 'impossible to regard belief as a relation of the mind to a single object, which could be said to be believed'.[1] For if propositions are disqualified, the only candidates for this role are facts, and they are ruled out by the possibility of false belief. Even if a false belief can be said to correspond, in its way, to the fact which makes it false, this fact can evidently not be the object of the belief, in the sense of being what is believed.

Having decided that belief, or judgement, could not consist in a relation of the mind to a single object, Russell adopted the view that it consisted in a relation of the mind to several objects. His procedure was, in effect, to replace propositions by their constituents. The resultant theory, which is set out in the essay 'On the Nature of Truth' and in *The Problems of Philosophy*, is that when one makes a judgement one's mind stands in a multiple relation to the various terms with which the judgement is concerned. This relation has a 'sense' in that it orders the terms in a certain fashion. When I judge that *A* loves *B* and when I judge that *B* loves *A*, the terms on which my judgement operates are the same in either case, but in the first case the relation of loving is before my mind 'as proceeding from *A* to *B*' and in the second case as proceeding from *B* to *A*. My judgement is true if the terms in question really are related in the sense in which they are judged to be, false if they are not. Russell does not say how this theory applies to judgements of other types, but presumably qualities are to be treated as monadic relations and existential judgements could be accommodated by counting quantified variables as terms. Whether logical operators like those of disjunction and negation are also to be counted as terms is not made clear. If they are not, the extension of the theory to judge-

---

[1] *The Problems of Philosophy*, p. 124.

ments of which the apparent objects are molecular propositions would present a problem.

But even if the theory can be adequately generalised, it has little to recommend it. In the first place, it does nothing to solve the problem of intentionality. Since the singular terms on which a judgement operates are taken to be actual individuals, the theory makes no provision for the cases in which one believes something to be true of a subject under one description but not under another. If I judge that the author of *Coningsby* was a romantic writer, I am construed as judging that Disraeli was a romantic writer, even though I think of Disraeli only as a statesman and am entirely ignorant of the fact that he also wrote novels. Professor Geach has, indeed, suggested an emendation of the theory which meets this difficulty. In his version, it is my Idea of the author of *Coningsby* that is a romantic writer, where it is understood that my Idea of the author of *Coningsby* may or may not comprise any Idea of Disraeli. So, according to Geach, when I judge that some knife is sharper than any spoon, my Idea of some knife stands in the relation 'sharper than' to my Idea of any spoon.[1] This sounds like a violation of the proverb that hard words break no bones, until it is realised that what is meant here by speaking of Ideas as standing in such and such relations to one another is that the intentional objects which figure as the subjects of our judgements are judged to stand in these relations. But while there may be no harm, and may even be some advantage, in having recourse to this sort of paraphrase, it can hardly be said to present us with an analysis of judgement. The same applies to Russell's theory, of which the most that can be said is that it does deliver us from propositions; but even this will be no great gain if we are obliged to put intentional objects in their place.

In *The Analysis of Mind*, Russell reverts to saying that propositions are believed, but having discarded the notion of mental acts, he now conceives of propositions as furnishing the contents rather than the objects of beliefs. 'The content of a belief', he says, 'may consist of words only, or of images only, or of a mixture of the two, or of either or both together with one or more sensations.'[2] He also says that 'We may identify propositions in general with the contents of actual and possible beliefs',[3] but in fact appears to conceive of them more narrowly as consisting wholly of words, or wholly of images. In the first case they are spoken of as word-propositions and in the second as

---

[1] P. T. Geach, *Mental Acts*, pp. 54–6.
[2] *The Analysis of Mind*, p. 236.   [3] Ibid., p. 241.

image-propositions. In either form, a proposition which expresses a belief refers to the fact which Russell calls the objective of the belief in question. If the belief is true, the proposition points towards this fact, and if it is false it points away from it. How this pointing is thought to be achieved is a question which I shall reserve for my discussion of Russell's theories of truth.

In the meantime, it is clear that we have not yet arrived at a theory of belief. To say that someone is in the state of believing or judging that something is so must be to say something more than that a sequence of words or images is occurring at that point in his mental history. This was, indeed, denied by William James who held that images were *ipso facto* taken for external objects, unless this was found to conflict with some other experience. But although Russell thinks 'It must be conceded that a mere image, without the addition of any positive feeling that could be called "belief", is apt to have a certain dynamic power',[1] he argues, in my view rightly, that even if we restrict ourselves to image-propositions, we cannot account in this way for all cases of belief. He also considers the view that 'The differentia of belief consists in its causal efficacy',[2] but rejects it on the ground, first, that a belief 'often exists actively (not as a mere disposition) without producing any voluntary movement whatever'[3] and secondly, that since the effect of believing a proposition and that of merely considering it may be different, while the content remains the same, there must be some intrinsic difference in the nature of believing and considering to account for the difference in their effects. His own theory is that belief is 'constituted by a certain feeling or complex of sensations, attached to the content believed'.[4] The variation in these feelings or sensations accounts, in his view, for there being 'at least three kinds of belief, namely memory, expectation and bare assent'.[5] Thus if I believe, for example, that it is now raining, the content of my belief may be a present sensation, or complex of sensations, giving rise perhaps to a word-proposition attached to a feeling of assent. On another occasion, the content may be a set of images, 'interrelated, roughly, as the sensations would be if it were raining',[6] and attached to the feeling of familiarity which Russell takes to be characteristic of memory, so that my belief would be that it was raining at some previous time. Alternatively, the same content might be attached to a feeling of expectation, in which case the belief would be that it was going to rain. Russell

---

[1] Ibid., p. 249.   [2] Ibid., p. 244.   [3] Ibid., p. 246.
[4] Ibid., p. 250.   [5] Ibid.   [6] Ibid.

sees that it is not sufficient that the content and the belief-feeling should merely coexist. 'It is necessary that there should be a specific relation between them, of the sort expressed by saying that the content is what is believed.'[1] Unfortunately, we are given no account of what this relation is.

It may be unkind to say that this analysis of belief comes to an end at the point where it should begin, but surely we require some explanation of the way in which a feeling and a set of images can combine into the belief that something is the case. For one thing, it is obvious that assenting to a proposition cannot be equated with having any sort of feeling towards a set of words or images considered in themselves. The words, or images, have to be functioning as signs, and what one is assenting to is not the words or images as such but rather whatever it is that one is taking them to be signifying. But then in the case where what they are taken to signify is not any actual state of affairs, all the old problems about intentional objects reappear. This is not to say that the idea of a feeling of assent has no part to play in the analysis of belief, though I should suppose that assenting normally consisted rather in the disposition to speak and act in certain ways than in the presence of any specific feeling; nor is it to say that assent may not figure in the analysis simply as the favourable reception of certain signs, considered merely as marks or noises. Indeed, it seems clear that it must so figure if intentional objects are to be avoided. The point is that the analysis of belief must then somehow be married to a non-intentional account of the interpretation of signs.

Russell makes a half-hearted attempt to do this in his *Inquiry into Meaning and Truth*. He refers with approval to what was then a recent article on the question 'Must there be propositions?' by Kaplan and Copilowish.[2] The authors had introduced the expression 'implicit behaviour' to designate 'whatever happens to or "in" an organism when it uses signs'. They had defined a sign as a class of 'sign-vehicles' which fulfilled the same law of interpretation, where the interpretation itself consisted in some kind of implicit behaviour, and had defined the interpretation as being correct if the law conformed to some pre-established standard. The implicit behaviour of an organism O was then said to be 'appropriate' to a situation S if it was caused by S and O recognised S, and a sentential sign was said to be true 'if and only if there exists a situation of such a kind that a correct interpretation of any sign-vehicle of the sign is appropriate to the situation'.[1]

---

[1] Ibid.   [2] Published in *Mind* (Oct 1939).   [3] *An Inquiry into Meaning and Truth*, p. 185.

Russell's first comment on this theory is that the term 'sign-vehicle' needs to be defined. His own view is that what makes one event a sign-vehicle of another is 'similarity in its effects', and this leads him to propose the following definition: 'A class of events S is, for an organism O, a *sign* of another class of events E when, as a result of acquired habit, the effects of a member of S on O are (in certain respects and with certain limitations) those which a member of E had before the habit in question was acquired.'[1] Russell expresses some doubt whether the use of a sign cannot be an unconditioned reflex as well as an acquired habit, and he admits that his definition is incomplete so long as 'the respects and limitations' with which he qualified it are not specified, but says that this is not an objection of principle.

Here I think that he makes things too easy for himself. His theory that signs are substitute stimuli is evidently false if stated without qualification. For instance, one's reaction to a propositional sign which relates to a past event is unlikely to be the same as that which the event would produce if one were currently observing it. It might, however, be argued that the theory did apply to the most primitive use of signs to refer to present objects, and that once the connection between words and things has been established at this level, we can accommodate the more sophisticated use of language by bringing in grammatical theory. But even in the case of present objects, the effect of a sign will not be entirely the same as that of perceiving what it signifies. For one thing, it makes all the difference whether the person who interprets the sign merely envisages the object or believes that it is present: for it is only when the uses of the sign arouses or expresses a belief in the presence of the relevant object that it is likely to act as a substitute stimulus. But then it may be objected that we fall into a circle, on the ground that one needs already to understand the sign in order to have the belief. I do not say that this objection cannot be met, but it is already clear that any account of meaning along these lines which is going to be at all plausible will need to be very much less simple than Russell appears to have supposed.

Commenting further on Kaplan and Copilowish's theory, Russell argues that they need not have troubled about 'correctness'. 'In fundamental discussions of language, its social aspect should be ignored, and a man should always be supposed to be speaking to himself, or, what comes to the same thing, to a man whose language is precisely identical with his own.'[2] Russell also suggests that the theory can be

---

[1] Ibid.   [2] Ibid., p. 186.

simplified by absorbing the definition of 'appropriate' into the definition of 'sign-vehicle'. Accordingly he arrives at an account of truth whereby 'A sentential sign present to an organism O is *true* when, *as sign*, it promotes behaviour which would have been promoted by a situation that exists, if this situation had been present to the organism'.[1] Once more, he overlooks the fact that the sign requires to be believed, and his definition is anyhow open to the more radical objection that we have no guarantee that different existent situations would, if they were present to the organism, promote the same behaviour in it, so that the truth of a sign might, in terms of the definition, become separated from what would ordinarily be taken to be its meaning.

With these emendations, Russell accepts Kaplan and Copilowish's theory. He says that what they call implicit behaviour is exactly what he means by a proposition. Propositions, he now thinks, 'are to be defined as psychological occurrences of certain sorts'.[2] In this sense, they are not of course what sentences are used to assert, but Russell wants to say that they are what sentences signify. He takes it for granted that 'Sentences signify something other than themselves, which can be the same when the sentences differ' and he infers that 'this something must be psychological (or physiological)' from 'the fact that propositions can be false'.[3]

This is carelessly put, since Russell presumably does not wish to predicate truth and falsehood of implicit behaviour, but the direction of his thought is reasonably clear. His problem is to give an analysis of statements of the form 'S means P to A', where A is a person, S is a sentence and P is what S is understood by A to state. He thinks that his old theory, whereby P is an objective entity, a proposition, which A designates by means of S, is vitiated by the fact that what A understands S to state may be false. The only alternative which he finds plausible is that S's meaning P to A should somehow be made to emerge out of the psychological accompaniments of A's use of S. This is a promising idea, but Russell does very little to develop it. He does make an effort at this point to connect significance with belief, but gets no further than saying that 'A spoken sentence is "significant" when there is a possible belief that it "expresses"' and that 'a heard sentence "S" is significant if it can cause any of the three kinds of states expressed by "S", "not-S", and "perhaps S"'.[4] But, apart from the fact that it is not at all obvious that only a significant sentence can have such effects, these suggestions are of no help to us in default of a satisfactory analysis of belief and of what it is for a sentence to express one. On the question of the analysis of belief, Russell goes back on the position which he took in *The Analysis of Mind* to the point of saying that 'perhaps the only definition is causal'.[1] He does not try to dispose of his previous objections and the best that he has to offer in the way of a causal definition is the suggestion that 'We may say that two states are instances of the same belief when they cause the same behaviour',[1] this being understood, in the case of those who possess language, to 'include the behaviour that consists in uttering a certain sentence'. He admits to being not entirely satisfied that this definition is adequate, and indeed it very plainly is not, since two persons who hold the same belief may behave very differently in consequence, if they have different purposes or characters, or their other beliefs are different, and this may equally be true of the same person at different times.

It cannot be said, then, that Russell has succeeded in getting rid of propositions as intentional objects by analysing meaning in terms of belief. Nevertheless I think that his intuition here may have been sound. A theory, which I have tried to develop elsewhere,[2] is that we can connect meaning with belief by saying that *S* means *P* to *A* just in case *A*'s assenting to *S* is a criterion for his believing that *P*. The idea is that *A*'s believing that *P* might be shown, in a concrete instance, to consist in a pattern of behaviour in which his disposition to respond positively to the presentation of *S* would be an essential factor. The behaviour need not be entirely overt, but if it includes the having of images or unspoken thoughts, they must figure only as mental occurrences, and not as the signs of anything other than themselves: otherwise the analysis would be circular. There are well-known objections to any theory of this kind which I do not claim altogether to have met.[3] If they cannot be disposed of, I am inclined to think that it may not be possible to give a non-intentional account of meaning. At least I cannot think of any other theory which would stand a better chance of success.

In spite of the fact that his own theory of belief would do the work if it were valid, Russell himself remains doubtful whether an extensional analysis can be given of propositions of the form '*A* believes that *p*'. He quotes Wittgenstein's mysterious dictum that 'It is clear that "*A*

---

[1] Ibid.
[2] In my essay on 'Meaning and Intentionality', in *Metaphysics and Common Sense*, pp. 35–49, and in *The Origins of Pragmatism*, pp. 173–9.
[3] See *The Origins of Pragmatism*, pp. 40–9.

believes that p", "A thinks that p", are of the form "'p' says p",[1] but objects that when we say, for example, that A believes that B is hot we are not saying anything about the words 'B is hot', 'but only about what they signify'.[2] For the same reason he thinks it correct to say 'p is true' rather than ' "p" is true'. He does, however, consider the suggestion that 'In "A believes that B is hot" the words "that B is hot" *describe* what is *expressed* by "B is hot" when this is a complete sentence',[3] and thinks that this may provide a way of escape. But in fact this only restates the problem. It tells us that the words 'B is hot', in this context, are to be taken as a description of A's state of belief; but what has still to be shown is that such a state of belief can be adequately described without the use of some intentional term.

D. HIS THEORIES OF TRUTH

The succession of Russell's theories of judgement carries with it the succession of his theories of truth. He began, as we have seen, with the simple theory that propositions are true or false, just as roses are red or white. When he ceased to believe in propositions as objective entities on which judgements were directed, and instead analysed judgement as a relation of the mind to a multiplicity of objects, he adopted something very like Aristotle's account of truth, according to which 'To say of what is that it is not, or of what is not that it is, is false, while to say of what is that it is, or of what is not that it is not, is true'.[4] For Russell, as we have seen, a judgement was true if its constituents were related in the way it represented them as being, and false if they were not.

The Aristotelian theory is commonly described, to my mind misleadingly, as the correspondence theory of truth, and Russell also at this stage spoke of truth as consisting in correspondence. He said that a judgement was true if there was a complex object corresponding to it and false if there was not.[5] But in saying this he misrepresented his position. To talk of correspondence is to imply that there are two sets of entities between which some relation holds. On Russell's view, however, the constituents of judgements were the very same objects as

---

[1] L. Wittgenstein, *Tractatus Logico-Philosophicus*, 5.542.
[2] *Inquiry into Meaning and Truth*, p. 270.   [3] Ibid., p. 271.
[4] Aristotle, *Metaphysics*, 7.27.   [5] *Philosophical Essays*, p. 158.

the constituents of facts. The only correspondence that there could be was between the arrangement of the objects in a judgement and their arrangement in reality, and in the case where the judgement was true, this correspondence was an identity.

It is worth making the point that this theory of Russell's is misrepresented as a correspondence theory of truth, because at a later stage he came to hold what was a correspondence theory, in the most literal sense. This theory is most fully set out in the article 'On Propositions: what they are and how they mean', which was first published in a supplementary volume of the *Proceedings of the Aristotelian Society* in 1919 and is reprinted in *Logic and Knowledge* as a sort of appendix to the lectures on Logical Atomism. It was written at a time when Russell was again in communication with Wittgenstein and it seems to bear the influence of the pictorial theory of language which Wittgenstein set out in his *Tractatus*.

At this period, as we have seen, Russell believed in the existence of both positive and negative facts and in this article at least he consistently used the term 'proposition', to refer not to an abstract object which a set of signs was understood to signify, but to the set of signs itself. These signs could take the form either of words or images. Word-propositions could be either positive or negative but image-propositions could only be positive. The reason for this was that whereas one could, in a favourable instance, express the statement that ARB by having an image of A standing in the relation R to an image of B, one could not express the negation of this statement by having an image of A which failed to stand in the relation R to an image of B, since there would be nothing to show that one was denying that A and B were related by R rather than by any other relation in which the images also failed to stand. Thus the doctrine of the Logical Atomism lectures that every fact has two propositions corresponding to it, the proposition which it verifies and the negation of that proposition, does not apply to image-propositions, since they have no negations. It does not apply to word-propositions either if these are to be identified with signs, since even if these signs are treated as types rather than tokens, a fact would still have as many propositions corresponding to it as there were different sets of signs, whether in the same or different language, which could be used to assert or deny it. A fact might, however, be said to have two word-propositions corresponding to it, if a proposition were taken to be a class of types of sign, the members of which all had the same meaning. Russell himself overlooks this difficulty, which is anyhow not of major importance for his theory of truth.

Since it is only of image-propositions that it is in the least degree plausible to say that they are pictures of the facts which verify them, Russell takes image-propositions to be more basic than word-propositions, in the sense that they alone directly correspond to facts. He says that 'Word-propositions may, in simple cases, be legitimately spoken of as "meaning" image-propositions',[1] forgetting that if the word-proposition is negative there will be no image-proposition for it to mean. However, he could say that the meaning of a negative word-proposition was determined by, though not of course identical with, the image-proposition which was meant by its contradictory. If a word-proposition either means or has its meaning determined by an image-proposition, in this sense, let us say that it is associated with the image-proposition. Then Russell's correspondence theory of truth is that an affirmative word-proposition is true if it is associated with a true image-proposition, that a negative word-proposition is true if it is associated with a false image-proposition, and that an image-proposition is true if and only if there is a fact which it resembles.

Russell admits that this definition applies only to a limited class of propositions, but if this class were coextensive with the class of atomic propositions and their negations, and if it could be shown that the truth or falsehood of all other propositions depended on the truth-values of atomic propositions, he could claim to be giving a general definition of truth. It is, indeed, certainly not the case that every atomic word-proposition is associated with an image-proposition, if that is understood to imply that the image-proposition is actually formulated, but it might be argued that there was a virtual association, in the sense that any world of sensibilia, which was described by a set of atomic propositions, could always in principle be pictorially represented. Even this would be doubtful if the pictures had to be mental images, but the point is not worth pursuing as this theory is anyhow untenable. The objection on which it founders is that the existence of a physical resemblance between two sets of objects can never in itself be sufficient to make one a representation of the other. There has to be a convention according to which one party to the relation is interpreted as signifying that there exists something which resembles it in certain respects. But then this convention is only one among others. There are many different methods of pictorial representation, and many methods

[1] *Logic and Knowledge*, p. 315.

of representation that are not pictorial. For certain limited purposes, a pictorial method may be more convenient, but there is no ground for saying that it takes us any closer to the facts. Moreover, even when a pictorial sign is used to make a true statement, it is a mistake to regard the resemblance of the sign to what it signifies as determining its truth. What the resemblance determines is the meaning of the sign. What makes the sign the expression of a true statement is the existence of the state of affairs which it signifies, and for this it is immaterial whether it signifies by resemblance or in any other manner. So if the correspondence theory of truth is taken literally, in the sense that correspondence is treated as a physical relation, we can only conclude that it is false.

The attraction which this false theory had for Russell is still apparent in *The Analysis of Mind*. It is shown by his speaking both of a belief and of the meaning of a proposition as pointing towards a fact if the proposition is true and pointing away from a fact if the proposition is false, and by his retaining a category of image-propositions the truth of which consists in their resembling facts. He is, however, doubtful whether it is possible to form image-propositions which can represent all the types of relation that may obtain between two imaged terms, on the ground that the act of comparison, which is implied, in such a judgement as that the sun is brighter than the moon, 'is something more than the mere coexistence of two images, one of which is in fact brighter than the other'.[1] He therefore adopts a different theory of truth according to which an affirmative atomic proposition is true if the replacement of each word by its meaning yields a fact. This suffers from the difficulties of Russell's denotative theory of meaning. Apart from this, it may be regarded as a restatement of the Aristotelian theory of truth, and, as such, correct so far as it goes.

In *An Inquiry into Meaning and Truth*, as we have seen, Russell marries his account of truth to his causal theory of meaning. The results of this are sometimes unfortunate, as in the instance of the definition in terms of behaviour which I have already quoted. Neither is it correct to say, as Russell also does, that 'The correspondence of truth and fact is causal':[2] for even if it is the case, on his narrow view of atomic propositions as limited to the description of their author's present experience, that the production of an atomic proposition is always caused by the fact which it indicates, it is still just the existence of the fact in question and not its casual relation to the propositional sign

---

[1] *The Analysis of Mind*, p. 277.   [2] *An Inquiry into Meaning and Truth*, p. 244.

that makes the proposition true. Russell himself appears to recognise this when he comes to propositions which are predictive of one's future experiences. Belief in such propositions takes the form of expectation, and an expectation, he says, may be defined as being true 'when it leads to confirmation',[1] which is as much as to say that it is true just in case the expected experience occurs. Not only that, but he shows some willingness to generalise this definition, so that it applies to all propositions which refer to one's own experiences. He speaks of the possible experiences to which such propositions refer as their verifiers, and is at times disposed to say that a proposition of this kind is true just in case its verifier exists.

Again there is no fault to be found with this definition so far as it goes; though like all such definitions of truth, it is not very illuminating so long as the accompanying questions about meaning have not been settled. Apart from these questions about meaning, the problem with which Russell was chiefly concerned was whether such a definition could be further generalised. Could one apply it to propositions which referred to events outside the domain of one's own experience? To put it more technically, could one hold that a proposition of the form 'for some x, fx' had a verifier, in the sense that there existed a state of affairs which made it true, even though one could never be in a position to assert or even to formulate any proposition of the form 'fa', the reason for this being, in Russell's view, that 'a' would have to be a name and that the only things for which one could have names were items of one's own experience? Russell's answer is that one should hold such propositions to be true, on the ground that the sceptical arguments which might lead one to give the opposite answer would end by confining truth 'to propositions asserting what I now perceive or remember', and that 'no one is willing to accept so narrow a theory'.[2] The question which then arises is what these events, which lie outside one's own experience, can be taken to be. For example, must the objects which figure in them be of the order of sensibilia, or can we rationally suppose them to have properties which do not enter into our experience? In this way, Russell's explanation of the concept of truth turns into a problem of ontology. What are the sorts of things in the existence of which we have any good reason to believe?

[1] Ibid., p. 216.   [2] Ibid., p. 305.

5 Russell's Conception of What There Is

A. HIS NEUTRAL MONISM

(i) *The Constitution of Minds*

In the first chapter of *The Analysis of Mind*, which was published in 1921, Russell gives it as his opinion that 'The stuff of which the world of our experience is composed is ... neither mind nor matter, but something more primitive than either'.[1] This more primitive stuff was thought by him to consist mainly of the sense-data, or sensibilia, out of which, as we have seen, he then believed the physical world to be constructible. These elements were also supposed to enter into the construction of minds, so that one and the same sense-datum might, as a member of one group, be a constituent, say, of a table, and as a member of another group, be a constituent of a mind in whose biography a perception of the table occurred. Apart from the fact that there were also images and feelings, which entered only into the construction of minds, the difference between mind and matter was not a difference of substance, or content, but a difference in the arrangement of common elements. Whether a group of sense-data constituted, or helped to constitute, a mind or a physical object depended on the ways in which its members were related. The different groups were distinguished also by their being subject to different causal laws.

This theory, which has come to be known by the name of Neutral Monism, had already been put forward by William James. It constituted what James called his Radical Empiricism. Such differences as there are between James's and Russell's versions of it are differences in interest rather than differences of doctrine. Russell makes a much more serious attempt than James to show how the neutral elements have to be related in order to constitute a physical object. I have, indeed, argued that Russell's actual theory is not satisfactory[2] and the theory

---

[1] *The Analysis of Mind*, p. 10.   [2] See above, pp. 57–64.

which I have proposed that we should substitute for it is, in fact, very largely based on James's construction of space.[1] Even so, it has to be admitted that James's own treatment of this question is very cavalier. On the other hand, James, with his greater interest in psychology, makes the more serious attempt to show how the elements have to be related in order to constitute a single mind. His theory is not fully worked out, but, as I have tried to show elsewhere,[2] it can be developed so that it gives, if not an entirely convincing, at least a respectable account of personal identity.

On this question, it is Russell who is cavalier. His ground for rejecting the Ego in which he had formerly believed, is that, as a particular or system of particulars, it must be known, if it can be known to exist at all, either by observation or by inference. At the time when he wrote *The Problems of Philosophy*, he was inclined to think that it could be known by observation, in the form of introspection. 'We are not only aware of things,' he maintained, 'but we are often aware of being aware of them. When I see the sun, I am often aware of my seeing the sun; thus "my seeing the sun" is an object with which I have acquaintance. When I desire food, I may be aware of my desire for food; thus "my desiring food" is an object with which I am acquainted.'[3] But in such cases, he goes on to argue, 'it seems plain that I am acquainted with two different things in relation to each other'.[4] In the case of my seeing the sun, he takes one of these things to be a sense-datum; but what can the other be if not myself? Furthermore, besides being acquainted with this sense-datum, I also know the truth that I am acquainted with it, and, he continues, 'It is hard to see how we could know this truth, or even understand what is meant by it, unless we were acquainted with something which we call "I". It does not seem necessary to suppose that we are acquainted with a more or less permanent person, the same today as yesterday, but it does seem as though we must be acquainted with that thing, whatever its nature, which sees the sun and has acquaintance with sense-data. Thus, in some sense it would seem we must be acquainted with our Selves as opposed to our particular experiences.'[5] Russell, however, admits that there are arguments on the other side, and therefore will not say that acquaintance with ourselves undoubtedly occurs; but he concludes that its occurrence seems probable.

This is an odd conclusion, since the question whether one is or is

---

[1] See my *Origins of Pragmatism*, chap. 3.   [2] Ibid., pp. 263–88.
[3] *The Problems of Philosophy*, p. 49.   [4] Ibid., p. 50.   [5] Ibid., p. 51.

not acquainted with oneself is represented as a question of fact: and in that case it would seem that a careful attention to our mental processes should settle it definitely one way or the other. But the truth is that this is not a question of fact. A philosopher who denies that one is acquainted with oneself is not to be taken as denying that such propositions as that one is aware of seeing the sun, or aware that one desires food, are very often true: to that extent, the facts are not in dispute. The problem is how they are to be analysed. Do we give an adequate account of self-consciousness, if we are content to say simply that it is a matter of the self becoming an object to itself? This is the question which is really at issue. So when Russell later comes to agree with Hume that he has no perception of himself, he is not revising his views about the findings of introspection. He is implying rather that the phenomena of self-consciousness cannot be satisfactorily analysed in terms of subject and object, and in saying that the Ego does not exist, he is saying that there is no need in such an analysis for the introduction of the Ego as an independent entity. His denial that the Ego is known by observation is therefore at one with his denial that it is known by inference. What it comes to is that the Ego is reducible: it succumbs to the principle that constructions are to be substituted for inferences.

This being so, it is incumbent on Russell to show how the construction can be carried out: but this he hardly attempts to do. In the course of his reply to criticisms in *The Philosophy of Bertrand Russell* he says that 'There are a number of causal connections between the mental occurrences which we regard as belonging to one person, which do not exist between those belonging to different people: of these memory is the most obvious and the most important. To these,' he continues, 'must be added compresence, a relation which holds between any two simultaneous contents of a given mind, as well as between any two events which overlap in physical space-time.'[1] In fact, as I have tried to show elsewhere,[2] we need the relation of sensible continuity as well as compresence, and these are the main foundations on which a Humean theory of self-identity can be built. Even so, they are not sufficient, because of the possibility of gaps in consciousness, and the problem of finding a way to bridge the gaps is not easy to solve. Memory is the obvious candidate, but in appealing to memory there is the danger of circularity. It must not here be presupposed that the experiences which one 'remembers' are one's own. On the other hand, if one tries

[1] *The Philosophy of Bertrand Russell*, p. 699.   [2] See *The Origins of Pragmatism*, pp. 266 ff.

to define one's own experiences as those which one seems to remember, one will in certain cases get an unacceptable result. A similar difficulty arises in the resort to causal connections. It is by no means clear that it is possible to discriminate the causal relations that hold between one's own experiences, unless these experiences have already been identified as one's own.

(ii) *His Account of Causality*

If we look for a solution of this problem to the chapters in *The Analysis of Mind* which Russell devotes to Memory and to Causal Laws, I am afraid that we get very little help. In the chapter on causal laws, he begins by asserting that such sequences as were sought by believers in the traditional form of causation, in which an event of type *A* was necessarily followed after a finite interval by an event of type *B*, 'have not so far been found in nature'. What we call one event, he continues, turns out to be a process and 'if this event is to cause another event, the two will have to be contiguous in time: for if there is any interval between them, something may happen during that interval to prevent the expected effect'.[1] This argument is one that Russell had already advanced in an essay 'On the Notion of Cause', his presidential address to the Aristotelian Society for the session 1912–13, which was published in their *Proceedings* and reprinted in *Mysticism and Logic*; and it seems to me fallacious. If one believes that causes necessitate their effects, an idea which Russell rightly repudiates, one can consistently infer that once the cause has occurred, then even though there is ample time for the effect to be prevented, it in fact cannot be. If one agrees, as Russell does, with Hume that the relation between cause and effect can be no more than a *de facto* conjunction, one can equally hold that the possibility which the time-interval allows for something to prevent the effect will not in fact be realised. We do, indeed, suppose that by diminishing the time-interval we increase the likelihood that the event, which we speak of as a cause, will be sufficient to produce the effect in question; but this is only a matter of degree. Even in the absence of any time-interval, there will still be negative conditions for which we have tacitly or explicitly to make provision.

It is all the more strange that Russell should advance this argument,

[1] *The Analysis of Mind*, p. 94.

since we shall see that, at least in the domain of mental events, he himself is prepared to allow for action at a distance. Not only that but in the essay 'On the Notion of Cause' he also produces an argument to show that cause and effect cannot be contiguous in time. 'No two instants', he says, 'are contiguous, since the time-series is compact', and from this he infers that if the causal relation is defined in such a way that the effect has immediately to follow the cause, which is both necessary and sufficient for it, one or other or both of them must be assumed to endure for a finite time. 'But then', he continues, 'we are faced with a dilemma: if the cause is a process involving change within itself, we shall require (if causality is universal) causal relations between its earlier and later parts; moreover, it would seem that only the later parts can be relevant to the effect, since the earlier parts are not contiguous to the effect, and therefore (by the definition) cannot influence the effect. Thus we shall be led to diminish the duration of the cause without limit, and however much we may diminish it, there will still remain an earlier part which might be altered without altering the effect, so that the true cause, as defined, will not have been reached, for it will be observed that the definition excludes plurality of causes. If, on the other hand, the cause is purely static, involving no change within itself, then, in the first place, no such cause is to be found in nature, and in the second place, it seems strange – too strange to be accepted, in spite of bare logical possibility – that the cause, after existing placidly for some time, should suddenly explode into the effect, when it might just as well have done so at any earlier time, or have gone on unchanged without producing its effect. This dilemma, therefore, is fatal to the view that cause and effect can be contiguous in time; if there are causes and effects they must be separated by a finite time-interval.'[1]

It can now be seen that what Russell is doing is attempting to construct a Kantian antinomy. He seeks to discredit the traditional notion of causality by showing that it makes it impossible for there either to be or not to be a time-interval between cause and effect. It seems to me, however, that his argument fails on both counts. We have already seen that no good reason is given why the events which a causal law conjoins should not be separated in time, and equally there appears to be no good reason why they should not in certain cases be temporally contiguous, in the sense that the interval between them can be taken to be as small as we please. The argument that if the cause lasts for a

[1] *Mysticism and Logic*, pp. 184–5.

finite time, the earlier parts of it cannot be relevant to the production of the effect, is surely not valid. If the causal law with which we are concerned is such as to correlate an event of type *A* with an immediately successive event of type *B*, then these are the types of event which it correlates; we have neither the right nor the obligation to infer that an event which is merely a part of an *A* will do just as well. It may or may not be that we can explain the operation of a type *A* event in terms of relations between its parts, but this makes no difference to the argument, since the same question will arise with respect to the parts if they are credited with any temporal duration. Neither does it appear to make any difference whether or not the event is taken to be qualitatively homogeneous throughout its length. Russell talks of its seeming strange in such a case that the event, after being quiescent for some time, should suddenly explode into the effect, but this is to overlook the fact that any event which enters into a causal law must have some duration. We can, indeed, ask why the law applies to events of just that length and not to shorter events, and then the answer may be that the existence of events of that kind, which are shorter than a given length, is not determinable, or it may be that we are reduced to saying that that is just how things are. If our causal law is such as to imply that events of such a kind as to have a minimal duration *d* are invariably accompanied after a time-interval *t* by events of such and such another kind, there is surely no *a priori* limitation on the values that can be given to *d* and *t*. If there is an objection to action at a distance, it is not that we have any *a priori* reason to believe that generalisations serving to connect events which are not contiguous in space or time will not hold good, but only that we feel that such generalisations leave more to be explained.

The conclusion which Russell draws from his alleged antinomy is that causal laws of the sort which philosophers have tried to foist on science must give way to differential equations. 'A physical law', he says in *The Analysis of Mind*, 'does not say "*A* will be followed by *B*" but tells us what acceleration a particle will have under given circumstances, i.e. it tells us how the particle's motion is changing at each moment, not where the particle will be at some future moment.'[1] And in the essay 'On the Notion of Cause' he says that the nearest approach to a 'Law of Causality' that can be stated in non-mathematical language would be as follows: 'There is a constant relation between the state of the universe at any instant and the rate of change in the rate

[1] *The Analysis of Mind*, p. 95.

at which any part of the universe is changing at that instant, and this relation is many–one, i.e. such that the rate of change in the rate of change is determinate when the state of the universe is given.'[1] He was, however, soon persuaded, mainly, I think, by the development of quantum physics, that this account of causality was too restricted, and in *The Analysis of Matter*, which was published in 1927, he goes to the other extreme. 'There is', he there says, 'a causal relation whenever two events, or two groups of events of which one at least is co-punctual', in the sense that there is a region common to its members, 'are related by a law which allows something to be inferred about the one from the other.'[2] In *Human Knowledge: Its Scope and Limits*, which appeared in 1948, this definition is maintained. 'A "causal law",' he there says, 'as I shall use the term, may be defined as a general principle in virtue of which, given sufficient data about certain regions of space-time, it is possible to infer something about certain other regions of space-time.'[3] It is a feature of this, as indeed of Russell's previous accounts of causality, that it is not made necessary that causes should precede their effects. As Russell said of the law of causality which he formulated in the essay 'On the Notion of Cause', 'The law makes no difference between past and future: the future "determines" the past in exactly the same sense in which the past "determines" the future.'[4] This may sound shocking to common sense, but if we take what seems the natural course of identifying causes either with necessary or with sufficient conditions, or both, it is the only logical conclusion. We can of course refuse to call anything 'a cause' unless it precedes the event of which it is the necessary or sufficient condition, but there appears to be no logical ground for making this restriction. There may, however, be an empirical ground, as Russell later admits, in view of the prevalence in modern physics of irreversible processes. We have also a motive for making it when we think of the causality which is involved in our own actions. We try to bring about events in the future, but it would seem absurd for anyone to try to bring about something that had already happened. I admit that I share this attitude, but the reason for it is not clear to me. The best explanation that I can think of, which I do not find entirely satisfactory, is that it is because we have, or think we have, considerable knowledge of the past and very little knowledge of the future.

If there is a criticism to be made of Russell's formal definition of

---

[1] *Mysticism and Logic*, p. 195.   [2] *The Analysis of Matter*, pp. 367–8.
[3] *Human Knowledge: Its Scope and Limits*, p. 308.   [4] *Mysticism and Logic*, p. 195.

causality, it must be that it is too general. Not every true generalisation that allows us to make inferences from what happens in one region of space-time to what happens in another would ordinarily be counted as a causal law. It may, indeed, be argued that the word 'cause' is commonly used so loosely that a meticulous investigation of its occurrences in ordinary language would not repay the labour. Even so, there are some distinctions that ought to be made. We need to distinguish between causal laws, in one of the narrower senses of the term, and statistical laws; between dynamic laws, qualitative laws and functional laws; between laws which correlate events at the same observational level and laws which explain the behaviour of objects in terms of their underlying structure: we need to consider whether there is any justification, or necessity, for admitting a special category of teleological laws: above all, we need to find some way of distinguishing between generalisations of law and accidental generalisations of fact.

I do not say that Russell was unaware of these problems, but he makes no attempt to deal with them, beyond giving, in *Human Knowledge*, a rather summary account of the distinction between differential equations, statistical regularities, and what he calls the law of quasi-permanence. This law of quasi-permanence is of special interest as 'it is designed to explain the success of the common-sense notion of "things" and the physical notion of "matter" (in classical physics)'.[1] The law is that 'Given an event at a certain time, then at any slightly earlier or slightly later time there is, at some neighbouring place, a closely similar event'.[2] Events which obey this law are said to form a causal line, the characteristic of a causal line being that the events which form it are 'so related that, given some of them, something can be inferred about the others whatever may be happening elsewhere'.[3] Thus causal lines are intended to do the work of substances in securing identity through time. They constitute what we ordinarily speak of as persistent things. In particular, Russell conceives of memory as generating one kind of causal line. To oneself, it guarantees personal identity.

(iii) *His Analysis of Memory*

I think it is true that memory generates a causal line, inasmuch as the occurrence of a memory-experience is, or is anyhow taken to be,

[1] *Human Knowledge*, p. 458.   [2] Ibid.   [3] Ibid., p. 459.

a reliable, and in certain cases the most reliable, indication that the event, or something very like the event, of which it purports to be a memory actually occurred. It is not an infallible indication, but the occasions on which we find reason to believe that our memory is playing us wholly false are comparatively rare. This is especially so when the events which we claim to remember are in the fairly recent past. To a lesser extent, the converse inference also holds. Not many of our experiences are consciously remembered over a long period of time, but I suppose that most of them are at least accessible to memory for a short period after their occurrence. Whether they are all memorable, in the sense that they leave traces which under the influence of the appropriate stimuli will later activate memories of them, is a question into which I shall not enter. Russell himself, in the *Analysis of Mind*, considers that the empirical evidence does not entitle us to draw the conclusion that 'Past experience only affects present behaviour through modifications of physiological structure',[1] and therefore prefers to account for the phenomena of memory in terms of what he calls 'mnemic causation'. The suggestion is that the past experience combines with some present stimulus and the present psychological and physiological states of the subject to cause a present memory. Russell remarks, correctly, that if we are regarding causal laws as '*merely* observed uniformities of sequence', which is 'all that science has to offer',[2] we have no *a priori* ground for objecting to the suggestion of a causal law in which part of the cause has ceased to exist. The only legitimate objection that we could have would be that this particular form of action at a distance is one that seems to us to call for further explanation. Russell also remarks that those who wish to secure the independence of psychology from physics will be well advised to fasten on to mnemic causation as a way of preserving them from psycho-physical parallelism. This would, indeed, be accomplished if it could be shown that the resort to mnemic causation was the only way of accounting for the phenomena of memory, for then it would follow, *ex hypothesi*, that memory-experiences did not have physiological counterparts with which they could be reliably correlated. This is, however, a very strong requirement. It is hard to see how one could be in a position to claim that experiences of any kind did not have physiological correlates. The most that could be reasonably said would be that, in the present state of our knowledge, we were not justified in assuming that they had them. And this is, in fact, as far as

[1] *Analysis of Mind*, p. 92.   [2] Ibid., p. 89.

Russell goes. In his later works he becomes less cautious, but in the other direction, since he identifies experiences with events in the brain. This is not, however, the concession to physicalism that it might appear to be, since he also maintains that 'The brain consists of thoughts – using "thought" in its widest sense, as it is used by Descartes'.[1] I shall have more to say about this later on.

In any case, if one adopts the position of neutral monism, the question of psycho-physical parallelism is not so very important. It comes down to the question whether one set of sensibilia can be systematically correlated with another set which also incorporates images and feelings. A more interesting question, philosophically, is how this second group is put together. Is the fact that it includes what I have been calling memory-experiences sufficient to bind its elements together so that they constitute the biography of a single mind? That one's awareness of one's own identity through time depends on memory is not, I think, to be disputed. But this is not to say that memory, even when allied to compresence and sensible continuity, is sufficient to constitute a mind's identity.

In fact, I think it is clear that it is not sufficient. The function which memory is needed to perform is to bridge the gap in consciousness which sensible continuity does not cover. It fails to perform this function because it can supply no guarantee that the experiences which it annexes are one's own. Admittedly, we most commonly speak of memory in such a way as to imply that the experiences which we remember must have been our own, but to rely on this usage would here be of no service, since the attempt to found identity on memory would then become circular. The ownership of a past experience would already have to be established before we were justified in saying that it was remembered.

Russell does not discuss this difficulty but his analysis of memory brings it out clearly. The first point to which he draws attention is that 'Everything constituting a memory-belief is happening *now*, not in that past time to which the belief is said to refer'. It is, therefore, 'not logically necessary to the existence of a memory-belief that the event remembered should have occurred, or even that the past should have existed at all. There is no logical impossibility in the hypothesis that the world sprang into being five minutes ago, exactly as it then was, with a population that "remembered" a wholly unreal past.' This follows from the fact that there is no logically necessary

[1] *My Philosophical Development*, p. 25.

connection between events at different times. 'Hence', Russell concludes, 'the occurrences which are *called* knowledge of the past are logically independent of the past; they are wholly analysable into present contents which might, theoretically, be just what they are even if no past had existed.'[1]

I think this is obviously true, and the consequence, as I have tried to show elsewhere,[2] is that no non-circular justification of memory can be given. We check one memory-belief against another, and against historical records, our reliance on which itself depends in part on memory-beliefs, but it is vain to ask for a general proof that memory is trustworthy. This would not, however, be a bar to our founding personal identity upon memory, if there were in fact a one–one relation between the characteristics of a veridical memory-experience and those of the past experience of which it is a memory. But unfortunately, this is not so. If the memory-experience consists, as Russell suggests, in the occurrence of an image conjoined with a 'feeling of familiarity' and a belief which may be expressed in the words 'This existed', it is clear that these conditions could all be satisfied when the experience, which corresponded to the image, was in fact, although of course not taken to be, the experience of another person. As it happens, Russell's conditions are neither necessary nor sufficient: not necessary, because the presence of an image is not essential for the recollection of a past event, and not sufficient because one might hold a true belief about a past experience of one's own, combined with an appropriate image and a feeling of familiarity, even though one did not remember the experience. This could happen, for instance, if one's belief that one had had the experience arose from one's having been told about it. This objection could, perhaps, be met by construing Russell's 'feeling of familiarity' as a feeling which was distinctive of a memory-experience, although the analysis could hardly then be said to be very informative. In any event, our difficulty remains. We have not excluded the possibility that the memory-belief is true of what was in fact the experience of some other person.

The obvious way to try to meet this difficulty is to require that the memory-experience be linked to the experience of which it is a memory by a causal relation which holds between what would ordinarily be taken to be the experiences of the same person, but not between what would ordinarily be taken to be the experiences of different persons. I think that this may be feasible, though a causal

[1] *The Analysis of Mind*, pp. 159–60.   [2] See *The Problem of Knowledge*, chap. iv.

relation which satisfies this condition will not be easy to define. But even if we are able to discover such a relation, we shall still not be able to constitute a person out of the series of his experiences, since it seems obvious that the only way in which this relation can achieve what is required of it is by linking different experiences with processes that take place in the same body. And in general I think it has to be admitted that no adequate account of personal identity can be given that does not depend, at least in part, upon the criterion of bodily identity.[1]

This is not a fatal objection to neutral monism, since it leaves open the possibility that bodily identity can itself be defined in terms of relations between sensibilia. What it does show is that in any system of this kind the construction of physical objects must be the primary step. The question which we have now to consider is how far Russell continued to believe that this construction could be carried out.

B. THE LOCATION OF PERCEPTS

An assumption to which Russell consistently adhered is that we are entitled, on the basis of our experiences, to infer the existence of things, or events, or processes which we do not experience. As we have already seen, he takes this to cover the experiences which we attribute to other persons and also things which do not actually enter into any experience at all. The critical question is whether or not he regards the things which lie outside any actual experience as being of the same character as those that lie within it.

So long as he adheres to the theory of neutral monism, the answer is almost undoubtedly that they are intended to be of the same character. It is true that he allows for the possibility that sensibilia, as they are in themselves, may differ from what they are when they become sense-data, because of the causal dependence of sense-data upon factors which include the observer's body, but he does not develop this suggestion, and the fact that he is willing to identify a physical object with the class of its actual and possible appearances strongly suggests that he did not take it seriously into account. I believe, therefore, that I was being faithful to his intention when I represented the physical object of common sense as what I called a standardised percept. We have also

[1] See *The Origins of Pragmatism*, chap. 3, B.2.

seen that the locations which he assigned to objects in physical space were a function of the locations of their appearances in perceptual space. I have indeed argued that his construction of physical space is not satisfactory, but I believe, as I said, that the theory which I substituted for it is also faithful to his intention: and there the location of the physical object is identified with that of the standardised percept. So our problem is to determine whether, and, if so, how far and for what reason, Russell departed from this main position.

On this point the textual evidence is conflicting. Thus, in the *Analysis of Matter*, he says that the construction of physical objects out of real and 'ideal' percepts 'remains valid and important', and objects to it only on the rather weak ground, if he is still adhering to a Humean view of causation, that it is hard to see how merely ideal elements can enter essentially into the formulation of causal laws.[1] On the other hand, he says, in the same book, that 'The physical world, it seems natural to infer, is destitute of colour',[2] which would evidently not be the case if physical objects were compounded out of percepts, and elsewhere, in connection with the example of one's seeing a glowing gas, he allows only of there being important similarities between the percepts and the physical event, the shape of the percept being said to correspond 'to the shape of the region in which the upheavals are taking place' and its colour 'to the amount of energy lost by each atom in an upheaval'.[3] In yet another passage he says that 'The gulf between percept and physics is not a gulf as regards intrinsic quality, for we know nothing of the intrinsic quality of the physical world and therefore do not know whether it is, or is not, very different from that of percepts'.[4] This is not so much at variance with neutral monism as the preceding passages which I quoted, but it is still inconsistent with it, since if neutral monism were true there would be no mystery about the intrinsic qualities of physical objects: they would simply be defined in terms of the qualities of percepts.

There are similar discrepancies in what Russell has to say in this book about the construction of physical space. At times he adheres to the theory which he developed in *Our Knowledge of the External World*, as when he speaks of our being able to form 'groups of percepts connected approximately, though not exactly, by laws which may be called laws of "perspective" 'and goes on to say that 'by means of these laws, together with the changes in our other percepts which are

---

[1] *The Analysis of Matter*, pp. 210–17.   [2] Ibid., p. 133.   [3] Ibid., p. 339.
[4] Ibid., p. 264.

connected with the perception of bodily movement, we can form the conception of a space in which percipients are situated, and we find that in this space all the percepts belonging to one group (i.e. of the same physical object, from the standpoint of common sense) can be ordered about a centre, which we take to be the place where the physical object in question is. (For us, this is a definition of the place of a physical object.)'[1] At other times, however, he speaks as though physical space were something inferred to which we were entitled to assign no more than a structural correspondence with perceptual space. 'I am concerned', he says in one passage, 'to point out that we can only infer the logical (or mathematical) properties of physical space, and must not suppose that it is identical with the space of our perceptions. Indeed, as I shall try to prove later, the whole of a man's visual space is, for physics, inside his head: this will follow from causal considerations.'[2] These causal considerations are to be found in the causal theory of perception, which Russell takes to be so well established on scientific grounds that it cannot seriously be questioned. 'Whoever', he says, 'accepts the causal theory of perception is compelled to conclude that percepts are in our heads, for they come at the end of a causal chain of physical events leading, spatially, from the object to the brain of the percipient. We cannot suppose that, at the end of this process, the last effect suddenly jumps back to the starting-point, like a stretched rope when it snaps.'[3] From this, Russell draws the startling conclusion that everything that we perceive is inside our own heads. 'What the physiologist sees when he examines a brain is in the physiologist, not in the brain he is examining.'[4] The brain which the physiologist examines, in the sense that it is causally responsible for the processes in his own head that he actually sees, is said to have included among its contents, while its owner was alive, the owner's percepts, thoughts and feelings. Since it also consisted of electrons, Russell infers that if an electron is in a human brain 'some of the events composing it are likely to be some of the "mental states" of the man to whom the brain belongs'.[4] And conversely, he infers that 'A percept is an event or a group of events, each of which belongs to one or more of the groups constituting the electrons in the brain'.[4] Again, this is not the concession to physicalism that it might appear to be, since the suggestion is rather that electrons have the qualities of percepts than that percepts have the qualities which are commonly attributed to electrons.

[1] Ibid., pp. 216–17.   [2] Ibid., pp. 252–3.   [3] Ibid., p. 320.   [4] Ibid.

In the book on *Human Knowledge: Its Scope and Limits*, and in a lecture on 'Physics and Experience' which Russell delivered at Cambridge in 1945, the trend away from neutral monism is still more pronounced. He remarks, in this lecture, that many people who rightly reject naïve realism in general, still adhere to it to the extent of identifying the spatial relations of their percepts with those of physical things. 'But this identification', he continues, 'is indefensible. The spatial relations of physics hold between electrons, protons, neutrons, etc., which we do not perceive: the spatial relations of visual percepts hold between things which we do perceive, and in the last analysis between coloured patches.'[1] And again, in *Human Knowledge*, having spoken of 'the construction of one space in which all our perceptual experiences are located' as 'a triumph of pre-scientific common sense', he calls it a 'serious error, committed not only by common sense but by many philosophers', to suppose that this space can be identified with the inferred space of physics'. 'The coloured surface', he continues, 'that I see when I look at a table has a special position in the space of my visual field; it exists only when eyes and nerves and brain exist to cause the energy of photons to undergo certain transformations. . . . The table as a physical object, consisting of electrons, positrons and neutrons, lies outside my experience, and if there is a space which contains both it and my perceptual space, then in that space the physical table must be wholly external to my perceptual space. This conclusion is inevitable if we accept the view as to the physical causation of sensation which is forced on us by physiology.'[2] It is also in the light of 'the development of physics and physiology' that Russell here takes the view that there is only a structural correspondence between percepts and physical objects. 'At best the resemblance between the (astronomer's) sensation and the astronomical fact cannot be closer than that between a gramophone record and the music that it plays, or between a library catalogue and the books that it enumerates.'[3]

Though Russell still writes in *My Philosophical Development*, which came out in 1959, as if he thought that physical space could be constructed out of perceptual space, in the way that he had suggested in *Our Knowledge of the External World*,[4] we have seen that the evidence mainly points to the supersession of the view that physical objects, and the space which they inhabit, are logical constructions by the view

---

[1] *Physics and Experience*, pp. 16–17.   [2] *Human Knowledge*, etc., pp. 220–1.
[3] Ibid., pp. 48–9.   [4] See *My Philosophical Development*, pp. 24–5.

that they are inferred entities. To see how this change comes about and whether it is justified, let us begin by looking at the question of the location of percepts.

It may be remembered that in his original construction of physical space out of the space of perspectives, Russell distinguishes between the place *at* which a percept is and the place *from* which it is. The place at which the percept is, in perspective space, is identical with the place which is occupied by the physical object which it helps to constitute, and the place from which it is locates the percipient, whom it also helps to constitute by its association with a different series. What Russell does, when he transforms physical objects from logical constructions into inferred entities, is to identify the place at which the percept is with the place from which he previously took it to be, that is to say the place which is occupied by the brain of the percipient; and his reason for doing this is that he thinks that he is committed to it by his acceptance of the standard physical theory about the way in which percepts are caused. The question is whether this is a good reason.

I think that it is a good reason for relocating the percept but a bad reason for relocating the corresponding physical object. The argument on which Russell relies is, as we have seen, that according to the scientific account of the process of visual perception, the physical object and the percept are separated by a spatio-temporal interval, the distance in space which the light travels from the object to the eye, and the length of time which it takes to travel this distance, together with the time occupied by certain occurrences in the brain. The percept appears at the latter end of this process and we have no justification for catapulting it to the beginning. As I shall explain later, I think that this is a good reason for locating percepts in the brain, if they are to be located anywhere at all, once we have developed our physical theory, and when we are reinterpreting our primary data in terms of the theory which we have used them to construct. But the point to which I now wish to draw attention is that the position which the object itself is assumed to occupy is its position in perceptual space, the position which is assigned to the standardised percept in my primary system. When my seeing the row of books in front of me is explained in terms of the passage of light from the books to my eye, the assumption is that the books are there where I see them, in the space which I perceive, not somewhere I can have no inkling of in a space which is only inferred and never perceived by anyone. It is true that we sometimes distinguish between the place where an object really is and the place where it appears to be. To take one of Russell's favourite examples, the sun looks much nearer to us than it really is, and because of the velocity of light we shall at best be seeing it not where it now is but where it was eight minutes ago. This does not, however, disprove what I have been saying. The position of the sun is determined by calculation, and the calculations are based on the assumption that various other objects are where they appear to be. It is only because we start by equating the physical positions of the things around us with the observed positions of standardised percepts that our more sophisticated methods of locating objects like the sun can lead to verifiable results.

Admittedly, the fact, if I am right in taking it to be so, that the causal account of perception is founded on the identification of physical and perceptual space is not itself a proof that this identification is correct. It may, in any case, be argued that the basis of the causal account is rather the naïve realism of common sense than the more sophisticated theory which I am advocating, and I certainly should not wish to maintain that the acceptance of the causal theory of perception, in its scientific aspect, entailed the acceptance of naïve realism. Russell, indeed, goes to the other extreme of maintaining that it entails its rejection. 'Naïve realism', he says in the *Inquiry into Meaning and Truth*, 'leads to physics, and physics, if true, show that naïve realism is false. Therefore, naïve realism, if true, is false; therefore it is false.'[1]

This argument, which much impressed Einstein,[2] is marvellously concise, but it is not so clear that its premisses are true. I do not want to defend naïve realism as a theory of perception, where I take it to consist in the purely negative thesis that the perception of the physical objects of common sense cannot be analysed in terms of the presentation of sense-qualia. On the contrary, I entirely agree with Russell that such an analysis can be given, though I have raised some serious objections to the form which his analysis takes. Naïve realism, however, is also a theory about what there is. It consists, as Russell puts it, in such beliefs as that grass is green, that stones are hard, and that snow is cold, and I am not persuaded that physics shows these beliefs to be false, in the way that common sense interprets them. Russell says that 'Physics assures us that the greenness of grass, the hardness of stones, and the coldness of snow are not the greenness, hardness, and coldness that we

---

[1] *Inquiry into Meaning and Truth*, p. 15.
[2] See *The Philosophy of Bertrand Russell*, pp. 281–3.

know in our own experience, but something very different'.[1] This is true in a way, but it may come to no more than that physics explains the greenness of grass, the coldness of snow, and so forth, in terms of the behaviour of entities which have very different properties, and the acceptance of this explanation may not be inconsistent with our continuing to hold a naïvely realistic view of what there is.

I shall return to this question in a moment. What I now wish to dispute is that the naïve realistic way of locating objects is incorrect, except in so far as it shirks the task of showing how perceptual space is organised. And one reason why I wish to dispute it is that the alternative theory, to which Russell believes that we are committed by the causal account of perception, appears to me quite unacceptable. I do not press the point that the postulation of unobservable entities as causes of our percepts is inconsistent with Russell's own derivation of the concept of cause from observed regularities, and with his principle that a concept is intelligible to us only if it is exemplified in our experience or is reducible to concepts which are so exemplified. I see no objection to the postulation of unobservable entities, so long as the hypotheses into which they enter have consequences which can be empirically tested, and it is quite customary to speak of such entities as causes of the phenomena which they are invoked to explain. If Russell's principle forbids us to speak in such a way, I think that it shows itself to be too stringent. What I do find objectionable, on the other hand, is the notion that these unobservable entities are located in an unobservable space. I cannot see that we have any justification for the inference that there is such a thing as unobservable space; and indeed I am not at all sure that I find the idea of it intelligible. I can conceive of there being spatial relations between unobservable objects, but only if these objects are located in a spatial system which fundamentally consists of the spatial relations which obtain between objects that are observable.

But how then can we accommodate the causal account of perception? How can we reconcile the objectivity which we are attributing to perceptual space with the fact that, as Russell puts it, 'The observer, when he seems to himself to be observing a stone, is really, if physics is to be believed, observing the effects of the stone upon himself'?[2] The answer, I maintain, is that it is possible, without any logical inconsistency, first to identify a physical object with a standardised percept, and then, at the theoretical level, to distinguish the object as it is in itself from the various perceptions that different observers have of it. What happens, as I have tried to show in the last section of my book *The Origins of Pragmatism*, is that having developed the common-sense conception of the physical world as a theoretical system with respect to a basis of sense-qualia, we can interpret into this system the elements upon which it was founded. The physical object which was originally constructed out of percepts acquires, as it were, a life of its own. Since the perceptual qualities with which it is credited in the theory are supposed to be constant, or at least not to change without a physical alteration in the object, they come to be contrasted with the fluctuating impressions which different observers have of them. In other words, the standardised percept comes to be set over against the actual percepts from which it was abstracted, and indeed regarded as causally responsible for them. A primitive distinction having been made between what in *The Origins of Pragmatism* I call the main story, the organisation of those of one's experiences that seem to fit into a regular pattern, and the subsidiary stories to which are relegated the experiences that do not fit in, the identification of other observers, with the same main story but their own subsidiary stories, permits the distinction to be sophisticated to the point where the main story itself is contrasted with any particular relation of it and all experiences, including those that furnish the main story, are regarded as subsidiary. So all percepts, whether veridical or delusive, come to be thought of as subjective, and as coming at the end of a causal process of which some physical object, itself no more than a standardised percept, is the source. There is a sense, therefore, in which our physical theory denies its starting-point, but it is rather the sense in which a self-made man may repudiate his humble origins. I cannot see that there is any logical incoherence in the process which I have outlined.

The distinction between standardised and actual percepts, which comes to be drawn at the theoretical level in the way that I have tried to explain, may also now be extended to their respective locations. My own view is that it is neither necessary, nor perhaps desirable, to find room in our physical theory for percepts as entities: they can be represented as ways in which persons are affected, and therefore as not requiring to be assigned a physical location. If we insist on there being a place where mental processes occur, the obvious candidate is indeed the brain. I am, however, somewhat reluctant to follow Russell in identifying the mental processes, into which I am suggesting that percepts become transmuted, with events in the brain. I am not disposed to question the hypothesis that these processes are causally dependent upon events in the brain, but I doubt if the evidence is sufficient for us to be justified in translating this causal dependence into a factual identity. Since it is not at all clear to me what evidence would be sufficient, I shall not pursue this question further here.

In my view, then, Russell is right in thinking that the things which we put first in the order of being need not be the same as those that we put first in the order of knowledge, but wrong in denying to the theoretical entities with which he furnishes the world the benefits of their phenomenal origin. If the view which I have outlined is correct, there is no call for any such paradox as that one only perceives what is inside one's own head. At the theoretical level, the process of seeing is to be located in the observer's head, if we choose to locate it anywhere at all, and the same applies at this level to his actual percepts, if we choose to treat them as entities. But the object which he sees can be external to his body in exactly the same sense in which the corresponding standardised percepts are external to each other in the system of phenomenal space; and this relation is directly derived, in the way I showed earlier, from the spatial properties of the sense-qualia from which they are abstracted.

C. THE PHYSICAL WORLD

If my argument is correct, the locations which we have to assign at least to the physical objects in our immediate environment are very much the same as those that are assigned to them by common sense. It does not follow, however, that we also have to represent them as having the qualities with which common sense endows them. Even if Russell is mistaken in thinking that the scientific theory about the causation of percepts obliges us to hold that we never see physical objects *where* they really are, it may still be thought to entail that we never see them *as* they really are. Many philosophers, indeed, before Russell, have thought that it had this consequence. They have, explicitly or tacitly, accepted Locke's distinction between the primary qualities of a physical object, which are roughly speaking those that are featured in the physics of their day, and its secondary qualities, which are only powers to produce sensations in us. At all periods, sounds, tastes, smells, and, most importantly, colours have been counted as secondary qualities. So in the contemporary version of this theory, the thing which I take to be the continuous, coloured, stationary surface of the desk at which I am writing is really a discontinuous group of darting colourless electrons. Except for denying that the electrons are where the desk appears to be, this is also the view that Russell takes.

I find this view difficult to assess, mainly because it is not made clear what criteria are being used to determine what a thing really is. We may, however, get a clue to this by considering why it is thought that physical objects do not possess the property of being coloured in the literal way in which it is ordinarily ascribed to them. The answer which is often given is summed up in Bradley's saying that things are coloured only to an eye:[1] the ground for maintaining that they are not literally coloured is that their appearing to be so is due, at least in part, to our own physical constitution. This argument obviously cannot be used to differentiate between perceptual qualities – as Berkeley pointed out in his attack on Locke, it applies no less to what Locke regarded as the primary quality of shape than it does to colour – but it might be used to differentiate all the perceptual qualities which we ascribe to the object from the purely theoretical properties which are supposed to account for its affecting us as it does. Even so, the argument proves too much, for our seeing the object where we do is also partly due to our physical constitution.

The argument can, however, be reformulated in a way that may make it more acceptable. We may begin by distinguishing between the causal properties of an object and its intrinsic properties. Its causal properties are those that are defined by reference to the effects that it has, or under the appropriate conditions would have, upon other things. Its intrinsic properties are those which it can be said to have without the implication that it is related to anything else: intrinsic properties may also have effects – indeed, if they are not perceptual properties they must have effects if we are to have any reason to believe in them – but they are not defined in terms of their effects. There are also properties, like spatio-temporal position, which are neither causal nor intrinsic. Now if we were to say that the only properties that a physical object literally has are its intrinsic properties, we should, from the point of view of the argument we are considering, again be in danger of proving too much. For instance, the energy which is attributed to electrons would appear to be not an intrinsic but a causal property: and indeed it is not easy to find examples of properties which

[1] F. H. Bradley, *Appearance and Reality*, p. 12.

are clearly intrinsic, outside the properties of percepts. We can, however, introduce a weaker sense of the term, in which a property is said to be intrinsic, if, and only if, it is not defined in terms of the effects which it has or would have upon an observer. Again, it is necessary that the property should at least have some remote effects which are detectible by an observer, if we are to have any reason to believe in its existence: what is required is just that it not be defined in terms of them. In this sense the colour which common sense ascribes to physical objects, as opposed to percepts, is not an intrinsic property, since the colour of an object is defined as the colour which it would appear to have to a normal observer under normal conditions of perception. On the other hand, the energy of an electron may be intrinsic to it.

The procedure then will be to say that the properties which are intrinsic to an object in this sense are the only ones that it literally has: and then if we substitute 'really' for 'literally' we reach the position which the followers of Locke have derived from the causal theory of perception. The result, at the common-sense level, is that the only properties that an object really has are those that are ascribed to it on the basis, not of straightforward observation, but of measurement; and this seems a very tenuous distinction on which to found a criterion of reality. Whether it can be made less tenuous will depend on the view which is taken of the status of the objects which enter into scientific explanations. Such things as electrons are sufficiently remote from observation to make it seem more reasonable to credit them with intrinsic properties, in the sense I have defined: and if it can be held that they are literally parts of the physical objects of common sense, one can perhaps follow Locke in identifying what he called the 'real essences' of these objects with the properties of their 'minute parts'. This view is not without its difficulties – it would entail, for instance, that this desk does not really have a continuous surface – but I think that it may be tenable.

If we do come to hold it, we should, however, be clear about what we are doing. We are not discovering what there really is. We are laying down a criterion of reality. It is not like the question whether the snakes which the drunkard sees are real or imaginary, or whether a pearl is real or artificial. In these cases there are established criteria for the respective uses of the word 'real', so that in answering the questions we are describing matters of fact. But the question whether my desk is really coloured, if it looks for some other answer than the common-sense answer 'Yes, it is brown', is not, at this stage, an answerable

question. It becomes an answerable question only after we have decided to lay down some such rule as that the intrinsic properties of
physical objects alone are to be accounted real, in the sense of the term
that we are introducing, and have then perhaps gone on to identify the
intrinsic properties of objects with the properties of the electrons which
are taken to be their minute parts. There is a logical question as to
whether the identification is justified, and there is a scientific question
as to what properties electrons have, but beyond that this ascription
of reality is just a matter of how we choose to picture the world. It is a
choice which there may be respectable motives for making, but it is
still a choice.

As we have seen, it is one that Russell makes, though he does not
think of it in these terms. He takes himself to be putting forward a
probable theory about the composition of the world, overlooking or
disregarding the fact that once it goes beyond the question of scientific
truth or falsehood, there is no possible way, apart from the consideration of logical coherence, in which the validity of such a theory could
be decided. In Russell's system, as it is set out in the chapter entitled
'My Present View of the World', in the last of his philosophical works,
My Philosophical Development, he takes as fundamental the notion of
'event'. Physical continuants are equated with events in causal lines,
and by a technique which Russell borrowed from Whitehead and set
out in *Our Knowledge of the External World*, point-instants, if they are
needed, are found to be constructible out of assemblages of overlapping
events. I believe that these constructions are feasible and illuminating,
though I cannot agree with Russell that in failing to make them we
should be giving unnecessary hostages to fortune. The only sense which
I can give to the question whether there really are point-instants is
whether they are logically eliminable.

In the opening words of his *Principia Ethica*, Moore says that it
appears to him 'that in Ethics, as in all other philosophical studies, the
difficulties and disagreements of which its history is full are mainly
due to a very simple cause: namely to the attempt to answer questions
without first discovering precisely *what* question it is which you desire
to answer'.[1] Whether or not this is true of ethics, and it is likely that it
is, it is undoubtedly true of ontology: and it is a charge from which
Russell does not altogether escape. He is not always clear what issue
is involved when he raises the question whether or not a certain type
of entity is to be regarded as part of the furniture of the world. Never-

[1] G. E. Moore, *Principia Ethica*, p. vi.

theless, his actual handling of these questions does often result in giving us a clearer understanding of their nature. No more in Russell's neutral monism, than in his theory of descriptions, do the doubts that one may feel about the official purpose of the analysis detract from the logical importance of the results that he achieves.

G. E. Moore

6 The Refutation of Idealism

A. MOORE'S LIFE AND WORKS

In the first volume of his autobiography, Bertrand Russell describes the impression which G. E. Moore made on him when they first met as undergraduates at Cambridge. He speaks of the purity of Moore's intellect and character and the intensity of his passion for truth, and says of him that 'for some years he fulfilled my ideal of genius'.[1] Neither was Russell alone in receiving this impression. It was fully shared by the next generation of Cambridge intellectuals, men like Lytton Strachey and Maynard Keynes and Leonard Woolf, who respected Russell as a philosopher but took Moore for their mentor. This group, with the principal addition of Roger Fry, Clive Bell, and the daughters of Leslie Stephen who became Vanessa Bell and Virginia Woolf, were the nucleus of what came to be known as the Bloomsbury set, and they found in Moore's *Principia Ethica*, and especially in its doctrine that the mental states which consisted in the love of beautiful objects and good persons were the only things perfectly good in themselves, a justification for a somewhat precious attitude to life. Russell remarks of this generation, unkindly, that whereas he and his friends had 'believed in ordered progress by means of politics and free discussion', 'they aimed rather at a life of retirement among fine shades and nice feelings, and conceived of the good as consisting in the passionate mutual admirations of a clique of the élite',[2] and adds that they fathered this doctrine quite unfairly upon Moore. There is some truth in this, but also some injustice. Keynes himself gives a more judicious account of what he and his friends owed to Moore in 'Early Beliefs', one of *Two Memoirs* which he published under that title in 1949. He admits that they treated Moore's ethics selectively, but argues, I think rightly, that their attitude had a basis in Moore's own unworldliness and his indifference to the 'qualities of a life of action'.

Principia Ethica was Moore's first book. It was published in 1903,

[1] *The Autobiography of Bertrand Russell*, I 64.   [2] Ibid.

towards the end of the six-year period during which he held a Research Fellowship at Trinity College, Cambridge. He was born in 1873, the son of a doctor of some independent means who had already retired from practice. His mother, originally a Miss Sturge, came from a well-known Quaker family. He was the fifth of eight children and one of his elder brothers, Thomas Sturge Moore, achieved some celebrity as a poet. He went as a day-boy to Dulwich College, where he distinguished himself as a classical scholar. The most interesting thing that he relates about his schooldays, in the autobiography which he contributed to *The Philosophy of G. E. Moore*, is that at the age of eleven or twelve he underwent 'an intense religious phase', even to the point of actively trying to make converts to the Salvation Army type of Christianity to which he had himself been converted. This phase lasted for about two years, after which Moore became and remained 'a complete agnostic'. In this he resembled Russell but without the militancy which led Russell to publish such works as *Why I am not a Christian*. Almost all that Moore thought it necessary to say about the grand metaphysical questions of God and Immortality is contained in one short paragraph of the essay, 'A Defence of Common Sense', which he contributed to the second volume of *Contemporary British Philosophy* in 1925:

'I have just explained', he says, 'that I differ from those philosophers who have held that there is good reason to suppose that all material things were created by God': the explanation being that he sees no good reason to suppose that every physical fact is either logically or casually dependent upon some mental fact. 'And it is', he continues, 'I think, an important point in my position, which should be mentioned, that I differ also from all philosophers who have held that there is good reason to suppose that there is a God at all, whether or not they have held it likely that he created all material things.

'And similarly, whereas some philosophers have held that there is good reason to suppose that we, human beings, shall continue to exist and to be conscious after the death of our bodies, I hold that there is no good reason to suppose this.'[1]

From Dulwich, Moore went in 1892 to Trinity College, Cambridge. At that time he knew next to nothing about philosophy. 'I came up to Cambridge,' he relates, 'expecting to do nothing but Classics there, and expecting also that afterwards, all my life long, my work would consist in teaching Classics to the Sixth Form of some Public School – a pro-

---

[1] 'A Defence of Common Sense', in *Philosophical Papers*, p. 52.

spect to which I looked forward with pleasure.'[1] It was only in his second year at Cambridge, when he got to know Russell well, that he became interested in philosophical questions and discovered that he had an aptitude for them: and it was Russell who persuaded him to specialise in philosophy for the second part of his undergraduate course. He graduated in 1896 and two years later was elected to a prize-fellowship at Trinity, having submitted a dissertation on Kant's Ethics. This dissertation has never been published but the substance of it is said by Moore to be contained in two articles which appeared in *Mind*, one on 'Freedom' in 1898 and the other on 'The Nature of Judgement' in 1899. Neither of these articles was thought by him to be worth reprinting, but the one on 'The Nature of Judgement' has a certain historical importance and I shall be saying something about it later on.

During the six years' tenure of his Fellowship, Moore was mainly occupied first in writing a number of articles for Baldwin's *Dictionary of Philosophy* and then in writing *Principia Ethica*. When the Fellowship lapsed in 1904, he had sufficient private means to enable him to continue working at philosophy without holding any official position. The main fruits of this period away from Cambridge, which lasted for seven years, were a small book on *Ethics*, which Moore wrote for the Home University Library, and his largest philosophical work, *Some Main Problems of Philosophy*. *Ethics*, which was published in 1912, is a more popular and less ambitious work than *Principia Ethica*, but commenting on it thirty years later, Moore said that he liked it better because it seemed to him 'much clearer and far less full of confusions and invalid arguments'.[2] *Some Main Problems of Philosophy* was not published until 1953, but, with a few minor verbal alterations, it is a reproduction of two series of lectures which Moore delivered at Morley College, a working-men's college in London, in the years 1910–11. At the time when he published it, Moore feared that it might be out of date, but in fact, though its tone is less sophisticated than that of some of his later work, the range of questions which it covers, the method of its approach to them, and the views which he expressed in it, all set a course from which he never deviated very far. The lectures were chiefly concerned with what Professor John Wisdom, in his foreword to the book, called the problem of the external world and the problem of general ideas, and these, together with certain questions in the philosophy of logic, are the problems with which Moore was mainly occupied for the remainder of his career.

<hr />

[1] *The Philosophy of G. E. Moore*, p. 13.   [2] Ibid., p. 27.

In 1911 he returned to Cambridge as a University lecturer, and he remained there, lecturing every term, for the next twenty-eight years. He married Miss Dorothy Ely, one of his pupils, in 1916 and had two sons. In 1925 he succeeded James Ward as Professor of Philosophy and again became a Fellow of Trinity. After he retired from the professorship in 1939, to be succeeded by Ludwig Wittgenstein, he gave a series of lectures at Oxford and then, in 1940, accepted an invitation to become a Visiting Professor for a year at Smith College. He remained in the United States, lecturing at various universities, until 1944, when he returned to live privately in Cambridge. He was editor of *Mind* from 1921 to 1947, and, in addition to one or two academic honours, was awarded the Order of Merit in 1951, an occasion on which he is reported to have been shocked by the fact that King George VI had never heard of Wittgenstein. He died in 1958, at the age of eighty-five.

Apart from the three books already mentioned, *Principia Ethica*, *Ethics*, and *Some Main Problems of Philosophy*, the only other of Moore's books which was published in his lifetime was a collection of articles called *Philosophical Studies*, which came out in 1922. Another collection of articles, called *Philosophical Papers*, was in proof at the time of Moore's death and was published in 1959. Between them these two volumes contain all the most important of Moore's articles, the great majority of which first appeared in the *Proceedings* or *Supplementary Proceedings of the Aristotelian Society*. Among the papers which Moore left to his executors was a series of notebooks, ranging in date from 1919 to 1953, in which he had entered brief reflections on a fairly wide range of philosophical problems. These notes were edited by Casimir Lewy and published in 1962 under the title of *The Commonplace Book of G. E. Moore*. Lewy also edited some of Moore's lecture notes and published them in 1965 under the title *Lectures in Philosophy*. This volume contains selections from three courses of lectures, one given in 1928-9 on the topic of perception and the reality of the material world, another given in 1925-6 on questions belonging to the philosophy of logic, and especially those arising from Russell's treatment of classes, and the third given in 1933-4 on the aims and methods of philosophy and the nature of philosophical analysis. Finally, *The Philosophy of G. E. Moore*, which was published in 1942, in Dr Schilpp's 'Library of Living Philosophers', achieves the purpose of the editor, to prompt the philosophers chosen to clarify their views, better, in my opinion, than any other volume in the series. Quite a high proportion of the critical essays are interesting and pertinent: Moore's replies to them are painstaking and informative, and his autobiography, on which I have been drawing freely, well displays the simplicity and charm of his personality.

An interesting admission which Moore makes in his autobiography is that in his case the main stimulus to philosophise came not from direct reflection on 'the world or the sciences' but rather from what other philosophers had said about them. And he adds that the problems which the writings of those other philosophers had suggested to him were, in his own words, 'mainly of two sorts, namely, first, the problem of trying to get really clear as to what a given philosopher *meant* by something which he said, and, secondly, the problem of discovering what really satisfactory reasons there are for supposing that what he meant was true, or, alternatively, was false'.[1] On this last point, he is certainly unfair to himself: he nearly always has a contribution of his own to make to the elucidation or the solution of the particular question at issue. It is, however, true that very often he takes some remark made by another philosopher as a starting-point: and the extent to which his work did depend on this sort of stimulus may account for the fact that so much of it takes the form of articles on specific questions, rather than the more general argument of a book. In his early writings, apart from his work on ethics, the provocation usually came from the neo-Hegelians, Bradley and McTaggart. Later on, it was often in relation to Russell, explicitly or tacitly, that he developed his own positions. The fact that so much of his writing hangs on the work of contemporary or near-contemporary British philosophers may also help to explain why, even now, his philosophy is not at all well known outside the English-speaking world.

Within the English-speaking world, on the other hand, Moore has had a very strong philosophical influence; a stronger influence, indeed, than could reasonably be ascribed to his published work, considered on its own. As Professor Broad put it, in his obituary notice of Moore which is reprinted as a foreword to the *Philosophical Papers*, 'It was by his lectures, his discussion-classes, his constant and illuminating contributions to discussion at the Cambridge Moral Science Club and the Aristotelian Society, and his private conversations with his colleagues and pupils that he mainly produced his effects on the thought of his time'.[2] In addition, his literalness, of which we have already seen an instance in his objecting to Russell that Scott might have been the author of *Waverley* without writing it, his circumspection in the use of technical terms, his insistence on taking the statements of metaphysicians

[1] Ibid., p. 14.   [2] *Philosophical Papers*, p. 12.

at their face value, his championship of the common-sense view of the world, and his occasional tendency to appeal to considerations of ordinary English usage, have led the disciples of Wittgenstein and Austin to venerate him, rather than Russell, as the precursor of their way of doing philosophy. I think that they have some justification for this, in that the implications of Moore's defence of common sense do tend to limit philosophy to the practice of conceptual analysis, although this is not a conclusion that he himself accepted. On the other hand, we shall also see that Moore is very little of a linguistic philosopher in the current acceptation of the term.

As a literary stylist, Moore cannot be compared with Russell, but his style has merits of its own. If he does not write with Russell's grace and fluency, he is never guilty, as Russell sometimes is, of achieving elegance at the expense of accuracy and precision. I doubt if there has ever been a philosopher who went to such lengths to make his meaning clear. Sometimes his precautions seem excessive: qualifications are made and distinctions drawn which the reader might think he could have been allowed to take for granted. But then one reflects that the style is the measure of the philosopher: and to be in any way slapdash was not in Moore's philosophical nature. It is a style that with its convolutions and frequent resort to italics reminds one, not at all of William, but of Henry James, and like Henry James's style it grows upon you. Moore's writing, however, is never affected in the way that Henry James's sometimes is. The impression which it gives is one of great subtlety but also of a fundamental simplicity and of complete intellectual honesty.

Although two of the three books which Moore published in his lifetime, apart from the collections of essays, deal with ethics, I shall not be concerned with him as a moral philosopher. This is a more serious omission than the corresponding omission in the case of Russell, since Moore did make an important contribution to ethical theory. My excuse is that his work on ethics, which, apart from his reply to his critics in *The Philosophy of G. E. Moore*, is confined to the earlier part of his career, is not a principal factor in his contribution to what I am calling the analytical heritage, and that in any case I have nothing new to add to the criticism which I have made elsewhere of his central ethical doctrine that good is a simple non-natural quality.[1] I shall, however, have something to say about his exposition of the so-called naturalistic fallacy, that is to say, the fallacy of supposing that good can

[1] See 'On the Analysis of Moral Judgements' in my *Philosophical Essays*.

be identical with any natural quality, since the arguments which he uses to arrive at this conclusion raise a fundamental question about the nature and validity of any definition.

B. HIS INTERPRETATION OF THE PRINCIPLE THAT TO BE IS TO BE PERCEIVED

Moore relates in his autobiography that of all his teachers at Cambridge, McTaggart was the one who had the most influence upon him. At the same time it was he who led the attack, in which Russell later joined, on the neo-Hegelianism of which McTaggart, with Bradley, was the leading English representative. Russell once spoke to me of the very strong impression which Moore's essay 'The Nature of Judgement' made on him when he first heard Moore read it: but this essay, as we shall see, exhibits the extreme form of Platonism which Moore took up when he had already rejected idealism, rather than the process of this rejection itself. The *locus classicus* for his refutation of idealism is an essay which appeared under that title in *Mind* in 1903. Though Moore himself confessed, nineteen years later, in his preface to *Philosophical Studies*, that this essay appeared to him 'to be very confused as well as to embody a good many down-right mistakes',[1] he reprinted it as it stood because of its historical importance. For the same reason I shall go through its argument in some detail.

'Modern Idealism,' Moore begins, 'if it asserts any general conclusion about the universe at all, asserts that it is *spiritual*.'[2] What Moore takes this to mean is at least that the universe is very different from what it seems to be, in that things like chairs and tables and mountains which appear to be inanimate are really conscious: and not only that but the universe has, or the things within it have, 'what we recognise in our-selves as the *higher* forms of consciousness'.[2] Here I think that Moore is being unfair to most of the Absolute Idealists in making them attribute consciousness to things like tables and mountains, rather than to the universe as a whole: but it is true that McTaggart held that what we misperceive as physical objects in spatio-temporal relations are really selves in some form of timeless mental communication with each other.

Moore does not profess to be able to prove that any such idealist doctrine is false. What he does undertake to prove is that no one has

---

[1] *Philosophical Studies*, p. viii.   [2] Ibid., p. 1.

any good reason for believing it. The reason why he thinks that this can be proved is that the arguments on which idealists rely always, in his view, involve the assumption of a principle which he believes that he can show to be unwarranted. This is the Berkeleyan principle that *esse est percipi* – to be is to be perceived – where *percipi* may be taken not just in the narrow sense of being sensibly perceived, but also as comprising being an object of thought, so that a better rendering of the principle, as Moore envisages it, might be that to be is to be experienced.

Now the first question that arises is how this principle is to be interpreted. Moore says that there are three different meanings which the statement of it might be taken to bear. In the first place, it might be construed as asserting that the words '*esse*' and '*percipi*' are synonymous. Of this interpretation Moore is content to say that he thinks he need not prove 'that the principle that *esse* is *percipi* is *not* thus intended merely to define a word; nor yet that, if it were, it would be an extremely bad definition'.[1] A second possible interpretation is 'that what is meant by *esse*, though not absolutely identical with what is meant by *percipi*, yet *includes* the latter as *part* of its meaning'.[2] Again, this proposition does not seem to Moore to be worth discussing. 'I do not, indeed, think', he says, 'that the word "reality" is commonly used to include "*percipi*": but I do not wish to argue about the meaning of words.'[2] He then makes the point that whether or not *esse* is correctly taken as containing *percipi*, it must include some other factor, or set of factors, which he proposes to call X, so that the question arises how *percipi* is related to X. Now there would, Moore maintains, be nothing in the principle that *esse* is *percipi* to arouse any interest if it implied only that X and *percipi* were contingently related: the claim has to be that there is a necessary connection between them. It cannot be an analytic connection, since *ex hypothesi* X does not overlap with *percipi*, but it could be synthetically necessary. For the sake of convenience, Moore next proposes that '*esse*' be construed as denoting X alone. Then the third, and in his view the only interesting interpretation of '*esse est percipi*' is that *esse*, in this sense, stands to *percipi* in a synthetically necessary relation.

At this point, Moore has to concede that if '*esse est percipi*' is put forward as a synthetic *a priori* proposition it cannot be refuted. 'If the Idealist chooses to assert that it is merely a self-evident truth, I have only to say that it does not appear to me to be so.'[3] At the same time he does not think that any idealist would take this proposition for a self-evident

[1] Ibid., p. 9.   [2] Ibid.   [3] Ibid., p. 11.

truth if he apprehended it distinctly. In his view, the reason why idealists believe that the words *'esse est percipi'* express a necessarily true proposition is that they confuse the proposition which he has just interpreted them as expressing with a different proposition which he thinks that he *can* refute, and that is the proposition that *esse* and *percipi* are analytically connected, in the sense that there logically could not be an object which was not an object of experience. Moore's ground for saying that he can refute this proposition is that he can show it to be self-contradictory. The result is that even if it cannot be proved that the idealists' doctrine is false, it can at least be proved that they are not justified in believing it, since the only reason which they have for holding an essential part of it is based on a self-contradictory mistake.

Before I set out the argument by which Moore seeks to show that the idealists are guilty of such a mistake, I want to say something about his interpretation of the Berkeleyan principle that *esse est principi*. I do not think that Berkeley himself meant it to be what Kant was to call a synthetic *a priori* proposition, nor do I think that it has to be taken in this way, in order to be of any philosophical interest. I believe that Berkeley did think of his principle as being logically necessary, but that he did not suppose that its necessity arose from the fact that the Latin word *'esse'*, or its equivalent in other languages, was commonly used in such a way as to be synonymous with or to comprehend *'percipi'*. If he had supposed this, I agree that he would have been mistaken.

In my view, the correct interpretation of Berkeley's principle is rather more complicated. It can be carried out in three stages. The first stage is to note that there are certain terms which are such that from the fact that they are exemplified it follows that something is experienced. For instance, if there is an occurrence of a headache it follows that something is being felt. It is to be remarked that the analytical connection here is not between being and being experienced, but between being an object of such and such a sort, a headache, a dream, an after-image, or whatever, and being experienced. His neglect of this point was one of the things that led Moore astray. It is also to be remarked that while, in speaking of any such object, one is certainly saying more than that something is being felt, it does not follow, as Moore seems to have assumed, that what one must be saying is that a feeling is conjoined with some other factor. It is, indeed, arguable that the ascription to anything of a bodily feeling carries a causal implication, but if we may leave this out of account, then to identify a feeling as a headache is not to make the separate statements that something is being felt, and that something is going on in someone's head: it is rather to specify the feeling by giving its location.

The second stage in Berkeley's argument is to extend this class of terms so that it covers all perceptual qualities. Thus, in the case of any colour, or shape, or sound, or taste or smell, or any tactile quality, the fact that it is exemplified in some particular instance is taken to entail that something is being experienced. Now, if this were meant to be an account of the way in which such terms are commonly understood, one would have to say that it was false. For anything to be coloured, it must indeed be visible, at least in principle, but it need not be actually seen: sounds must be audible, but they can exist without being actually heard; and similarly with the other perceptual qualities. But Berkeley was not giving an account of ordinary usage: he was engaging in semantic legislation, though he himself may not have been fully aware of this. Having introduced the technical term 'sensible quality', he reclassifies colours, sounds, and the rest as sensible qualities, and then stipulates that for a sensible quality to be instantiated is for it to be experienced. It may be noted that even here the logical connection is not between being and being perceived, but between being a sensible quality and being perceived. And it may also be noted that the reclassification of what I have been calling perceptual qualities as sensory qualities is not a very great departure from ordinary usage. There is a good case for saying that perceptual qualities, like that of being coloured, are dispositional properties, which are defined by reference to instances in which the colour, or whatever it may be, is actually perceived. If Berkeley distorts the usage of terms which designate these dispositional properties, it is only to the extent of making them refer to the corresponding instances.

The point of this manœuvre becomes clear when we pass to the third stage in our development of Berkeley's principle. For what he next maintains is that it is logically impossible that there should be anything which is not either (i) a sensible quality, or collection of sensible qualities, in the sense defined or (ii) a substance to which these qualities are presented. In putting his conclusion in the form of the proposition that *esse* is *percipi*, Berkeley limits the discussion to the first of these alternatives. What he is saying is that things, other than minds, consist of sensible qualities, and from the way in which he defends this proposition, it is reasonably clear that he takes it to be logically necessary. This does not commit him to holding that when people talk about material things, they intend to refer to sensible qualities: if it did he would be obviously wrong. His position is rather that it is only to the extent that they can be replaced by statements about sensible qualities that the statements that we make about material things can have any truth-value: and his ground for this is that, given that they have some legitimate reference and that they do not refer to minds, there are no other conceivable candidates.

If my interpretation of Berkeley's principle is correct, it would appear to be open to two kinds of attack. One can try to show that his notion of a sensible quality is incoherent or wrongly applied. Alternatively, one can dispute the contention that things are composed of sensible qualities. The second line of attack is, to my mind, the more promising, but the first is more ambitious, in that, if it succeeds, the second does not arise.

C. HIS CRITICISM OF THIS PRINCIPLE

Moore takes the more ambitious course. The allegedly self-contradictory error which he rather surprisingly thinks that 'no previous philosopher has ever yet succeeded in avoiding'[1] is just that of taking the first two steps in my exposition of Berkeley's argument. The example which he uses to prove that these steps are self-contradictory is that of the sensation of colour: with less than his usual attention to English idiom, he speaks of the consciousness of blue and the consciousness of green. Such states are analysed by him into two elements: on the one hand, consciousness, in respect of which all sensations are alike, and on the other, the object of consciousness, in respect of which they differ. Thus, when I have a sensation of blue, or green, or sweet, blue, green, and sweet are the objects of my consciousness. But then, Moore argues, it follows that consciousness is different from blue, since consciousness is present also in the consciousness of green or sweet, whereas blue is not. And if consciousness and blue are different, he continues, it must be self-contradictory to say that 'blue exists' is equivalent to 'blue and consciousness exist'. So, he concludes, 'If anyone tells us that the existence of blue is the same thing as the existence of the sensation of blue he makes a mistake and a self-contradictory mistake, for he asserts *either* that blue is the same thing as blue together with consciousness, *or* that it is the same thing as consciousness alone'.[2]

[1] Ibid., p. 19.   [2] Ibid., p. 18.

What this argument comes down to is that since blue and consciousness are different, it must be logically possible that they should exist independently: if it were to be logically impossible for blue to exist independently of consciousness, it would have to be identical with it. But as a general principle, this is plainly false. For instance, being red is not identical with being coloured, yet to be red is the same thing as to be coloured red; waltzing is not identical with dancing, yet there cannot be a waltz without a dance; there are card games other than bridge, yet one cannot play bridge without playing cards. And similarly, I should say, although a headache is only one sort of feeling, there cannot be a headache without its being felt.

Moore's argument would work, at least for his examples, if the relation of blue to the sensation of blue were that of part to whole. For in the case of any whole, it is logically possible that the parts should exist independently. But if this applied to consciousness and its objects, it would follow not only that the objects could exist uncognised but also that consciousness could exist independently of any object. It is not clear to me whether Moore accepts this conclusion. He talks in one place of the element of consciousness as being 'extremely difficult to fix' and as seeming to be transparent,[1] but later he says that this diaphanous element 'can be distinguished if we look attentively enough, and if we know that there is something to look for'.[2] Yet, whatever Moore may have thought that he found when he undertook this introspection, it is hard to understand how there could be a state of consciousness which had no 'object', or as I should prefer to put it, no content at all.

The suggestion that blue should be said to be the content of the sensation of blue is one that Moore does discuss. He begins by asking what is meant by saying that one thing is the content of another, and answers that the word 'content' is being properly used when it is said that blue is part of the content of a blue flower. Since he takes this to mean that blue is one of the qualities of a blue flower, he concludes that to say that blue is the content of the sensation of blue is to say that it qualifies the sensation in the way that it qualifies a flower or a bead when we speak of a blue flower or a blue bead. The sensation of blue must, indeed, also have the quality of being a sensation: or if we think of the element of consciousness as the common substance which is differentiated in different sensations, it must still be represented in the sensation of blue by some factor which is other than blue, so that blue

[1] Ibid., p. 20.   [2] Ibid., p. 25.

cannot in any case be the whole of the content of the sensation; however, it might be part of it.

Moore allows that this suggestion is logically possible, but no more than that. We have no reason whatever, he says, to suppose that the sensation of blue is itself blue, and even if it were its being blue would not make it a sensation *of* blue, any more than the fact that an image is blue is sufficient to make it a representation of a blue object.

This last point is valid, but the reasoning which leads Moore to it is perverse. I doubt if we ever speak of qualities like the colour of a flower as contents of the things which they qualify, and even if we did it would not be the usage which was intended by anyone who spoke of colours as the contents of sensations. The sense in which he would be using the word 'content' would be that in which, when someone has a feeling of excitement or lassitude, one can speak of this excitement or lassitude as the content of his feeling. It would not be incorrect, I think, to speak of them as different species of feeling, but a better way of putting it would be to say that the contents of feelings, in this sense, are cognate to the experiences into which they enter. This would be understood to entail that they cannot exist apart from being experienced, any more than a game of cards can take place without being played.

As I have already pointed out, it is not difficult to find examples of things which we ordinarily speak of as being cognate to experience. I doubt, for instance, if anyone would wish to say that dreams existed apart from being dreamed. On the other hand it is also true, as I have said, that we do not ordinarily speak of colours in this way. We speak of colours as qualities of objects and, with the exception of mental images, the objects which are said to be coloured are thought to exist independently of being perceived. But this does not settle the argument. As we have seen, the question is whether there is any logical objection to Berkeley's proposal to use colour-terms in such a way that colours become cognate to being seen: and on this point it seems to me that Moore has offered no valid argument at all.

The suggestion that colours, and other such perceptual qualities, are cognate to the experiencing of them was put forward by Professor C. J. Ducasse in his contribution to *The Philosophy of G. E. Moore*, though he treated it not as a proposal to revise our usage of colour terms, but rather as if it called attention to a matter of fact. In his reply Moore argued that in defending the view that the *esse* of sensible qualities was

percipi, Ducasse had come to what might very well be the right conclusion for the wrong reason. The reason was wrong because the view
that colours were similar to headaches, in respect of being cognate to
experiences, was inconsistent with the fact that being coloured was a
property of objects. On the other hand, Moore believed that the ascription of colour to material things was derivative from its ascription to
sense-data, and he was also inclined to think, by this time, that no sense-
datum could possibly exist except while it was being sensed, and indeed
that none that he sensed could possibly exist except while he was
sensing it, although he still said that he was unable to see where the
contradiction lay in supposing the opposite.[1] On this point, therefore,
he may be said to have come round, or almost to have come round, to
Berkeley's position.

I shall have something to say later on about Moore's conception of
sense-data. We shall find that some of the difficulties which it raises are
due to his failure to allow sufficiently for the fact that he is introducing
a technical term for which the rules of usage need to be specified. Such
a question as whether a sense-datum can exist without being sensed is
one that these rules should not leave in doubt. In fact, it is fairly clear
to me that Moore's use of the term 'sense-datum' is, among other things,
a device for reconciling the positions which he held to be inconsistent,
in his answer to Ducasse. It enables him both to speak of perceptual
qualities, like colours, as properties of objects, and to treat them as
cognate to experience. This is effected simply by introducing sense-
data as objects which are cognate to experience and attributing
perceptual qualities to them. The legitimacy of this manœuvre has
indeed been questioned, but for reasons which I have set out at length
elsewhere,[2] I do not think that it succumbs to any of the main objections
which have so far been brought against it.

To accept the second stage in my exposition of Berkeley's argument
does not commit one to accepting the third. And indeed, if the thesis
that things consist of sensible qualities is understood to imply that the
statements which we make about what we consider to be physical
objects can be adequately replaced by statements about sensible
qualities, I believe it to be false.[3] On the other hand, as I have
attempted to show in my discussion of William James's Radical

---

[1] *The Philosophy of G. E. Moore*, p. 660.
[2] See *The Problem of Knowledge*, chap. v, and my essay 'Has Austin Refuted the Sense-
Datum Theory?' in *Metaphysics and Common Sense*.
[3] See *The Problem of Knowledge*, chap. v.

Empiricism in my book on *The Origins of Pragmatism*,[1] it is possible to exhibit our common-sense conception of the physical world as a theory with respect to a primary system of sense-qualia. To this extent, therefore, I believe that Berkeley's position can be upheld. This is not, however, a vindication of idealism, since the programme requires that the qualia be treated initially as neutral and not as mental entities. They can be represented as mental entities only when they are reinterpreted into the theory which has been developed out of them, but since the theory is realistic this counts against idealism rather than for it.

A familiar objection to Berkeleyan idealism is that it leads to solipsism: if we start with the assumption that we are acquainted only with our own 'ideas', we can never find reason to believe that there is anything beyond them. This is indeed true, but it does not set the problem in the proper light. I agree that it is a mistake in the theory of knowledge to start with private entities, but the reason why it is a mistake is not just that it leads to awkward consequences but that it only makes sense to talk of privacy with respect to a universe of discourse which contains different persons, and persons are not to be reckoned among our primitive data. They are to be 'constructed' along with other physical objects. This is not, of course, to deny that even at the level of a realistic theory, there is still a sceptical problem about one's knowledge of other minds. We shall, however, see in a moment that the point that the problem arises only at this level is very important.

In concluding his argument against the principle that *esse* is *percipi*, Moore makes short work of the threat of solipsism. He maintains first that 'the only thing that is common and peculiar to all experiences' is the relation of being aware of something and secondly, that 'this awareness is and must be in all cases of such a nature that its object, when we are aware of it, is precisely what it would be, if we were not aware'.[2] Once this point is taken, 'It becomes plain that the existence of a table in space is related to my experience of *it* in precisely the same way as the existence of my own experience is related to my experience of *that*. Of both we are merely aware: if we are aware that the one exists, we are aware in precisely the same sense that the other exists: and if it is true that my experience can exist, even when I do not happen to be aware of its existence, we have exactly the same reason for supposing that the table can do so also.'[3]

The assumption that we are 'directly aware of the existence of

---

[1] See *The Origins of Pragmatism*, chap. 3, section C.   [2] *Philosophical Studies*, p. 29.
[3] Ibid., pp. 29–30

material things in space' would not have been regarded by Moore as necessarily inconsistent with his later view that in all cases of sense-perception we are directly aware of sense-data, since he took it to be an open question whether sense-data were not in some cases identical with parts of the surfaces of material things. I shall explain later on that this was a mistake on his part but it can be allowed to pass for the moment, as his contention that everything of which we are aware exists independently of our awareness of it is anyhow unacceptable. Not only does it leave us with objective headaches and the like, but since awareness is here taken to cover all forms of thought, it commits us, if not to the existence of fictitious and imaginary objects, which we shall see that Moore tries to resolve into concepts, at least to that of every conceivable type of abstract entity.

How far Moore continued to believe in the existence of abstract entities is a question which I shall discuss later on in detail. All that I wish to say about it now is that to the extent that he did continue to believe in their existence, it was not just on the ground that they were objects of awareness. On the contrary, in an essay on 'The Conception of Reality', which was first published in the *Proceedings of the Aristotelian Society* for 1917–18 and is also reprinted in *Philosophical Studies*, he explicitly makes the point that being thought of does not entail existing. He contrasts the proposition 'Lions are hunted', from which he says it does follow that there are lions, with the proposition 'Unicorns are thought of', from which it does not follow that there are unicorns. The example is ill chosen in that hunting does not necessarily entail the existence of what is hunted – I could truthfully report that an expedition had been organised to hunt abominable snowmen, without thereby implying that there are such things – but the point which it was intended to illustrate is sound. There is only a limited number of cases in which one can legitimately infer, from the truth of what is expressed by a sentence of the subject–predicate form, that there are things of the sort of which the subject is said to be, and the cases in which the predicate is that of being thought of are not among them This is not, of course, a proof that there are not abstract entities; it is a proof only that what Moore calls our apprehending them is not a sufficient reason for concluding that there are.

When it comes to predicates which are used for the attribution of the various forms of sense-perception, the position is not so clear. We do, I think, have a tendency to use verbs like 'see' and 'hear' in such a way that if something is seen or heard it follows that it exists, but most of us do not follow this usage consistently. If we did follow it consistently, we should feel obliged, in telling the story of Macbeth, to say not that he saw a visionary dagger, but that he only thought he saw a real one: if we did not believe in the reality of Joan of Arc's voices, we should have to say, not that she heard voices, but that she only thought that she did. This would not be inaccurate, but equally I do not think that someone who attempted to make the same statements by speaking of Macbeth as having seen an unreal dagger or of Joan of Arc as having heard non-existent voices could be rightly accused of misusing the English language. The fact is that both these ways of speaking are permissible, and this is one reason why some philosophers, including Moore, have spoken of there being different senses of verbs like the English verb 'to see'. The peculiarity of the sense-datum theory is that it combines these different usages. It allows us to speak of Macbeth's experience as an instance of seeing, and at the same time maintains the rule that if someone sees something, there is something which he sees. The objects which in such cases would otherwise be lacking are supplied by the introduction of sense-data. Why it is thought necessary to supply such objects and how they come to be represented as the only objects of which we are directly aware in sense-perception, whether or not the perception is delusive, are questions to which I shall return at a later stage.

The introduction of sense-data, to which Moore had become committed by the time that he composed his lectures on *Some Main Problems of Philosophy*, thus enabled him to hold that sense-perception was always directed upon an existent object. It did not, however, entail that these objects always existed independently of being perceived. On the contrary, as I have already remarked, he was inclined to take the view that they never did. This was not a capitulation to idealism, because Moore also held, as we shall see, that it was quite certain that our claims to perceive physical objects, which did exist independently of being perceived, were very often true. This may look like a contradiction, but the contradiction is avoided by distinguishing different levels of perception, so that the perception of physical objects is made to depend upon the direct perception of sense-data. The problem, then, is to show exactly how these two levels of perception are related, and to this problem, as we shall also see, Moore never found a satisfactory answer.

At an intervening stage, in a long essay on 'The Nature and Reality of Objects of Perception', which appeared in the *Proceedings of the*

Aristotelian Society for 1905–6, and is reprinted in *Philosophical Studies*, Moore took the view that the objects of sense-perception might not exist. He in fact appears to oscillate between saying of cases like that of Macbeth's perception of a dagger that they are not real perceptions and saying that they are not perceptions of real objects. At the same time, he advances a strong *ad hominem* argument to prove that the objects of perception must sometimes be real, where their being real is understood to imply that they exist independently of being perceived. The argument is *ad hominem*, in the sense that it is directed against an idealist, or indeed anyone else, who thinks that he is entitled to believe in the existence of experiences which are not his own. Moore takes it for granted that if anyone ever is entitled to hold such a belief, it must be on the basis of an argument from analogy, and he admits that such an argument can legitimately support a probable inference. 'I am willing to allow', he says, 'that my observations of the fact that my perception of a certain movement in my own body is preceded by a certain feeling of pain, *will* justify the generalisation that my perception of any such movement, whether in my own body *or* in that of another person, is generally preceded by a similar feeling of pain.'[1] But he then points out that if an inference to the existence of an unobserved *B* from that of an observed *A* is to be justified on the ground that *A*s and *B*s have been generally found to be associated, it is essential that the relation in which *B* is taken to stand to *A* in this instance should be the same as in the preceding case. We can infer that an observed egg has been laid by an unobserved hen, but only by a hen which has been in the appropriate spatio-temporal relation to it. Consequently, if it were the case that the objects of my perception never existed independently of my perceiving them, so that what I described as the perception of another person's body was in fact the perception of a sense-content private to myself, then the most that a perception of this sort could justify me in inferring would be the existence of an unconscious pain of my own. This follows from the assumption that the only things that I can ever have observed to be associated are my own experiences. On the other hand, the position is quite different if the perceptions which enter into the argument are taken to be perceptions of real, independently existing, objects. For then 'There is no reason why I should not be justified in inferring that another person's feelings stand *in the same relation* to the real movements of his body, in which I observe my own feelings to stand to similar real movements of mine'.[2]

---

[1] *Philosophical Studies*, p. 81.   [2] Ibid., p. 83.

There are, indeed, notorious difficulties about the use of an argument from analogy, even on the most favourable assumptions, to justify belief in the existence of other people's experiences, but this is not a question into which I propose to enter here. It is enough for our present concern that Moore's argument is clearly valid *ad hominem*. If I do not believe that it commits us to a naïve realist view of perception, it is only because I think it possible, as I have already said, to start with neutral data, and then 'construct' the physical world as a theory with respect to them. The two points which emerge are, first, that the question whether one has good reason to believe in the existence of other minds has no hope of being answered affirmatively unless it is posed at a theoretical level at which provision is already made for the existence of physical objects, and, secondly, that this level cannot legitimately be reached if our primary data are taken to be private, not merely in terms of the physical theory which is based upon them, but on their own account from the start. So while I do not agree that Moore's argument proves all that he thinks it does, I do think that in this instance he has shown one common idealist position to be untenable.

D. THE DOGMA OF INTERNAL RELATIONS

Historically, Moore was no doubt right in assuming that the two propositions which a philosopher is required to hold in order to be fairly classified as an idealist are, first, that there is at least one spiritual substance and, secondly, that apart from this spiritual substance, or substances, nothing exists independently of being experienced. There is, however, another thesis to which the Absolute Idealists, whom Moore was mainly concerned to criticise, attached an equally great importance, and that is the thesis that reality is an organic whole. Exactly what they meant by this was never made entirely clear, but they took it as implying that any reference to an object which was abstractive, in the sense that it failed to specify all the relations in which it stood to other objects, was bound to misrepresent it. From this it was inferred that all the propositions of ordinary or scientific discourse were at least partially false, and that the one and only truth consisted in reality's being what it was, a truth which could not be stated, since the abstraction of the symbols which would be required to state it would itself be a falsification of it.

This conclusion may be thought sufficiently absurd for the thesis hardly to be worth discussing, but it depended on a proposition which is of a philosophical interest. This is the so-called dogma of internal relations, which Bradley expressed by saying that every relation is intrinsical in the sense that it 'essentially penetrates the being of its terms'.[1] What this comes to is that every relation in which an object stands to any other is necessary to its being the object that it is. On its own, this principle does not entail that any attempt to refer to an individual object is a piece of vicious abstraction: one has to combine with it the false assumption, which philosophers like Bradley also made, that what is not explicitly asserted is implicitly denied. Without this assumption, and with the true assumption that everything in the world is somehow related to everything else, the principle entails rather that in making a successful reference to any particular object one is covertly asserting the existence of every particular object that there is. If one added to this the Leibnizian doctrine that all qualities are internal to their subjects, the result would be that any self-consistent proposition about any particular object entailed every true proposition about every object, with the further consequence that all these propositions were equivalent. I do not know that any philosopher who believes in the internality of all relations has drawn this conclusion, but in default of some good reason for distinguishing in this regard between relations and qualities, I do not see how he can legitimately avoid it. In any event, even without this final absurdity, the consequences of the doctrine are clearly unacceptable.

There is no question, then, but that the dogma of internal relations is false. What is of interest is how it has come to be held. Moore addresses himself to the problem in an essay on 'External and Internal Relations', which first appeared in the *Proceedings of the Aristotelian Society* in 1919–20, and is the latest in date of those reprinted in his *Philosophical Studies*. Bradley is again the principal target, and the essay may be said to complete Moore's attack on the idealist position.

Moore begins by distinguishing between relations, like that of fatherhood, and relational properties, like that of being the father of such and such a person, and argues that the dogma of internal relations should be construed as a thesis with respect to relational properties. What he takes it to imply is that 'In the case of every relational property, it can always be truly asserted of any term A which has that property, that any term which had not had it would necessarily have been different

[1] F. H. Bradley, *Appearance and Reality*, p. 392.

from A'.[1] He notes that this formulation leaves it unclear whether the difference is intended to be qualitative, or merely numerical, and remarks that if qualitative difference is intended, then, so far from its being the case that all relations are internal to their terms, it is doubtful if any are. In order to get an example, he thinks it would be necessary to assume that qualities themselves, and not merely the things that had them, differed in quality: it could then be said, for instance, that the quality orange had the internal relational property of being intermediate between the qualities yellow and red. This would not, however, be an internal property of anything that had the property orange unless it were a necessary fact that the object in question was of this colour: and this would not in general be true. It might, I think, be argued that it was sometimes true, for instance in the case of an afterimage, but this raises a more general question about the identification of particular objects about which I shall have something to say later on.

Moore does not dwell on the thesis that any two terms which differ in their relational properties must of necessity be qualitatively different, because he thinks that he can refute the weaker thesis that they must of necessity be numerically different, and from the falsity of the weaker thesis that of the stronger thesis follows. He allows that some relational properties are internal, in the weaker sense, and gives as an instance the property which is possessed by a coloured patch, half of which is red and half yellow, of containing the red portion as a part. He thinks, however, that the same example can be used to show that some relational properties are not internal. For, as he says, 'It seems quite clear that though the whole could not have existed without having the red patch for a part, the red patch might perfectly well have existed without being part of that particular whole.'[2] And plainly one could adduce many other examples in which it is 'a mere matter of fact' that an object possesses some relational property, in the sense that its not having had it would not have affected its identity.

But how could anyone have supposed otherwise? Moore suggests that this may have come about through a failure to distinguish a necessarily true proposition from one that is generally false. For the expression of these propositions he found that he needed a term to express the converse of the relation which holds between two propositions when one follows logically from the other, and chose the term 'entails' for this purpose. So far as I know, it was its first introduction into philosophical literature. Then the necessarily true proposition is

[1] *Philosophical Studies*, p. 284.   [2] Ibid., p. 288.

that the possession by an object A of a relational property P entails that in the case of any object X, if X has not got P it is not identical with A. The generally false proposition, with which the true one is confused, is that if A has P, then in the case of any object X the proposition that X has not got P entails that X is not identical with A. In short, the confusion is between a proposition of the form 'p entails (if q then r)' and one of the form 'if p, then (q entails r)'. To show that this is a confusion, Moore substitutes for p, q and r respectively, the propositions 'All the books on this shelf are blue', 'My copy of the *Principles of Mathematics* is a book on this shelf', and 'My copy of the *Principles of Mathematics* is blue'. Then it is certainly true that 'All the books on this shelf are blue' entails that if my copy of the *Principles* is a book on this shelf, my copy of the *Principles* is blue. This is not, however, to say that if all the books on the shelf are blue, then 'My copy of the *Principles* is a book on this shelf' entails 'My copy of the *Principles* is blue'. For from the fact that the proposition 'My copy of the *Principles* is a book on this shelf' entails the proposition 'My copy of the *Principles* is blue' in conjunction with the premiss that all the books on my shelf are blue, it certainly does not follow that it entails it by itself; and indeed, it evidently does not.

There is no doubt that Moore's argument is valid so far as it goes, and it may well be that the confusion which he attributes to those who have accepted the dogma of internal relations is one of which they have in fact been guilty. Nevertheless his own treatment of the question is not entirely satisfactory. The reason why it is not is that he overlooks the crucial fact that the question whether any property is or is not internal to a particular object may be taken to depend on the way in which the object is described. Thus it is not an internal property of Scott to have been the author of *Waverley*, neither is it an internal property of the author of *Ivanhoe*, but what of the author of *Waverley*? Is the proposition that the author of *Waverley* composed *Waverley* necessarily true? On one obvious interpretation of it, it surely is. Even so, one can attach a sense to saying that the person who was in fact the author of *Waverley* might not have been so. All that is needed for this is that he be capable of being otherwise identified.

The fact is that no property is internal to an individual, if its being internal implies that one can find no way of referring to the individual which is logically consistent with denying it the property. In the case of Moore's colour patch, if we begin by describing it as a patch which is half red and half yellow, we are logically committed to assigning it the property of containing the red patch as a part. But this would not be so, if we had described it initially as the patch which occupied such and such a spatial position. It might, indeed, still be argued that its containing this red part was essential to its being this particular colour patch, but that is only because in speaking of it as a colour patch we are implying that it is to be identified by its colour. If we were considering it, say, as a piece of cloth, the false hypothesis that the red part of it had been dyed a different colour would not be contradictory.

What we must not do, however, is be misled by the fact that none of an individual's properties are internal to it into supposing that we can affirm or deny anything whatsoever of it, while still maintaining its identity. For then we should be left with the untenable conception of an object as a bare particular. There is no item in the actual biography of an object that could not be denied to it without self-contradiction, but if we deprive it of the whole of its biography we shall find at some point that its identity has been lost. The object which I now identify as the inkpot in front of me might conceivably have been elsewhere, but if I am conceiving of it only as this inkpot, I cannot consistently ascribe to it a totally different spatio-temporal path from that which it has actually followed. I can go so far as to say that it might not have been an inkpot, but only if I mean to assert some such proposition as that another sort of object might have been made out of the same actual materials. The question of causal possibility also enters here. I do not think it can be true that this inkpot might have been a giraffe, except in the very weak sense that certain things which are true of it – for instance, that it is used to illustrate a point in such and such an argument – might conceivably not have been true of it and might have been true of some giraffe instead. But the difficulty with any discussion of this kind is that while it can safely be said that we have to maintain some anchorage in reality if our references to individual objects are to remain successful, there appear to be no general rules for deciding how firm the anchorage has to be. The requirements vary with the context of our statements, and perhaps also with the character of the objects in question. I think it to be true in general that the identity of an object does not survive complete spatio-temporal dislocation, but an exception may be made for objects which are qualitatively unique in some conspicuous way. For instance, the false proposition that the Parthenon was built in Corinth in the third century B.C. is at least not evidently self-contradictory. But then, does it follow that the Parthenon might, without loss of identity, have existed at any place and at any time; that it is, for example, logically possible that the very same building should be first erected in New York next year? And if this is not admissible, what are the limits? How far is our imagination allowed to travel in space and time, before a merely factual error becomes a logical one? I doubt if these questions have any definite answer.

The fact that such questions do not appear to have any definite answer may be taken as showing that the question whether a proposition is synthetic or analytic is not always decidable. It is also true that these puzzles about identity do not arise if one eliminates singular terms, since what is logically possible will then be determined by the answer to the more straightforward question whether or not certain predicates are mutually compatible. Moore himself, as we have seen, did not pursue the argument to the point where these difficulties are encountered, but he never expressed any doubts about the universality of the analytic–synthetic distinction, and while he accepted Russell's theory of descriptions he did not see it as leading to the elimination of singular terms. This is not to say that he would have rejected this possibility, but only that it did not occur to him to develop it. Though it is true that he operated mainly within the framework of ordinary language, this was not, in his case, a matter of principle. It was rather that he effectively reduced philosophy, at least in its constructive aspect, to a form of analysis, and that the analysis which he practised was intended to be descriptive rather than revisionary. The meaning of these remarks, and the justification for them, will, I hope, become clearer when we have examined his defence of common sense.

7 The Defence of Common Sense

A. THE COMMON-SENSE VIEW OF THE WORLD

In the first of the lectures which he entitled *Some Main Problems of Philosophy*, Moore says that he is going to try to give a description of the whole range of the subject. He adds, truly, that 'This is not at all an easy thing to do, because, when you come to look into the matter, you find that philosophers have in fact discussed an immense variety of different sorts of questions',[1] but he undertakes at least to begin by picking out the more important and interesting of them. He then at once goes on to say that it seems to him that 'The most important and interesting thing which philosophers have tried to do is no less than this; namely: To give a general description of the *whole* of the Universe, mentioning all the most important kinds of things which we *know* to be in it, considering how far it is likely that there are in it important kinds of things which we do not absolutely *know* to be in it, and also considering the most important ways in which these various kinds of things are related to one another.'[2]

This sounds a very large undertaking. How large it is will depend upon what is counted as an important kind of thing. It may look at first sight as if Moore thought of philosophers as being engaged in compiling a vast encyclopaedia, in which every known type of object, of scientific or historical interest, was listed and cross-classified. This would be a useful enterprise, in its way, though if the consideration of the most important ways in which the various kinds of things are related to one another were taken to include the whole of current scientific theory, the rapid advance of science might make it difficult to keep up to date. But the truth is that with the exception of the eighteenth-century French Encyclopédistes, who at any rate thought of themselves as *philosophes*, and with the less relevant exception of the Logical Positivists, who, at the instigation of Otto Neurath in the late 1930s, produced a number of interesting brochures under the general

[1] *Some Main Problems of Philosophy*, p. 1.   [2] Ibid.

heading of 'The Encyclopaedia of Unified Science', this is not the sort of thing that philosophers have mostly tried to do: and Moore did not suppose that it was. Though he does not lay down any criteria of importance, it soon becomes clear that he is concerned only with very broad classifications. This is sufficiently indicated by the fact that the first example that he gives of what he considers to be an important philosophical question is that of the truth or falsehood of what he calls the common-sense view of the world.

The principal feature of the common-sense view of the world, as Moore conceives it, is the belief 'that there are in the Universe enormous numbers of material objects'.[1] Moore does not, at this point, define what he means, or what he takes common sense to mean, by a material object, but he gives as examples human bodies, animals, plants, mountains, stones, grains of sand, minerals, soils, drops of water in rivers and seas, things manufactured by men, such as houses and chairs and tables and railway engines, and 'besides all these things upon the surface of the earth',[2] the earth itself and the sun and the moon and the stars. Every material object, in the common-sense view, is situated somewhere or other in space, which means, according to Moore, at least that 'each of them is, at any given moment, at some definite *distance* from all the rest' and that they are distant 'in some one or other of a quite *definite* set of directions'.[3] Every material object is also located in time, in the sense that 'each of them either did exist in the past, or exists now, or will exist in the future';[4] or else, as Moore characteristically adds, '*both* did exist at some time in the past, do exist now, and will exist in the future'.[5] Later in the book, when he defines a material object as 'something which (1) does occupy space, (2) is *not* a sense-datum of any kind whatever and (3) is not a mind, nor an act of consciousness',[6] he leaves out the property of being located in time, but presumably this is only an oversight, or because he thinks that it can be taken for granted.

The second of the main beliefs which enter into the common-sense view of the world, as Moore conceives it, is the belief that men, and possibly some other animals, have minds: and what Moore takes this to mean, at least in part, is that they perform what he calls acts of consciousness. Again, these acts of consciousness are not defined by Moore but he implies that they include hearing, seeing, remembering, feeling, thinking and dreaming. These acts are located in time and, rather surprisingly, Moore also ascribes to common sense the belief

¹ Ibid., p. 2.   ² Ibid., p. 3.   ³ Ibid., p. 5.
⁴ Ibid., p. 11.   ⁵ Ibid., p. 12.   ⁶ Ibid., p. 131.

that they are located in space. Although he believes that most philo-sophers have taken the view that 'Acts of consciousness do not occur in any place at all', he maintains that 'We all commonly assume . . . that our acts of consciousness take place, at any moment, *in the place* in which our bodies are at that moment'.[1] For instance, the common-sense belief, which he says that he shares, would be that when he took the train to get to the place where he was giving his lecture, his mind and his acts of consciousness travelled with him. He does not think that we commonly 'have any definite idea as to exactly *where* in our bodies our acts of consciousness take place':[2] we merely believe that they take place somewhere in them. Moore speaks of acts of consciousness as being attached to bodies and says that what this attachment is princi-pally thought to consist in is just that they take place where the bodies are. He allows it, however, also to be a common-sense belief that acts of consciousness are attached to bodies, in the sense that they are causally dependent on them.

It is, then, part of the common-sense view of the world, that acts of consciousness are attached, in these senses, to some bodies, but it is also part of its view that 'To the vast majority of material objects, *no* acts of consciousness are attached'.[3] And while we believe that we are at times conscious of material objects, we also believe that material objects, including those to which acts of consciousness are attached, continue to exist when we are not conscious of them. This goes with the belief that material objects existed at a time when there were no men on earth, and perhaps no acts of consciousness anywhere in the universe, and that 'there *may* come a time in the future when this would again be so'.[4]

The third main belief which Moore attributes to common sense is the belief that we really do know that there are material objects and acts of consciousness, and that they have the properties that he has listed. Not only that but 'We believe that we *know* an immense number of details about particular material objects and acts of consciousness, past, present and future. We know', he continues, 'most, indeed about the past; but a great deal about the present; and much also (though perhaps this is only probable knowledge) about the future.'[5] Much of this knowledge is thought to come from the special sciences, the function of which is to give us detailed knowledge about material objects, or, in the case of history and psychology, about acts of consciousness as well. 'In the case of all these sciences there are . . . a great many [things], which were formerly believed, but are now definitely known to be

[1] Ibid., p. 7.   [2] Ibid.   [3] Ibid., p. 8.   [4] Ibid., p. 10.   [5] Ibid., p. 12.

errors: and a great many which we do not know and perhaps never shall know': but there are also 'we believe, an immense number of things which are now definitely known to be facts'.[1]

Whether there are other things in the universe besides material objects and acts of consciousness (together with space and time of which Moore says that while they are certainly something, they are not substantial things, in the way that material objects and acts of consciousness are) is a question which he believes that common sense leaves open. He himself thinks that 'there certainly are several other kinds of things, and that it is one of the objects of philosophy to point them out'.[2] He does not say what kinds of things he has in mind, but I assume that they are abstract entities of various sorts. Since he does not mention abstract entities in his account of the common-sense view of the world, it may be inferred that he did not think that they were included in it. But here he may well have been mistaken. No doubt, it is left to philosophers to believe in the existence of universals or classes or propositions, but I should have thought that a belief in the existence of numbers was a characteristic of common sense. Perhaps Moore omitted numbers on the ground that they were not thought to be a substantial kind of thing.

Another notable omission from Moore's account of the common-sense view of the world is the belief in the existence of God. He does consider whether it ought to be included, but decides that it should not be, on the ground that, although many people do still believe that there certainly is a God, so many people nowadays deny that we know there to be a God, even if there is one, that this is a question upon which common sense cannot be regarded as having any definite opinion. For the same reason he excludes the belief, which has been held by some believers in an after-life, that there are acts of consciousness which are not attached to any material objects. Both these beliefs are, however, regarded by Moore as being compatible with the common-sense view of the world and, therefore, as being possible additions to it. Another possible addition is the belief that there is, or may be, in the universe, besides material objects and acts of consciousness, at least one other substantial kind of thing, which is unknown to us, or even unknowable. The belief that there *is* such an unknown kind of thing is regarded by Moore as going a long way beyond common sense, but the belief that there *may* be only a little way beyond it.

This, then, being the common-sense view of the world, and 'the first and most interesting problem of philosophy'[3] being, in Moore's

---

[1] Ibid., p. 13.　　　[2] Ibid., p. 16.　　　[3] Ibid., p. 23.

opinion, that of giving a general description of the whole universe, one way of setting about this problem will be to inquire whether the common-sense view is true, and if it is found to be true, to consider what additions, if any, we are justified in making to it. And since it is part of the common-sense view that we know a great deal both about material objects and about acts of consciousness, this will also be a way of introducing another of the main problems of philosophy, which is that of determining *how* we know whatever it is, if anything, that we do know: a problem which, according to Moore, consists in asking first 'what sort of a thing knowledge is',[1] a question which he thinks that philosophy shares with psychology, secondly, what is truth, and thirdly, in particular cases, what reason there is for believing that the proposition in question is true. These are not the only main problems which Moore attributes to philosophy – there is also the problem of defining the things that we are talking about and the differences between them, and the problem, to which he thinks that moral philosophy is devoted, of saying what characteristics anything must have to be good or bad, right or wrong – but they are the ones to which, in *Some Main Problems of Philosophy* at least, he attaches the greatest importance.

The question whether the common-sense view of the world is true is most succinctly answered by Moore in the essay which he entitled 'A Defence of Common Sense'. In this essay he begins by giving a long list of propositions, every one of which he claims to know with certainty to be true. These propositions fall into three groups. In outline, the propositions of the first group are that there exists, and has for some time existed, a human body which is his body; that during the time that it has existed, this body has been 'in contact with or not far from the surface of the earth', that there have existed many other things, 'also having shape and size in three dimensions', from which it has been at various distances and with some of which it has been in contact, that among these things have been other human bodies of which the same propositions are true, that many of these bodies have ceased to exist, that the earth had existed for many years before he was born, and that during many of those years a large number of human bodies had at every moment been alive upon it, and had, in very many cases, ceased to exist before he was born. The second group of propositions consists, in outline, of the propositions that since his birth he has had many different experiences, that he has often perceived his own

[1] Ibid., p. 25.

body, and other things in its environment, including other human bodies; that he has often observed facts about these things, such as the fact, which he is observing as he writes, that a particular mantelpiece is nearer to his body than a particular bookcase, that he is aware of facts which he is not at present observing, such as that his body existed on the previous day and was then for some time nearer to the mantelpiece than to the bookcase, that he has had expectations with regard to the future, that he has held many beliefs, both true and false, that he has thought of imaginary things without believing in their reality, that he has had dreams, that he has had feelings of many different kinds, and that many other human beings have had similar experiences. Finally, the third group consists of the single proposition which states with regard to many other human beings, who resemble Moore in that, *mutatis mutandis*, the propositions of his first two classes are also true of them, that each of them has frequently known, with regard to himself and his body, propositions corresponding to those that Moore has listed.[1]

To avoid any possible misunderstanding, Moore goes on to make two further remarks. The first is that when he says that he and others have known such propositions to be true, he is using the word 'true' in a sense which is not compatible with their being even partially false, and the second is that what he means by the words which he has used to express these propositions is what would ordinarily be meant by them. The first of these remarks was directed against idealist philosophers who believed in degrees of truth, and the second against those philosophers who believe that the propositions which are ordinarily expressed by sentences like 'The earth has existed for many years past' are at least partially false, but are willing to use the same form of words to express propositions which they believe to be true. Presumably Berkeley would come into this category. A third set of philosophers with whom Moore also disagrees are those who imply that sentences like 'The earth has existed for many years past' do not have any ordinary meaning. 'They seem to think', Moore says, 'that the question "Do you believe that the earth has existed for many years past?" is not a plain question, such as should be met either by a plain "Yes" or "No", or by a plain "I can't make up my mind", but is the sort of question which can be properly met by: "It all depends on what you mean by 'the earth' and 'exists' and 'years': if you mean so and so, and so and so, and so and so, then I do; but if you mean so and so, and

[1] *Philosophical Papers*, pp. 32–5.

so and so, and so and so, or so and so and so and so, and so and so, then I don't, or at least I think it is extremely doubtful".[1] Moore thinks that this view is 'as profoundly mistaken as any view can be'. 'Such an expression', he says, 'as "The earth has existed for many years past" is the very type of an unambiguous expression, the meaning of which we all understand.'[2] He then, however, goes on to admit that although we all understand an expression of this sort, it does not follow that we know what it means, in the sense that we are able to give a correct analysis of its meaning. We shall see later on that this admission has very far-reaching consequences.

But what, one may ask, is the point of affirming this set of propositions, especially if, as Moore himself says, they are nothing more than a series of truisms? The answer is that, if they are all known to be true, they render it certain that there are in the universe the two kinds of things that common sense believes there to be: material objects and acts of consciousness. They achieve this in virtue of Moore's assumption that if human bodies, or bookcases, or mantelpieces, exist, it follows that there are material objects, and that if he perceives these objects, or remembers them, or dreams about them, it follows that there are acts of consciousness. It also follows, if we do know these propositions to be true and they have the implications which Moore thinks they have, that philosophers who have denied the existence of matter, or mind, or time, or motion, must have been mistaken. And if the content of these true propositions is to be determined by the ordinary meaning of the sentences by which Moore has expressed them, then not only has he refuted the metaphysicians to whom he attributes the view that there are no such things as human bodies, or mantelpieces, or bookcases, that nothing is at a distance from anything else, and that nothing occurs at any time, but he has also refuted philosophers like Berkeley who allow that there are human bodies and bookcases and so forth, but deny that there are material objects, and materialist philosophers who allow that people have thoughts and feelings and sensations but deny that there are acts of consciousness. It might be suggested that philosophers like Berkeley and the materialists had not been refuted, on the ground that they were not denying any proposition that Moore claims to know, but only offering an unconventional analysis of certain of these propositions: and, in fact, although Moore does mention Berkeley, in *Some Main Problems of Philosophy*, as one who held a position which was inconsistent with the common-sense view of the

[1] Ibid., pp. 36–7.   [2] Ibid., p. 32.

world, he says, in the essay on 'A Defence of Common Sense' and elsewhere, that the phenomenalist analysis of propositions about material
objects may very well be true. He does not discuss the physicalist
interpretation of propositions about acts of consciousness, but here too
he might have considered philosophers like Ryle to be offering an
unconventional analysis of propositions to the expression of which they
attached their ordinary meaning. Nevertheless, it seems strange to say
that what is commonly understood when one speaks about chairs and
tables is consistent with their being no more than 'permanent possibilities of sensation', or that what is commonly understood when one
speaks about thoughts, or sensations, or feelings is consistent with their
being physical events. The difficulty is that the distinction between the
question what a sentence means and the question how the proposition
which it expresses is correctly to be analysed is not at all a clear one and
Moore does not do very much to make it so. I shall return to this point
later on.

B. MOORE'S PROOF OF AN EXTERNAL WORLD

In support of his contention that there are and are known to be material
objects, Moore offers three arguments. The first two of them are negative, in the sense that they are directed, in the first case, against philosophers who deny that material objects exist, and, in the second, against
those who deny that we ever know that they do. The third is a positive
proof that material objects exist. Of the negative arguments, the first
is that if the view that material objects do not exist is true, it follows
that no philosopher has ever held it: for philosophers are themselves
material objects, albeit of a special sort. Evidently, the same argument
can be used against those who deny the reality of space and time; for
any opinion which any human being holds is held at some time or
other and by someone who occupies some position or other in space.
This argument is not a *reductio ad absurdum*, in the sense that it shows the
opponent's position to be self-contradictory, since, logically, a proposition might be true, even though it entailed that no one believed or even
thought of it, but it is a *reductio ad absurdum* in the sense that it shows
the opponent's position to be ridiculous. It also serves to absolve Moore
from attaching any weight to the fact that eminent philosophers have
rejected or even queried the common-sense view of the world, since

he takes the very fact that there are philosophers who have rejected or queried it to entail that it is true.[1]

The second of Moore's negative arguments is directed against the more numerous class of philosophers who do not deny the truth of the propositions on Moore's list but do deny that most of them are known to be true. They are represented by Moore as taking the position that each of us knows with respect to himself that he is having or has had such and such experiences, but that nobody knows for certain either that there are material objects or that there are other persons who also have experiences. This might appear to be a more modest position than that taken by those who deny the existence of material objects, and therefore harder to refute, but Moore thinks it easier to refute, on the ground that, unlike the other, it really can be shown to be self-contradictory. His argument is that the philosopher who says that each of *us* has knowledge of his own experiences, but not of the existence of material objects or of other persons, is implying by his very use of the word 'us' that he knows that there are persons besides himself who have experiences: and if he knows that there are other persons, then he knows that there are human bodies, and consequently that there are material objects. Put more succinctly, the argument is that it is self-contradictory to say that the beliefs of common sense 'are not matters of *knowledge*',[2] for merely in characterising a set of beliefs as the beliefs of common sense one is implying that one knows that many human beings hold them; and if one knows that there are many human beings, one knows that the common-sense view of the world is true.

Although it is more ambitious, this argument seems to me less powerful than the other. No doubt philosophers who hold that one's belief in the existence of other persons falls short of knowledge do often formulate their view in a way which assumes that other persons exist. There is, however, no need for them to do so. It is enough for a philosopher of this kind to say 'I know that I have experiences. I do not know that there are any other persons who also have experiences: but if, as I believe, there are such persons, then each of them is in the same position as I am, in that he may have knowledge of his own experiences, but can at best believe in the existence of persons other than himself.' This is in effect the position taken by Russell, and it is certainly not self-contradictory, in the way that Moore suggests. It would become self-contradictory if one's inability to know that there are other persons who had experiences were asserted on the ground, once taken by

[1] Ibid., p. 40.   [2] Ibid., p. 43.

Carnap, that since one could not observe the experiences of others, one could not significantly talk about them unless they were equated with physical events.[1] But this is not Russell's view, nor does Moore attribute it to the philosophers whom he is here trying to refute.

It should be said that Moore does mention this way of escaping his argument in the notes for a course of lectures which he gave in 1928–9. He says 'Nobody, in fact, means only: "I don't know, and, if other men have existed similar to me, they don't know either" '.[2] But even if this were true, it would mean only that his argument was valid *ad homines*. His opponents could still escape from it by taking this position.

The positive argument for the existence of material objects, which is already implicit in Moore's essay, 'A Defence of Common Sense', is fully set out in a lecture entitled 'Proof of an External World' which he delivered at the British Academy in 1939 and reprinted in his *Philosophical Papers*. He begins the lecture by quoting a remark made by Kant, in the preface to the second edition to *The Critique of Pure Reason*, that 'It still remains a scandal to philosophy . . . that the existence of things outside of us . . . must be accepted merely on *faith*, and that, if anyone thinks good to doubt their existence, we are unable to counter his doubts by any satisfactory proof', and then goes on to ask what is meant by 'the existence of things outside of us', where the word 'us' is intended, as it presumably is in this context, to refer to our minds. His answer is that, for his purpose, the existence of things outside of us can be equated with the existence of things which are to be met with in space, in a sense which includes common-sense material objects as well as such things as shadows, but does not include such things as after-images or double-images or pains, which, although they can be said to be presented in space, are not, in Moore's view, to be met with there. For anything to fall into the class of things which are to be met with in space, it is necessary both that it be perceptible to different people and that it be capable of existing unperceived, but these conditions, though necessary, are not sufficient, since they are satisfied by things like reflections in mirrors, or the sky, which Moore does not think it right to include among the things which are to be met with in space. He therefore admits that he has not been able to give 'a clear-cut definition' of the expression 'things to be met with in space', but he thinks that he has said enough about the intended extension of

[1] See Rudolf Carnap, 'Psychologie in physikalische Sprache', in *Erkenntnis*, II (1932) and *The Unity of Science* (1934).
[2] *Lectures on Philosophy*, p. 48.

this concept for it is to be safe for his argument to proceed. He then spends some time discussing the question whether the existence of things to be met with in space would entail the existence of things external to our minds, and decides that it would, on the ground, which he had indeed already assumed, that a necessary condition for anything to be met with in space is that it be capable of existing without anyone's perceiving it or thinking of it.

Moore's proof that there are such things, when he finally comes to it, is very simple. 'I can', he says, 'prove now, for instance, that two human hands exist. How? By holding up my two hands, and saying, as I make a certain gesture with the right hand, "Here is one hand", and adding, as I make a certain gesture with the left, "and here is another". And, if by doing this, I have proved *ipso facto* the existence of external things, you will all see that I can also do it now in numbers of other ways: there is no need to multiply examples.'[1]

Moore goes on to argue that his proof is perfectly rigorous. The three conditions which a rigorous proof must satisfy are, he says, first that the conclusion is different from the premiss, secondly, that the premiss is known to be true, and thirdly, that the conclusion really follows from the premiss: and he insists that in this case these three conditions are all satisfied. The conclusion is different from the premiss: it is less specific: it does follow from the premiss, and Moore does know the premiss to be true. 'How absurd', he says, 'it would be to suggest that I did not know it, but only believed it, and that perhaps it was not the case. You might as well suggest that I do not know that I am now standing up and talking – that perhaps after all I'm not, and that it is not quite certain that I am!'[2]

In the same way Moore claims to be able to offer any number of proofs that there have been external objects in the past. The one which he does offer runs as follows: 'I can say "I held up two hands above this desk not very long ago; therefore at least two external objects have existed at some time in the past, Q.E.D." '[3] Again, he maintains that this is a perfectly rigorous proof, provided that he knows what is asserted in the premiss, and again he insists that he does know it and that all the members of his audience know it too.

So Moore concludes that he has met Kant's challenge. He has given a proof of the existence of external objects, both in the present and in the past. All the same, he recognises that many philosophers will not be satisfied by his proof: and he thinks that one reason why they will

[1] *Philosophical Papers*, p. 146.   [2] Ibid., pp. 146–7.   [3] Ibid., p. 148.

not be satisfied is that he has not attempted to prove the premises from which the conclusions that there are, and have been, external objects follow. What these critics expect of him is not a proof of some particular proposition like 'Here are two human hands' or 'I did hold up my two hands a few minutes ago' but some general statement as to how any proposition of these sorts can be proved, and this is a demand which is not, in his view, capable of being met. Even to prove the particular proposition that he is holding up his hands, he would have to prove that he was not dreaming, and how is this to be achieved? 'I have,' he says, 'no doubt, conclusive reasons for asserting that I am not now dreaming; I have conclusive evidence that I am awake: but that is a very different thing from being able to prove it. I could not tell you what all my evidence is; and I should require to do this at least, in order to give you a proof.'[1] Nevertheless, Moore insists that it would be 'a definite mistake' to argue that because he cannot prove his premises, he does not know them to be true.

This, then, is as far as Moore goes: but I think that he could and should have gone a little further. No doubt he could not prove his premises, in the sense of being able to draw up a list of true propositions from which they logically followed, but he had reasons for accepting them, and these reasons can be generally described. His reason for accepting the proposition 'Here are two hands' was that he perceived them, and his reason for accepting the proposition 'I held up my hands a few minutes ago' was that he remembered doing so.

When stated in this way, these reasons are conclusive, since the word 'perceive' is ordinarily used in such a way that from the fact that something is perceived it follows that it exists, and the word 'remember' is ordinarily used in such a way that from the fact that something is remembered it follows that it occurred. It is, however, possible to reformulate them in a way that does not carry these implications. Let us say, more cautiously, that it seemed to Moore that he saw his hands, and that it later seemed to him that he remembered holding them up, where the words 'it seemed that' are not to be understood in the way they ordinarily would be, as actually suggesting that he was mistaken, but only as preventing our statements from entailing that he was not. This is a device to which some philosophers have, in my view quite wrongly, taken exception,[2] but Moore is not among them, at least with

[1] Ibid., p. 149.
[2] See, for example, J. L. Austin, *Sense and Sensibilia*, and my essay 'Has Austin Refuted the Sense-Datum Theory', in *Metaphysics and Common Sense*.

regard to sense-perception, since he held that perceiving a physical object entailed sensing some sense-datum, and was also inclined to hold that from the fact that the sense-datum was sensed it did not logically follow that the physical object existed. With respect to memory, the position is not so clear, since he thinks that memory is what he calls 'immediate knowledge', which I take to imply that he disagrees with Russell's view that the experience which gives rise to one's claim to recollect a past event is a present occurrence from which the existence of the past event cannot be logically deduced. But if Moore did disagree with Russell on this issue, I think that he was mistaken. On the point of logic, it seems clear to me that Russell was right.

But now, if the reasons which Moore had for asserting his premisses can properly be expressed in this more cautious way, it would appear that they were not conclusive; for a conclusive reason is surely one the truth of which guarantees the truth of the proposition for which it is a reason; and if this is to be an absolute guarantee, it would seem to be required that the proposition for which it is a reason should follow from it. This is, however, a conclusion which Moore denies. In a paper entitled 'Four Forms of Scepticism', which was composed about 1940, and first published in his *Philosophical Papers*, he takes issue with Russell on this point. Russell had maintained, in various passages in his works, that one never knows with complete certainty the truth of any proposition which attributes some experience to oneself, or that of any proposition which refers to a past event, or that of any proposition which attributes experiences to other persons, or that of any proposition which implies the existence of some physical object; and his reason for this in every instance was that what was asserted in the proposition went beyond the evidence on which it was based. This is, perhaps, not immediately obvious in the case of a proposition which attributes some present experience to oneself, but Russell took the view that the reference to oneself implied at least that the present experience was related in some special way to certain experiences in the past: and he argued that merely from the occurrence of the present experience one could not deduce that it had had any predecessors. His reason for denying that one can know for certain that even such propositions about oneself are true is substantially the same as his reason for denying that one can know for certain the truth of any proposition about a past event, and in both cases Moore, by claiming to have immediate knowledge of what Russell said could not be known, rejects the initial stage of Russell's argument. This is, however, irrelevant

to my present purpose, which is to bring out the fact that even when
Moore admits Russell's initial step he rejects his conclusion. He agrees
with Russell that our knowledge of the truth of propositions which
ascribe experiences to others, or imply the existence of material
objects, is not immediate, and that these propositions are not entailed
by the sensory propositions on which they are based. Even so, he maintains that there are occasions on which he knows with certainty that
some other person is having such and such an experience, and that
such and such a material object does exist. The only reason which
Russell gives for saying that such propositions cannot be certainly
known is that the sort of inference on which they depend is not
infallible; propositions which have been advanced on the basis of
similar experiences to those which prompt Moore's claims to knowledge have sometimes turned out to be false. But Moore's answer to
this is that from the fact that some other percepts, which were similar
to his own present percept, have not been associated with a percept
belonging to some other person, although they were thought to be, it
does not in the least follow that it is not known for certain that his
present percept is so associated, and that exactly the same applies,
mutatis mutandis, to the cases where, on the basis of a present percept,
he knows for certain that some physical object exists, or, on the basis
of a present experience, he knows for certain that there has been such
and such a past event. In none of these instances does Moore suggest
that his present experience, or percept, is significantly different from
those which occurred in the cases where the corresponding inferences
went astray. He merely asserts that he is more certain that he does know
what he thinks he knows than that Russell's argument is valid. He
points out that 'Russell's view that I do not know for certain that this
is a pencil or that you are conscious', rests on the 'four distinct assumptions: (1) That I don't know these things immediately; (2) That they
don't follow logically from any thing or things that I do know
immediately; (3) That, *if* (1) and (2) are true, my belief in or knowledge
of them must be "based on an analogical or inductive argument";
and (4) That what is so based cannot be *certain knowledge*':[1] and of these
assumptions he admits that he also thinks the first three to be true. Even
so, he is not so sure of their truth as he is that he knows for certain 'that
this is a pencil'. 'Nay more,' he continues: 'I do not think it is *rational*
to be as certain of any one of these four propositions, as of the proposition that I do know that this is a pencil. And how on earth is it

[1] *Philosophical Papers*, p. 226.

to be decided which of two things it is *rational* to be most certain of?'[1]

Moore does not answer this question, but he does take the argument a little further in a lecture on 'Certainty' which he delivered at the University of California in 1941 and first published in his *Philosophical Papers*. Once more he begins by giving a list of propositions which he claims to know for certain to be true. These propositions, on this occasion numbering seven, were that he was, at the time that he was speaking, in a room, that he was standing up, that he had clothes on, that he was speaking in a fairly loud voice, that he had in his hand some sheets of papers with writing on them, that there were a good many other people in the room, and that there were windows in one of its walls and a door in another.[2] These are all contingent propositions, and Moore argues at some length that the fact that they are contingent does not entail either that it is possible that they are false or that it is not absolutely certain that they are true. The next point which he makes about them is that they none of them imply anything about his mind, so that if he knows any of them to be true, he knows that there is an external world. Thirdly, he remarks that they are all propositions for which, when he asserted them, he had the current evidence of his senses, though this was not the only evidence that he had. He does not say what he takes this other evidence to be, but presumably it consisted in his memories of his past experiences. And his final remark about them is that 'if *they* were not certain, then no proposition which implies the existence of anything external to the mind of the person who makes it is ever certain',[3] since the case which he had for saying that he knew them to be true was as strong as such a case ever is.

Moore then turns to consider what can be said against his claim to know these propositions to be true, and concentrates this time on the argument that he might be dreaming. He remarks that even if he were dreaming it would not follow that these propositions were not true – for example, 'The story, about a well-known Duke of Devonshire, that he once dreamt that he was speaking in the House of Lords and, when he woke up, found that he *was* speaking in the House of Lords, is certainly logically possible'[4] – but it would follow that he did not know them to be true. Consequently, if he does know them to be true, he must also know that he is not dreaming. But many philosophers have argued that it is impossible to know for certain at any given moment that one is not dreaming. Can Moore show that their argument is not cogent?

[1] Ibid.   [2] *Philosophical Papers*, p. 227.   [3] Ibid., p. 244.   [4] Ibid., p. 245.

He begins by saying that one premiss which these philosophers would certainly use is that 'Some at least of the sensory experiences which you are having now are similar in important respects to dream-images which actually have occurred in dreams':[1] and he allows that this premiss is true. But even though it is true, it cannot, he thinks, consistently be used to support his opponents' argument. For what they imply in using it is that they know that dreams have occurred, and Moore argues that they could not know this unless they knew that they were not now dreaming. For otherwise they might only be dreaming that dreams had occurred.

This is an ingenious argument, but I do not think that it gives Moore what he wants. The objection to it is that it is not necessary for his opponents to assume the actual occurrence of dreams. It is enough that they should be able to argue that it is logically possible that a series of dream-images should be exactly similar to the percepts which furnish Moore's sensory evidence for the propositions which he claims to know. Admittedly, an argument of this sort is more persuasive, if one refers to actual examples of what one is claiming to be logically possible, but this is not essential for its validity. If one merely has the concept of a dream, one can derive this conclusion. It may, indeed, be argued that one must have had dreams, in order to possess the concept, but I doubt if this is logically necessary, and anyhow one could possess the concept without necessarily knowing that this was the way in which one had acquired it.

The proposition that 'It is logically possible that there should be dream-images *exactly like all* the sense-experiences I am now having'[2] is, in fact, formulated by Moore as the next step in his opponents' argument; and he does not deny that it is true: nor does he deny that, if this is so, it is also logically possible 'that all the sense-experiences I am having now should be mere dream-images'.[3] And from this he agrees that it would follow that he did not know that he was not dreaming, if these sensory experiences were the only experiences that he was currently having. But, besides these experiences, he also has memories of the immediate past, and he thinks that the two together may be sufficient to exclude the possibility that he is dreaming. He concludes, therefore, by saying that while the proposition that 'I *am* dreaming now' is not self-contradictory, when considered by itself, 'the conjunction of the proposition that I have these sense experiences

[1] Ibid., p. 248.   [2] Ibid., p. 249.   [3] Ibid., p. 250.

and memories with the proposition that I am dreaming does seem to me to be very likely self-contradictory'.[1]

Moore said, in the preface which he wrote for *Philosophical Papers* just before his death, that there were bad mistakes in this lecture which he could not yet see how to put right, and his editor explains that Moore was particularly dissatisfied with the last steps in his argument. He may have thought that he had conceded too much to his opponents in failing to deny that it was logically possible that his sense-experiences, at any given time, should be mere dream-images, and he may have lost confidence in his suggestion that the proposition that he was having the sense-experiences in question ceased to be compatible with the proposition that he was dreaming, when the proposition that he was also having such and such memories was added to it. If he had lost confidence in this suggestion, he was surely right: for if it is logically possible that one's sense-experiences, at any time, should be mere dream-images, there seems to be no good reason why this should not apply to one's memory-experiences as well.

In the light of this whole discussion, I think that we are forced to conclude that Moore never did succeed in proving that he knew the truth of the propositions which he claimed to know. Neither, in my view, is this at all surprising, since in trying to defeat his opponents on their own ground, he was, I think, attempting the impossible. If to prove that I am not now dreaming, I have to find some set of true propositions about my present experiences from which the proposition that I am not now dreaming logically follows, then I cannot prove that I am not now dreaming: and if the possibility that I am dreaming is a fatal obstacle to my being said to know the truth of any propositions of the sort that Moore takes as his examples, then I do not know the truth of any such propositions. Moreover, even if this obstacle were overcome, I still should not know the truth of any such propositions if this entailed my being able to deduce them solely from the content of my present experiences: for Russell is surely right in taking it to be a feature of any proposition which implies the existence of a physical object, or the experiences of another person, or the occurrence of a past event, that it goes beyond the immediate data upon which it is based. Moore was, therefore, better advised in taking his earlier position that such propositions as that he was holding up his hands were not, in this sense, susceptible of proof.

[3] Ibid., p. 251.

C. AN EXTENSION OF MOORE'S ARGUMENT

Does it follow that these propositions cannot be known for certain to be true? It does follow, if their being known for certain is taken, as Russell takes it, to imply that one is never in a position to say that the possibility of their being false is logically excluded. On the other hand, we quite commonly speak of knowing something for certain, when the possibility of our being mistaken is so remote that it would not be reasonable to entertain it: and in this sense, it might seem obvious that Moore did know for certain the truth of all the propositions that he claimed to know.

But how is even this to be demonstrated? Moore himself does not attempt to demonstrate it, but I suspect, perhaps unjustly, that he was tacitly relying on an argument which has since gained very wide currency. Its starting-point, which is the same as Moore's, is that we have sense-experiences which we unhesitatingly take as establishing the truth of such propositions as that I have a sheet of paper in my hands with writing on it, or that this room contains benches on which a certain number of people are sitting. The question is then raised whether such experiences can ever establish propositions of this kind, at least beyond reasonable doubt. But, so the argument runs, it is characteristic of the meaning of the sentences which express these propositions that the truth of the propositions which they express *is* established by these sorts of experiences. The rules which govern the use of sentences of this type are such as to correlate them with observable states of affairs; we understand the sentences when we know what observations would verify or falsify the propositions which they express. On certain occasions, indeed, we may have reason for distrusting what appear to be such observations; we may have grounds for thinking that the appearances are deceptive in one way or another. But in default of any such special reasons for mistrust, to have the appropriate experiences and to refuse to accept the proposition which is expressed by the sentence with which they are conventionally correlated is simply to violate the canons of the language which one purports to be using. In short, there are accepted criteria for deciding in particular cases whether these common-sense propositions are true or false, and the question whether the criteria are satisfied in any given instance is a question not for philosophical argument but simply for empirical observation.

It is plain that this argument can be generalised. For the propositions of common sense are not the only ones of which it is true that there are recognised criteria for deciding when they are true or false. This applies equally to the propositions which occur in the natural sciences, and also to the *a priori* propositions of logic and pure mathematics, although in their case the criteria are not empirical. Here too there are recognised standards of proof and recognised procedures for determining whether these standards have been met. If someone refuses to regard a favourable experiment as confirming a scientific theory, then, unless he has some special reason for mistrusting the experiment, unless he has grounds for suspecting that there has been an error of observation, or that there is some other special reason why the apparent result of the experiment is not to be taken at its face value, he simply has not understood what the theory is. If someone refuses to accept the result of a logical or mathematical demonstration, without having any special reason for thinking that the procedure which was employed in this instance was faulty or inaccurately carried out, he simply does not understand how logic and mathematics work.

This argument has serious consequences for philosophy. For what follows from it is that the truth or falsehood of all these propositions is not even a matter for philosophical discussion. It depends only on the satisfaction of the appropriate criteria: and whether the criteria are satisfied is always a matter of empirical or formal fact. There is no place here for philosophy to intervene. But then what is there left for it to do? The received answer is that while it is not equipped to estimate the truth or falsehood of these propositions, it can and should attempt to elucidate their meaning: it should devote itself exclusively to the task of analysis. Exactly what is analysed, whether it is words or concepts, sentences or propositions or facts, what purposes the analyses serve, and how their results are to be assessed, are all matters on which no very general agreement has been reached. There is just the feeling that philosophy must after all be good for something, and that the avenue of analysis, whatever that may be, is the only one left open to it.

As I said, Moore did not himself employ this argument, neither did he take the view of philosophy to which we have just seen that it leads. On the contrary, when Professor John Wisdom in his contribution to *The Philosophy of G. E. Moore*, spoke of 'Moore's conception of philosophy as analysis', with the implication that Moore thought that philosophy had no other function to fulfil, Moore replied that this was not so. 'It is not true', he said, 'that I have ever either said or thought or implied that analysis is the only proper business of philosophy! By practising analysis I may have implied that it is *one* of the proper businesses of philosophy. But I certainly cannot have implied more than that. And, in fact, analysis is by no means the only thing I have tried to do.'[1] This protest was, indeed, justified, since we have seen that Moore also looked to philosophy to determine what kinds of things there were in the universe and to answer the questions whether we know, and, if so, how we know, all the things that we should ordinarily claim to know. Nevertheless, the facts that he accepts the common-sense view of the world, that the only positive reason which he gives for accepting it is that he knows the truth of propositions which entail it, that his defence of these premises comes down to affirming that he just does know them to be true, and finally that while he thinks there can be no doubt of the truth of the common-sense propositions which he lists, he also thinks that there is considerable doubt as to what is their correct analysis, together lead to very much the same conclusion as the argument which I have just set out. The steps by which Moore arrives at this result may also be described as philosophical: but they are very straightforward, and the difficult work which is left for philosophy does, at any rate on the positive side, consist only of analysis.

Unlike some other philosophers I do not find this conclusion emotionally repugnant. It is, indeed, one that I have long accepted in theory, and to some extent in practice. I have, however, now come to think that the argument which leads to it is unsound. Let us look at it again more closely. At first sight it is very persuasive. How could a philosophical argument show that in these perfectly normal circumstances I am mistaken in believing in the existence of the physical objects which I can see around me. Of course I may fail to identify all of them correctly: it is conceivable even that I am the victim of some more serious illusion. But then there are ways of finding out whether this is so: and if they show that nothing is amiss, the question is settled, so far as it can be. It would be merely neurotic to embark on an endless series of further tests, when one had no reason at all to expect that they would yield any different result. It is true that I may be dreaming, in the sense that this is a hypothesis which I cannot logically exclude. But nothing in the character of my present experience gives me any reason to think that I am dreaming, or that if I were I should not sooner or later discover it by having the experience which I interpret as that of waking up: and if it can be argued that even this experience can occur as part of a dream, the answer is still that this can only be shown

[1] *The Philosophy of G. E. Moore*, pp. 675–6.

by its falling within a series of experiences which at some point gives way to a series which exhibits a different sort of order. The hypothesis that I pass my whole life in a dream is, indeed, significant, though not verifiable by me, if it is entertained at the level of physical theory: there is nothing contradictory in the idea of someone's sleeping for a lifetime, and if I observed, or thought that I observed, someone in this condition, I might vainly wonder whether other people were not making the same observation of myself. On the other hand, I cannot construct the theory, in terms of which this hypothesis makes sense, unless I can distinguish those of my experiences which fit into what I have called the main story from those which do not. One only has the concept of delusive experiences of any kind because one is able to contrast them with those that are declared to be veridical.

So far, then, the argument survives, although at the cost of some complexity. But now let us suppose that someone has been convinced by reading Berkeley that the things which he perceives are not material objects, as we understand the term, but only collections of ideas in his own mind. How would this argument serve to disabuse him? The answer is that it would not serve at all. There will never be an occasion on which we can show him that because of his fidelity to Berkeley his judgements of perception run counter to the evidence. In the relevant circumstances, he will be as ready as we are to admit the truth of such propositions as that this is a piece of paper or that the earth has existed for many years past. Of course he interprets them differently: he does not think that they commit him to holding that these objects exist when he is not perceiving them, except perhaps as permanent possibilities of sensation, or as ideas in the mind of another person, or in the mind of God: but this does not mean that we can expect his judgement to dissent from ours in any concrete situation. If he is making an error, it is not one that has any practical consequences.

It is, indeed, not easy to say what kind of error such a man would be making, if he were making one at all. It might even be argued that his position did not conflict with Moore's, on the ground that he was not denying the truth of any common-sense propositions but only accepting what might turn out to be a mistaken view of their analysis. There is some support for this interpretation in Berkeley's own writings, and I do not wish to rule it out of court, especially as the distinction between the meaning of an expression and the analysis of its meaning is anyhow not clear. It is, however, to be remarked that the more latitude we give to the province of analysis, the less is defended by the defence of common sense. It may in the end come down to no more than the claim that some fact or other is captured by a common-sense proposition – a claim which only a very few metaphysicians would wish to dispute. On the other hand, if we look to analysis to reproduce, in any literal sense, what is ordinarily meant by the expressions with which it is concerned, then I think that it would be doing Berkeley an injustice to represent him as an analyst, because it would at once put him in the wrong. For I do not see how it can be denied that our ordinary way of speaking about material objects is realistic. When the ordinary man speaks of a chair or a clock or a piece of paper, he plainly does so with the implication that these things exist unperceived in a way that amounts to something more than their just being permanent possibilities of sensation. Perhaps he ought not to, but that is another question. There is surely no doubt that he does. And if this is the common-sense view, then it seems to me that Berkeley is not analysing but attacking it. This is also the line that Moore takes in *Some Main Problems of Philosophy*, where he maintains that 'If it were self-evident, as Berkeley says, that nothing resembling a sense-datum can ever exist except in someone's mind, it would follow that no material object exists at all'.[1] In short, Berkeley is not elucidating the way in which we ordinarily systematise our experiences: he is putting up a rival system.

But how is this possible? How can the common-sense view of the world be open to attack? In trying to answer this question, we shall find it helpful to make use of the distinction which Professor Carnap has drawn between what he calls internal and external questions of existence. The reference is to an article of his entitled 'Empiricism, Semantics and Ontology', which originally appeared in the *Revue Internationale de Philosophie* in 1950, and has since been reprinted in various anthologies. Internal questions, as the name suggests, are questions that arise within the framework of a conceptual system and are settled by the application of the criteria which the system supplies. Thus, if we are speaking at the level of common sense, the questions whether there are chairs in the room, and whether there are elephants, can be settled by observation, the answer being yes in the one case and no in the other. If we are speaking at the level of physics, the question whether there are mesons, to which the answer is yes, and whether there is the ether, to which the answer is no, are questions which are decided in the last resort by observation, but also in terms of the acceptability of certain theories. If we are operating inside mathematics,

[1] *Some Main Problems of Philosophy*, p. 105.

there are formal procedures for deciding such questions as whether there is a rational square root of 2, which there is not, or a prime number between 11 and 15, which there is. If we are talking about mythology or literature, then such questions as whether there is a Greek god of the Underworld, which there is, or a woman married to Mr Pickwick, which there is not, are settled by looking up the relevant texts. Of course the answers are not always so easy. Even in mathematics there may be questions like that of the validity of Goldbach's conjecture, which no one has yet been able to decide. There may also be disputes concerning the criteria themselves: a mathematical example would be the disagreement about the status of *reductio ad absurdum* proofs. The point remains that once the criteria have been settled, the question whether they are satisfied is internal to the relevant discipline.

Now if we raise very general questions like 'Are there material objects?', 'Are there numbers?', 'Are there fictitious persons?' and treat them as internal questions, the answers to them are always obvious, either obviously yes or obviously no, according as the conceptual framework within which we are operating does or does not make provision for them. Yes, there are physical objects, this chair is a physical object. Yes, there are numbers, 2 is a number. Yes, there are fictitious persons, Mr Pickwick is a fictitious person. Or, if one is speaking within a universe of discourse where the criterion of existence is location in space and time, then of course there are no fictitious persons, and, for that matter, no numbers either.

But, Carnap goes on, these very general questions can also be treated as external questions. That is to say, they can be interpreted, not as questions arising within a given conceptual or linguistic framework, but as questions which bear upon the framework itself. Carnap's own view is that when they are treated in this way, they are to be construed as questions of policy. To ask whether there are numbers, or whether there are propositions, is to ask whether we wish to employ a language in which references to numbers, or to propositions, are made, or anyhow one that contains functions which have such entities for their arguments. Thoroughgoing nominalists will feel themselves obliged to restrict their discourse so as to avoid such commitments, but Carnap can see no good reason for their self-denial. There are, indeed, limits to his permissiveness. Statements which are not analytically true have to be empirically verifiable. But so long as this requirement is satisfied, Carnap is in favour of what he calls a principle of tolerance. We are free to employ any form of language that we find useful, no matter what sorts of entities it refers to. I shall show in a moment that there are at least respectable motives for not being quite so tolerant as this.

This distinction of Carnap's, which I find very illuminating, has been challenged by Professor Quine in an essay 'On Carnap's Views on Ontology', which was first published in 1951 in vol. II of *Philosophical Studies* and is reprinted in his book *The Ways of Paradox*. Quine argues that Carnap's distinction between external and internal questions of existence amounts to no more than a distinction between what he calls category questions and sub-class questions, the question 'Are there so and so's?' being a category question when the so and so's purport to exhaust the range of a particular style of bound variables, and a sub-class question when they do not. But then the distinction turns out to be fairly arbitrary. For instance, the question whether there are numbers would be a category, and so an external, question only with respect to languages which have a special style of variables which range over numbers. In a language like the language normally used in set theory, where the variables which take numbers for their values also range over classes which are not numbers, the question whether there are numbers would be a sub-class, and so an internal, question. So while the distinction is tenable, it would not appear to be of any philosophical interest.

I accept what Quine says about the distinction between category and sub-class questions, and would argue only that it misses the point. The point is that Carnap's distinction between internal and external questions is not just a distinction with respect to levels of generality. It is rather a distinction with respect to the ways in which existential questions can be answered. An internal question is one that can be settled by giving examples of the sort of entity whose existence is being queried. An external question is one that cannot be settled in this fashion. External questions are philosophically interesting when they are raised by philosophers who acknowledge examples of a certain sort of entity, but deny that any entity of that sort exists. Thus a philosopher like Berkeley will admit that there are chairs in the room but denies that there are material objects; a nominalist will admit that many things have the property of being red but denies that there are universals. There is no contradiction here because the philosophers in question are not denying, or anyhow straightforwardly denying, empirical or formal facts. They are engaging in conceptual criticism.

There may be various motives for this. One common line of argument against admitting the existence of objects of a given category is that the category in question is not ultimate; the things which fall under it have been mistakenly hypostatised; what really exists is something else. This leads to such assertions as that there are no material things but only sense-data, no numbers but only numerals, no universals but only sets of similar particulars, or alternatively no particulars but only sets of compresent universals, no propositions but only sentences, no mental events but only dispositions to behave in certain ways, and so forth. The motive for trying to get rid of one or other of these sorts of entities is that they do not fit in with a preconceived idea of what the world is really like. In general, the tendency, especially among analytical philosophers, is to try to eliminate the abstract in favour of the concrete, but it may also go the other way. Or it may be, as I said when talking about Russell's philosophy of mathematics, that certain types of entity, like numbers or universals, strike us as mysterious, and we wish to explain them in terms of other sorts of entities which we find less problematic. Epistemological considerations, as I then said, may also play a part. If it is believed, as it was by Russell and Moore and many others, in the case of material objects and sense-data, and by nearly everybody, in the case of propositions and sentences, that one type of entity is accessible only through another, then there may be an inclination to try to reduce the more remote entities to those that give us access to them. The vindication of all these claims is that the entities whose removal is desired should be successfully explained away, though it has to be admitted that it is not always made clear what are the criteria for deciding when this end has been achieved.

Another line of argument is that the category, or concept, which is put in question is somehow defective. This is the nerve of Parmenides's attack on the concept of plurality, or that of the neo-Hegelians on the categories of space and time, or Ryle's on the concept of mind. Sometimes this line of argument is joined to the reductive line, as in the case of Berkeley, whose reason for denying the existence of matter was principally that it was not verifiable. But this brings us back to the argument from which this discussion started. How can there be any hope of disqualifying a concept of which it is obvious that we make successful use? If it is a plain matter of fact that a concept has empirical application, then how can one think that it is radically defective?

The answer is that we have to distinguish between the practical operation of a concept and the theory which it carries with it. This distinction is not sharp, since it is arguable that the description of any phenomena incorporates some element of theory, but it will serve our present purpose. Thus, the concept of possession by evil spirits had empirical application: there were established criteria for deciding when people were so possessed, and they were very often found to be satisfied. At the time when the belief in good and evil spirits was part of popular culture, to deny the possibility of demonic possession might have seemed to be flying in the face of common sense. Nevertheless we now find it perfectly easy to dissociate the concept from the phenomena to which it was taken to apply. We simply account for the facts in a very different sort of way. Or again, to take a concept of more current interest, the concept of free-will has empirical application: there are accepted criteria for deciding whether one is doing something of one's own free-will as opposed, say, to doing it under duress. But the acceptance of such factual distinctions does not oblige us to accept the ideas about guilt and responsibility which the concept of free-will carries with it; and in fact I doubt if they can withstand rational criticism. In the same way, a philosopher may consistently allow that there are facts which are picked out by Moore's common-sense propositions, but still reject the construction which common sense puts upon them.[1]

The fact that this position is tenable takes much of the sting out of the stronger of Moore's negative arguments in favour of the common-sense view of the world: the argument that if the opinions of those who reject it are true, they cannot exist to hold them. I think that this argument is still effective against metaphysicians who try to dispense with space and time; for I do not see how any acceptable account of what makes it true that someone holds an opinion can avoid a commitment to some sort of spatio-temporal system. On the other hand, it is not effective against a philosopher who rejects the common-sense conception of material objects, whether on Berkeleyan grounds, or because, like Russell, he thinks it to be inconsistent with established scientific theories about the causation of percepts. We have, indeed, seen that there are serious difficulties in Russell's position, but it certainly cannot be refuted, on the naïve ground that it is in conflict with common sense.

In the essay on 'Metaphysics and Common Sense' in which I first set out this argument, I said that the salient features of Moore's technique was that it treated metaphysical questions internally, as though

[1] Cf. my essay 'Metaphysics and Common Sense', in the book of that title, where I develop this point at greater length.

they arose within the framework of common sense, and that while this gave him an easy victory over the metaphysicians, the victory was won on the wrong terrain. This is obviously true of many of Moore's followers, but I now think that although it is a charge which is borne out by much of what Moore says in *Some Main Problems of Philosophy*, it is in the end unfair to Moore himself, because the possibilities for which I have been arguing are admitted by him under the covering of analysis. The result of this is, however, that his defence of common sense is weakened to the point where it repels only the most extravagant forms of metaphysics. If it remains of value, it is because it provokes us into taking a more sophisticated view of the ends which the philosophers who have seemed to make light of common sense were really pursuing.

So our interest turns to Moore's conception of analysis. But before I embark upon this, I wish to complete my account of his inquiry into the general kinds of things that there are in the universe, by considering his treatment of abstract entities. Since the abstract entities with which I shall be most concerned are propositions and facts, this will also give me an occasion to say something about Moore's theory of truth.

8 Moore's Treatment of Abstract Entities

A. THE REALITY OF CONCEPTS

(i) Moore's Early Platonism

Moore was not always a champion of common sense. Although in the autobiography which he contributed to *The Philosophy of G. E. Moore* he said that when he first heard McTaggart propose 'his well-known view that Time is unreal' it must have seemed to him then, as it still did, 'a perfectly monstrous proposition',[1] the fact, to which Professor Ryle has drawn attention in his contribution to a recent volume entitled *G. E. Moore: Essays in Retrospect*, is that in Moore's earliest published paper, which appeared in *Mind* in 1897, as part of a symposium on the question 'In what sense, if any, do past and future time exist?', he writes of the temporal as being inferior in reality to the timeless, and that in an article on 'Freedom', which appeared in *Mind* the following year, he goes so far as to say that 'The arguments by which Mr Bradley has endeavoured to prove the unreality of time appear to me perfectly conclusive'. Ryle also remarks that in this article and in the article on 'The Nature of Judgement', which appeared in *Mind* in 1899, Moore professes a qualified allegiance to Kant. This comes out mainly in the respect shown for Kant's views about synthetic necessity: and in 'The Nature of Judgement' it is combined with the Platonic realism to which Moore then converted Russell. He takes it very much further, however, than there is any evidence that Russell ever did. Not only does he believe that there really are concepts, but in this article he tries to show that concepts are the only things that there really are.

The steps by which he arrives at this remarkable conclusion are not very easy to follow. He begins, as so often in his early work, by criticising a proposition of Bradley's. In this instance the proposition, which occurs in Bradley's *Principles of Logic*, is that the meaning of an

[1] *The Philosophy of G. E. Moore*, p. 14.

idea consists of part of its content 'cut off, fixed by the mind, and considered apart from the existence of the sign'.[1] Moore objects to this that the ideas which are used in judgements cannot be psychological contents, because in treating any such content as a sign we should already be making the judgement that it referred to something else, and since the same will be true of the idea which is used in *this* judgement, we should fall into an infinite regress. On similar grounds, he argues that concepts cannot be identified with physical existents. In both cases, the argument rests on the false assumption that one cannot use anything as a sign, without independently judging that one is so using it. It is true that no intrinsic quality of an event, or object, can make it into a sign – it has to be interpreted as such – but it may be possible, as I have argued elsewhere,[2] to analyse its significance in terms of its relation to other psychological or physical events. What is anyhow clear is that we explain nothing by treating meanings as objective entities, which is what Moore proceeds to do. Concepts are said by him, not actually to exist, since any talk of existence presupposes them, but just to be. In combination they form propositions which, like their constituent concepts, are unchanging, and have being independently of our being aware of them.

Having attacked Bradley's theory on the ground that it does not explain how an idea can refer to anything other than itself, Moore goes on to argue that concepts do not refer to anything other than themselves. They cannot refer to, or even be satisfied by, existent objects, because the concept of existence is subordinate to that of truth. One might well think that it went the opposite way, but Moore argues that truth cannot depend on a relation of a concept to anything existent, since the proposition by which it is so defined must itself be held to be true, and if the truth of this proposition is taken to consist in a relation to existents, we fall into a vicious circle. So truth and falsehood consist in relations between concepts, and since it cannot be the case that an object satisfies a concept unless the proposition that the object exists is true, the satisfaction of a concept itself becomes a matter of its having a certain relation to other concepts. So to say that this piece of paper now exists is to say that the concepts which combine to form the concept of 'a piece of paper' are also combined, in a specific manner, with the concepts of 'this' and 'now' and 'existence'. What the combination has to be in order that the proposition should be true is something

[1] F. H. Bradley, *The Principles of Logic*, I 4.
[2] See *The Origins of Pragmatism*, pp. 173–9.

that cannot be further defined. It is immediately recognisable, like red or the number two. This is the conception of truth which Russell took from Moore and defended, as we have seen, in his article on Meinong, together with the view that perception is just the knowledge of an existential proposition.

Not only did Moore conclude that the world consisted of concepts, but he also held that all propositions were necessary. The difference between propositions ordinarily thought to be necessary and those thought to be contingent was that the latter contained the concept of existence at particular times. This is a very strange view, but it is consistent with the rest. Matters of empirical fact are contingent, but it is hard to see how relations between concepts could be.

These views are so extraordinary, and so much at variance with Moore's later opinions, that it may seem hardly worth while exhuming them. Nevertheless the difficulties which they were designed to meet are genuine and have led others astray besides Moore. The idea that verifying an empirical proposition consists in making the judgement that some object exists was responsible for the coherence theory of truth, which was held not only by the Absolute Idealists, but also by Logical Positivists, like Carnap and Neurath, in the 1930s, when they argued that sentences could be compared only with one another, and that it was metaphysical to talk of comparing them with facts. It is easy to show that the coherence theory of truth is false, but not so easy to show what comparing sentences with facts consists in. We have to explain how we escape from the confines of language, not by assenting to any proposition but by actually having some experience. In the same way, even if we push our addiction to concepts to the point of eliminating singular terms, we shall need an operator to bring them down to earth; and the determination, in any concrete instance, that the demands of the operator are met is not just a matter of our using concepts to judge that they are met, but rather of our finding, as Peirce put it, that our experiences force this judgement upon us.

(ii) *His Conception of Reality*

In the ordinary way, the notion of existence plays the part of such an operator: and one of the principal mistakes which Moore made in 'The Analysis of Judgement' was to treat the predication of existence as a matter of combining concepts. It is because such a mistake is easily made that there is a point in saying that existence is not a predicate, or at any rate not a predicate of the subjects to which it is ascribed. There is no harm in treating it as a property of propositional functions, so long as it is realised that it is not a property, in the ordinary sense in which a property determines the character or condition of the things which have it, but only a marker for the fact that some set of ordinary properties is exemplified. This point is made by Moore himself, nearly twenty years later, in his essay on 'The Conception of Reality' where he says that 'what "Lions are real" *means* is that some particular property – I will say for the sake of brevity, *the* property of being a lion, though that is not strictly accurate – does in fact *belong to* something – that there are things which have it, or, to put it in another way, that the conception of being a lion is a conception which does apply to some things – that there are things which *fall under* it. And similarly,' he continues, 'what "Unicorns are unreal" means is that the property of being a unicorn belongs to *nothing*.'[1] From this Moore infers that, since 'The only conceptions that occur in the proposition "Lions are real" are the conceptions of being a lion and that of belonging to something, and since it is obvious that "real" does not stand either for the conception of being a lion or for that of belonging to something, inasmuch as in saying that lions are real we are not saying that lions themselves belong to something, there is a very important sense in which "real" and "unreal" do *not*, in this usage, stand for any conceptions at all'.[2] And it soon becomes clear that what he means by this is that they do not stand for any property in the way that 'being a mammal' does stand for a property when it is predicated of lions. 'The two propositions "Lions are real" and "Lions are mammalian",' he says, 'though grammatically similar, are in reality of wholly different forms; and one difference between them may be expressed by saying that whereas "mammalian" does stand for a property or conception, the very point of this usage of "real" is that it does not'.[2]

Moore returns to this question in his essay 'Is Existence a Predicate?' to which I have already referred in connection with Russell's view that it is not significant to attribute existence to an object which is designated by a logically proper name. Apart from its discussion of this point, this essay is of some historical interest, as it is one of the rare instances in which Moore explicitly relies on a linguistic argument. Professing not to understand what his fellow symposiast Professor Kneale meant by saying that existence is not a logical predicate, he

[1] *Philosophical Studies*, p. 212.   [2] Ibid.

suggests that one thing that may be meant is that there is a significant difference between the use of the word 'exists' in the sentence 'Tame tigers exist' and the use of the word 'growl' in the sentence 'Tame tigers growl': and he brings this out by remarking, first, that while it makes good sense to say 'Most tame tigers growl', it does not make good sense to say 'Most tame tigers exist', and secondly, that whereas 'Some tame tigers growl' 'asserts that more than one value of "x is a tame tiger *and growls*" is true', 'Some tame tigers exist' 'asserts, *not* that more than one value of "x is a tame tiger *and exists*" is true, but merely that more than one value of "x is a tame tiger" is true'.[1] I think that these linguistic observations are valid, but they do not do more than re-inforce the point which Moore had already made in his essay on 'The Conception of Reality'.

I have already said that I agreed with Moore in his contention that 'This exists' is significant, and that 'exists', in this usage, is not to be analysed in the Russellian way. Moore also suggests that this is true of its use in such sentences as 'This book exists'. Taking it for granted that the demonstrative 'this' refers to a sense-datum, he remarks that one might try to apply the method of the theory of descriptions by construing 'This book exists' as 'There is just one book which this is a sense-datum of', but that this would not be correct unless the word 'of' here stood for a relation, which he does not believe to be the case. I find this argument obscure as I should have thought that in all the analyses of propositions like 'This book exists' which we shall find that Moore regards as having some chance of being correct, the existence of factors other than the presented sense-datum would be something known only by description; but this point is not important in the present context, since it has already been admitted that the use of 'exists' in conjunction with a demonstrative which refers to a present sense-datum is not Russellian. Moore briefly considers the question whether we should say that 'exists', in this usage, stands for an attribute, and says that the only reason he can find why we should not is that whereas in the case of a sentence like 'This is red' only part of what is asserted is that 'This exists', in the case of 'This exists' it is the whole of what is asserted. Again, the argument is not very clear, but I think that it may be a way of making the valid point that, in this usage also, one is not in any way characterising an object in saying only that it exists.

In the notes for a course of lectures which he gave in 1928–9, Moore makes a passing reference to what I have called the 'external' use of

---

[1] *Philosophical Papers*, p. 123.

terms like 'exists' or 'real'. He remarks that when Russell says in his Logical Atomism lectures that material things are unreal, what he means is that they are not simple particulars. He thinks that Russell may very well be right about this, but maintains, without developing the point, that it is not inconsistent with the proposition that there are material things. He is, however, mainly concerned in these lectures with the ordinary, internal use of words like 'real' for which the theory of descriptions caters, and especially with the analysis of our talk about imaginary entities. For example, he considers the attempt to derive the conclusion that some material things are unreal from the premises that Aladdin's lamp was a material thing and Aladdin's lamp was unreal, and argues that the deduction is invalid, on the ground that what is meant by 'Aladdin's lamp was a material thing' is that 'Aladdin's lamp, *if* it had existed, would have been a material thing'.[1] Since he would not be prepared to analyse 'Florence Nightingale's lamp was a material thing' in the same hypothetical fashion, the moral of this is that we have first to decide whether we wish to claim reality for the thing which we are describing before we decide whether to bring the theory of descriptions to bear upon it. This is, perhaps, not objectionable in itself, but it does show that the theory of descriptions does not supply us with a straightforward criterion of existential commitment. I shall recur to this point later on.

An interesting question which Moore raises in these notes is that of our ability to use different descriptions to refer to the same imaginary entity. He thinks that what is meant by saying of two people that they are thinking of the same existent object, for instance Julius Caesar, under different descriptions, is that each of them knows with regard to the description he is employing that something uniquely satisfies it, and that, whether they know it or not, what satisfies both descriptions is in fact Julius Caesar. It is, however, clear that this analysis will not do in the case where they are both thinking of an imaginary object, like the god Apollo, simply because there is no description which Apollo in fact satisfies. So Moore suggests that what is meant, in cases of this kind, by saying that two people are thinking of the same object, is that their conceptions of it are derived from a common source, this being the conception of it which was entertained by the person who first invented the legend, or the story, in which the object figures.

It seems to me that both these analyses are faulty. We can successfully use a description to refer to an existent object, without knowing it to be a description which something uniquely satisfies, and in certain cases, as I said earlier, we can even make a successful reference, in the sense of directing the hearer's attention to the right existent object, by using a description which it does not in fact satisfy. It is enough, in either case, that the description be selected from a stock of descriptions, of which a sufficient number are conjointly satisfied by the object in question and by nothing else. This is, however, a minor emendation, whereas in the case of imaginary objects I think that the whole direction of Moore's approach is wrong. Not only is the suggested causal analysis very far-fetched, but I do not see how, among the common causes which the different conceptions may have, we are to find out the one that is to fix the reference. For example, our conceptions of Shakespeare's Hamlet are indirectly caused by Shakespeare's conception of Hamlet, but they are also indirectly caused by the thoughts of those chroniclers from whom Shakespeare took the outline of his story. It may be objected that even so our conceptions will have a common source, but I do not think that we can be satisfied with an analysis which accounts for the fact that different descriptions of an imaginary object can have the same ostensible reference in a way that fails to determine what this ostensible reference is. Neither does there seem to be any need for this complication. Here again, it seems to be enough to say that two people are thinking of the same imaginary object under different descriptions if each includes his description in a set of descriptions which jointly make up his conception of the object, and a sufficient number of descriptions are common to both sets. This solution is not, indeed, available to Moore because he holds that no two persons can conceive of anything under the same description. He does not say why he believes this, but it could be either on the ground that every description is anchored in sense-data, or on the ground that every description contains a reference to the speaker's unique spatio-temporal position. This is, however, to assume in either case that every description involves the use of a demonstrative; and this is an assumption which we have already seen that there is no good reason to accept.

The point that being thought of does not entail being real is applied by Moore, as we shall discover, to putative facts, but otherwise only to things like unicorns, which, if they were real, would be material objects. The question whether they are real or not comes down, as we have seen, to the question whether certain concepts are, or are not, satisfied. Whether, and if so in what sense, the concepts themselves are real is a question which he does not reopen. Indeed, there is little mention of concepts in any but his earliest works, except for a number of passages in which he speaks of concepts, in their role as the meanings of a certain class of expressions, as being among the things that one should try to analyse. This apparent neglect of concepts reflects no more, however, than a change of usage. He frequently speaks of properties in contexts in which he could equally well have talked of concepts, and in *Some Main Problems of Philosophy* he speaks of abstract or general ideas as being among the things that there are in the universe, though he prefers to designate them by what he calls the less familiar name of 'universals'.

B. THE NATURE OF UNIVERSALS

Since Moore never doubts that there are universals, the question which he is, in this context, chiefly concerned to answer is what sorts of universals there are. He discusses this question in considerable detail in the last two chapters of *Some Main Problems of Philosophy*. He begins there by distinguishing two kinds of universals, which he takes to be easily recognisable, and then raises the question whether there are any other kinds of universals besides these two. The two kinds which he takes to be easily recognisable are, first, relations, and secondly, 'properties which consist in the having of a relation to *something or other*'.[1] The first kind is subdivided into (1) direct relations between two terms, (2) indirect relations between two terms, where each has a relation to some third particular, and (3) indirect relations between two terms where each has a relation to some one or other of a group of particulars, to which are added two sorts of indirect relations between two terms, where each has a relation to one or other of the two recognised types of universal. The possibility to which Russell drew attention[2] of their being relations which are irreducibly n-adic, where n is greater than two, is not here considered. The second kind is subdivided into (i) properties which consist in having a relation to a particular, like the property of being in the neighbourhood of London, (ii) properties which consist in having a relation to some member or other of a group of particulars, like the property of being in the neighbourhood of some city or other, and (iii) properties which consist in being a member of a group of particulars, as London is a member of

[1] *Some Main Problems of Philosophy*, p. 325.   [2] See *The Problems of Philosophy*, pp. 124-5.

the group consisting of London and Paris. To these are added the three further sorts of properties which consist in having the corresponding relations, not to particulars but to universals of the recognised types. Moore thinks it important to distinguish relations from relational properties, a distinction to which we have already referred in discussing his refutation of the dogma of internal relations, and both from the fact that two objects stand to one another in such and such a relation. Two objects can have the same relational properties, and even when they do not have the same relational properties, they can be terms in the same relation, in the sense in which the relation which C has to the group consisting of B and C is the same as that which A has to the group consisting of A and B. Relational properties are said to be constituents of relations and relations to be constituents of facts. Facts are not universals, though they too, in Moore's opinion, are undoubtedly real.

The fact that there undoubtedly are universals of the kinds which he has so far distinguished is thought by Moore as being sufficient to show that Berkeley and Hume were wrong in denying the existence of abstract or general ideas. In this, however, I think that he is probably mistaken. As we saw when discussing Russell's treatment of universals, it is quite likely that all that Berkeley and Hume wanted to deny was the existence of universals which could not be wholly analysed in terms of relations between particulars, though they may also have held the dubious thesis that these relations could all themselves be analysed in terms of the single relation of resemblance. One thing which they anyhow wished to maintain, though they would not have put it in these terms, is that the possession by anything of what is ordinarily spoken of as a quality is to be equated with its possession of what Moore would call the relational property of being a member of a group: and on this point Moore is not certain that they were wrong. It is, indeed, only if qualities cannot be treated in this way, that he thinks it necessary to admit any other kind of universals than those which he began by listing.

I have already given what seem to me conclusive reasons against the view that in saying of an object A, for example, that it is white, what one is saying is that A is a member of the group of white things, where this group is constituted by enumeration. Moore also rejects this view after some hesitation, but the only reason which he gives for doing so is that it seems plain to him that a group such as that which consists of all the sense-data which we should unhesitatingly call white is, in some sense, a natural and not a merely arbitrary group; and that what is meant by saying that it is, in this sense, a natural group is 'that there *is* some other property, *beside* mere membership of the group, which *is* both common and peculiar to all its members'.[1] He restricts himself to sense-data, because he takes it for granted that when we ascribe a quality like that of being white to a physical object, part of what we are saying is that the physical object is somehow related to a sense-datum which has the quality. This point is debatable but it need not concern us here. If anyone queries our right to talk about sense-data, we can define the objects which occur in Moore's example as those of which the adjective 'white' is straightforwardly predicable. Then the question is what other property is common and peculiar to these things, besides that of just being members of the group of white things.

Moore considers three possible answers to this question, between which he finds it difficult to decide. The first of them is that the property which white things have in common is that there is one among them which they all resemble. In discussing this answer Moore concentrates on the case of pure white colour patches, where the resemblance can be said to be exact. He seems to think that there is a difficulty in extending the theory to other cases, on the ground that resemblance may not yield the groupings that we want: a yellowish-white patch may resemble a whitish-yellow patch in colour more closely than it resembles a pure white one. In the end, he disposes of this difficulty rather too summarily by saying that there may also be kinds of resemblance which fall short of being exact. The main objection which he finds to this theory is that the sense-datum which serves as the model of whiteness cannot be said to resemble itself. Consequently, being white will have to be the disjunctive property of being either identical with *A*, where *A* is the model, or resembling *A* in colour with some special degree of exactitude; and it will be a different disjunctive property, according as a different sense-datum is taken as the model. Moore finds this conclusion somewhat counter-intuitive, but does not regard it as a fatal objection to the theory.

Since resemblance in colour is a relation, the acceptance of this theory would not entail the admission of a new kind of universal. This is not true of the second theory he considers, which is that there is a thing called 'pure white' which has the property of being able to be in different places at once. So the common property which two pure white colour patches would possess would be that of being at a place

[1] Ibid., p. 330.

which pure white occupied. Again, Moore thinks that there is a difficulty in the case of two patches which are not of exactly the same shade
of colour, though there seems no obvious reason why a less specific
property like whitishness should not also have multiple location.
Moore remarks shrewdly that 'If this theory were true . . . there would
be no reason to suppose that there are any particulars at all except
particular places and times',[1] and he regards this as a serious objection
to it. But his main objection is based on a confusion between colours
and colour patches, as a result of which he attributes to the theory the
proposition that the same colour patch can have different properties in
different places, and not surprisingly finds this self-evidently false. He
himself adverts to what he calls this bad mistake in the Appendix to
Some Main Problems, which he wrote in 1952, and there says that the
view that 'When we have two sense-given "patches" . . . which are of
exactly the same shade of colour as one another, and each of them of
that particular shade *all over*, then . . . the colour of the one is *identical*
with the colour of the other',[2] is a view which he considers to be true.
And in one of his few later treatments of the question of universals, a
contribution to an Aristotelian Society symposium in 1923 which is
reprinted in his *Philosophical Papers* under the title 'Are the Characteristics of Particular Things Universal or Particular?', he relies on the
argument that the specific colour of a thing can be 'locally separated'
from itself[3] to refute Professor Stout's contention that the characteristics
of particular things are themselves particular.

Continuing the inquiry in *Some Main Problems of Philosophy*, Moore
points out that when two objects stand in some relation to one another,
it is a mistake to think that they are related not only to each other but
to the relation as well; for this would clearly lead to an infinite regress.
Having a relation is, he says, 'an ultimate notion',[4] and relational
properties simply 'belong' to the things which have them. Accordingly,
he thinks that one might adopt the theory that having a property like
the property of being white simply consists in being related in this
ultimate way to a thing which he calls *W*. Alternatively, it might be
held that what white patches had in common was not that they were
all related to *W*, but that *W* itself belonged to them. In either case, *W*
would be a universal of a new sort: it would not itself be a relational
property, though, on one version of the theory, white colour patches
would have the relational property of being related to it. If they were

---

[1] Ibid., p. 343.   [2] Ibid., p. 374.   [3] *Philosophical Papers* p. 26.
[4] *Some Main Problems of Philosophy*, p. 346.

all related to it, or if it belonged to them as a quality, they would resemble one another in this respect, but they would not resemble it. To suppose that they did would be to fall into Plato's mistake of regarding universals as models which particulars copied: for then, as Aristotle pointed out, if the resemblance between men consisted in their copying the form of man, the resemblance between a man and the form would itself have to consist in their copying a third entity, and so *ad infinitum*.

Moore refers to the universal which the theory postulates as W, rather than white, or whatever, because he thinks that it could not be seen, but only discovered by some act of mental intuition, and his objection to the theory is that he cannot perform this act: he cannot discover that he ever has such a thing as W before his mind. As a result, he comes down tentatively in favour of the first theory, that properties like that of being white are disjunctive properties, without, however, concluding that there are no kinds of universals other than the two that he first distinguished, since he thinks that numbers are universals, and that they are not either relations or relational properties. The property of being a number, like the number 2, or the number 3, may, he thinks, be a disjunctive relational property, like the property of being white, but he holds, ignoring Russell, that the property of being so and so many in number, the property which is common to all pairs or triads, is simply that the number 2, or the number 3, belongs to them. In fairness to Moore, it should, however, be added that when he wrote about numbers, some thirty years later, in his *Commonplace Book*, he was mainly disposed to regard a number as a property of properties, and in particular remarked that when one says 'That's one thing' one is not making what would be the nonsensical statement: 'That's a thing that has the property of being "one".'[1]

Moore had nothing more to say about universals in the lectures which became the text of *Some Main Problems of Philosophy*, but in the Appendix to the book he admitted that he had made 'a second gross mistake' in attributing to the proponents of his third theory the view that universals, like shades of colour, are not seen. 'The view', he says, 'which I express in these chapters that, if there are any "qualities" which "belong" to a patch in the same non-relational sense in which its relational properties belong to it, then these "qualities" must be things we never see, seems to me now to be quite absurd, and a view which nobody has ever held.'[2] We do see shades of colour, just as we see

---

[1] *The Commonplace Book of G. E. Moore*, p. 215.
[2] *Some Main Problems of Philosophy*, p. 375.

sizes and shapes, though Moore thinks that the sense in which we are said to see such abstract things cannot be quite the same as that in which we are said to see the concrete patches which they characterise. His objection to the third theory is therefore removed and he adopts it in the cases of size and shape, without actually saying whether he thinks that they simply belong to the sense-data which they characterise, or are related to them by the relation of predication, but seeming to imply that he thinks they simply belong. With regard to colour, on the other hand, he argues that a property like that of being white is a relational property, on the ground that 'In saying that a sense-datum is white, we are saying that every part of it is of *some shade* of white',[1] and that this entails that the sense-datum has to the shade of white in question the relation which consists in the colour's being '*spread over* the whole of it'.[2] At the same time he thinks that 'the property of being *a* white', which belongs not to sense-data but to colours, is not a relational property, in which case it would again have to be a disjunction in which one of the disjuncts was identity and the other defined in some way in terms of resemblance between colours, but a universal of the kind that he was looking for.

Moore takes up the question of shades of colour in a series of entries in his *Commonplace Book* which were written about 1919. He thinks that what is sensibly presented, when one sees a colour, is always a universal which is an *infima species* in the sense that no quality is subordinate to it, in the way that it is subordinate to red, or primrose-yellow, or whatever colour it may be. In the same way the shapes of the sense-data which are presented to us are absolutely specific. Moore says of these absolutely specific characters that they cannot be abstracted and therefore cannot be named, his reason for this being, first, that when two such shades of colour are not simultaneously presented it is impossible to say for certain that the one which you are seeing is not perceptually different from the one which you remember, and secondly, that even when they are simultaneously presented, and one can say that there is no perceptible difference between them, one still cannot say that they are not really different.[3] I should have thought, however, that the most that this proved was that one would in certain cases be uncertain about the extension of the predicates which were supposed to stand for the specific properties, and that sometimes when one had formed a view about this extension one might find occasion to revise it. But this is surely true of many predicates: it does not seem to me a good

[1] Ibid., p. 377.   [2] Ibid.   [3] *The Commonplace Book of G. E. Moore*, p. 52.

reason for holding that just these specific properties cannot be named. We shall see that this is a point of some importance when we come to Moore's theory of truth.

Moore also says in these notes that the fact that 'Two shades which have no common quality may be just as like as or more like than two others which have one' proves that 'likeness, in the sense of which we talk of more or less like between simple qualities, does not consist in possession of a common quality',[1] and he adds, possibly though not expressly on the same ground, that 'To refute Russell's theory of universals, it is sufficient to ask what is meant by the proposition: "Yellow is lighter than red" '.[2] I do not profess to understand this reference to Russell, but the answer to Moore's point is surely that if two simple qualities do seem to us to be alike in some degree, all that we have to do in order to endow them with a common quality is to invent an appropriate term.

In an entry in *The Commonplace Book*, dating from 1942–3, Moore asks how we can explain what is meant by saying 'So and so is a universal' and begins by saying that a universal is anything which can be asserted about each of two different things. It then occurs to him that 'That is Socrates' could have been asserted, mistakenly, about different people, but rather than admit 'Socrates' or even 'being Socrates' as a universal, he qualifies his answer by ruling that 'the sort of thing you *assert about* an object at which you point when you use a proper name' is not to count.[3] He mentions but does not answer Ramsey's argument that in the case of a proposition like 'Socrates is wise', you can just as well say that you are asserting of wisdom that it characterises Socrates as that you are asserting of Socrates that he is characterised by wisdom. I suppose that the answer is that what makes Socrates a particular and being wise a universal is the difference in the criteria of identity according to which being wise collects its instances and Socrates his biography.[4] It can, however, be shown that this is not a radical difference. As we saw when discussing Russell's theory of descriptions, it can be attenuated to the point where it remains only as a difference between demonstrative and descriptive signs.

I said earlier that there was no doubt that there are universals, if this is taken to mean no more than that we cannot dispense with expressions which pick out recurrent features of the world. I also said that most of those who insisted on the reality of universals probably meant something

---

[1] Ibid., p. 58.   [2] Ibid., p. 59.   [3] Ibid., pp. 205–6.
[4] Cf. 'Individuals', in my *Philosophical Essays*.

more than this, but that it was not clear what more they did mean. I think it likely that Moore is one of those who did mean something more, but for all the trouble that he takes in distinguishing different kinds of universals, he does not explain what he means by saying that there are such things. He may have continued to think, mistakenly, that being, in the sense here in question, was an ultimate notion which did not call for any explanation. To try to get a clearer idea whether this is so, let us see how he deals with the similar question whether there are classes.

C. THE EXISTENCE OF CLASSES

Apart from one entry in the earliest of his notebooks, where he argues against the existence of unit-classes on the ground that there is no reason to think that there is 'anything which is related to "eldest son of King Edward", in the way in which "men" is related to "human being" ',[1] all that Moore has to say about classes is to be found in the notes for a course of lectures which he delivered in the year 1925–6. He there makes the point that the proposition that there are classes can be taken in two different senses. The first of these senses is characterised by him as one in which the proposition that there are classes is not a proposition about symbols, the second as one in which it is. Of 'There are classes', in the first sense, he says that it seems to him 'something which is *logically equivalent* to saying that there are more than one proposition of a certain sort that are true: viz. "My fingers are a class", "The hairs of my head are a class". *If* there are classes, at least two different propositions of this sort must be true; and if *one* proposition of this sort is true then there is at least one class.'[2] Moore goes on to suggest that this can serve as a general explanation of this sort of existential statement. Whether, to use his own examples, it is a matter of there being men, or lions, or relations, or qualities, to say that there are things of the kind in question is to say that at least two propositions of the form '*x* is a so and so' are true. In other words, the question of existence, in this sense, is settled by giving instances.

There is, however, still a difficulty about deciding when an existential statement comes into this category. If 'There are men' follows from the fact that the propositional function '*x* is a man' is satisfied in at least

---

[1] *The Commonplace Book of G. E. Moore*, p. 14.   [2] *Lectures on Philosophy*, p. 122.

two different instances, then, as Moore remarks, 'you might think similarly that (1) "There are imaginary beings" will follow from "Ariel is an imaginary being" and "Oberon is an imaginary being"; and that (2) "There are fairies" will follow from "Oberon is a fairy" and "Titania is a fairy".'[1] His answer is that you would be wrong in thinking this because 'x is an imaginary being' or 'x is a fairy' is not a function of the same sort as 'x is a man' or 'x is a class'. To say that Oberon is an imaginary being, if it is not to be taken as expressing the self-contradictory proposition that a certain set of predicates both belongs to one individual and to nothing at all, must be interpreted as saying that a certain set of predicates has been imagined as belonging to one individual, without in fact being attributed to anyone. To say that Oberon is a fairy is to say that the attribute of being a fairy is one of those that have been attributed to a particular imaginary character. Moore sees, however, that this gives no rule for determining when the existential inference is legitimate. You have first to decide whether the subject exists before you can decide whether the expression which appears to attribute a predicate to it is to be interpreted according to the model of 'Shakespeare is a man' or according to the model of 'Oberon is a fairy'.

In the case of classes, as we have just seen, Moore does consider the existential inference to be legitimate, and he also considers it to be legitimate in the case of qualities, since he says that 'There are qualities' follows from the propositions 'Red is a quality' and 'Blue is a quality'. What we have now to see is whether he also thinks that there are classes in the second of the senses which he began by distinguishing: the one in which the sentence 'There are classes' is construed as expressing a proposition about symbols.

The account which we are given of this second sense in Moore's lecture notes is somewhat compressed, and not at all points easy to follow, but its outline is reasonably clear. It takes its origin from Russell's conception of classes, according to which every predicate can be used to determine a class. In this usage, as we have seen, the concept of class is an extensional concept: if two predicates are coextensive in their application, they determine the same class, which, in the case where the predicates are not satisfied, will be the null-class. Moore regards this as a queer usage, not because of the extensionality, to which he has no objection, but because he thinks that, in ordinary language, it is contradictory to speak of a class with less than two members. We

[1] *Lectures on Philosophy*, p. 123.

shall see in a moment that this is a point of more consequence to Moore than might at first appear.

Moore then adopts Russell's view of classes with the restriction that only predicates which are satisfied by at least two objects are to be said to determine a class. And in order to decide whether there are classes, in the sense in which the question is construed as a question about symbols, he brings in Russell's notion of an incomplete symbol, of which he gives his own definition. He first points out that what needs to be defined is not just '*x* is an incomplete symbol' but rather '*x in this usage* is an incomplete symbol', and then defines the expression as follows: 'In the case of *every* sentence, *p*, in which *x* occurs *with this meaning*, there can be formed another sentence, *q*, for which *p* is short, such that neither *x* itself nor any expression for which *x* is short occurs in *q, and p* always *looks as if* the rest of it expressed a propositional function, such that the proposition expressed by *p* is a value of that function, whereas in fact it never does.'[1]

Having given this definition of an incomplete symbol, Moore says that he construes the statement that there are no classes as meaning what Russell meant by saying that classes are logical fictions, and what he takes this to mean is that 'symbols for classes *are* incomplete and are *not* descriptions'.[2] He further explains that what this comes down to is that the expression 'determined by', in the sense in which classes are said to be determined by predicates, is an incomplete symbol. If there are no classes, this expression 'does not express any relation';[3] if there are, it does. Surprisingly Moore says that, in the sense in which Russell speaks of classes, 'hardly anyone would be disposed to question' that 'determined by' does not express a relation.[4] On the other hand, when it comes to classes in what he takes to be the ordinary sense of the term, he is disposed to go the other way; he inclines towards the view that 'having for a member' is an ultimate relation in which classes stand to their elements. But, so far as I can see, his only reason for adopting this position is that he just cannot bring himself to believe that there is such a thing as the null-class, or that there is an entity distinct from Scott, namely the class of which Scott is the only member, which is determined by the predicate 'wrote *Waverley*'; whereas he has no difficulty in believing that there are such entities as the classes constituted by the fingers on his right hand, or the pennies in his pocket. He fails, however, to explain what he thinks is meant by saying that these classes exist, over and above the fact that the predicates 'being a finger on

[1] Ibid., p. 119.   [2] Ibid., p. 124.   [3] Ibid.   [4] Ibid., p. 126.

Moore's right hand' or 'being a penny in Moore's pocket' at a given date are satisfied by such and such particulars. Consequently, we are not left very much wiser than we were over the question of the reality of universals. In the case of classes, we are at least given a criterion for saying that they are not real, but we do not know how to determine whether the criterion is satisfied.

D. ARE THERE PROPOSITIONS?

Some further light on Moore's attitude towards abstract entities is displayed in his treatment of propositions. I shall first show what he meant by a proposition and then consider whether, and if so in what sense, he believed in their reality.

We have seen that in his early paper on 'The Nature of Judgement', Moore simply deduces the reality of propositions from that of the concepts of which he takes them to be composed, but his treatment of it in *Some Main Problems of Philosophy* is more sophisticated. Having introduced them there, in the first instance, by mentioning a couple of sentences, and informing his audience that when they understood those sentences they were directly apprehending propositions, he assigns them a number of characteristics, of which the most important are that, in addition to being apprehensible, a proposition may be the object of the mental attitudes of belief or disbelief, in any of their various degrees, and that propositions are 'a sort of thing which can properly be said to be *true* or *false*'.[1] They are not, indeed, the only sort of thing of which Moore thinks this can properly be said. He thinks that it is also correct to say it of acts of belief. He holds that the sense in which propositions are true or false is different from that in which acts of belief are, but that the two senses are inter-definable. We can equally well say that an act of belief is true when it has for its object a true proposition, or that a proposition is true when it is the object of a true act of belief.

In *Some Main Problems of Philosophy*, Moore does not lay down any restriction on the sorts of signs that can express propositions, but in his later writings he limits them to declarative sentences: and in an entry in the notebook which he began at the end of the year 1947, he defines a declarative sentence in the following way: 'An English sentence is "declarative" if and only if *both* it makes sense, when the words and

---

[1] *Some Main Problems of Philosophy*, p. 62.

syntax are used in accordance with good English usage, and also *either*
(1) begins with "I know that", "I think that", "I feel sure that", "It's
certain that" or any other of the English phrases which mean the same
as one of these *or* (2) is such that the sentence formed by adding one of
these before it makes sense'.[1] He does not comment on the fact that if
we accept this definition we may be put into the position of having to
say either that not every declarative sentence expresses a proposition
or that not every proposition is either true or false. For instance, it is
clear that both sentences which are used to express moral judgements
and sentences like 'The present King of France is bald', which refer to
non-existent individuals, satisfy Moore's definition: yet with regard to
sentences of each of these kinds some philosophers have held that what
they express is neither true nor false. In the case of sentences which
refer to non-existent individuals, Moore himself accepted Russell's
theory of descriptions, which does assign a truth-value to what they
express. On the other hand, in his reply to his critics in *The Philosophy
of G. E. Moore*, he admits to being half-inclined to accept Professor Stevenson's 'emotive' theory of ethics, from which it would
follow that sentences which expressed moral judgements were not
used to assert anything of which truth or falsehood could be
predicated.[2]

The distinction between propositions and sentences is maintained
throughout Moore's writings on this topic. In the entry in *The Commonplace Book* which follows that in which he defines declarative sentences,
he remarks, truly, that ' "He asserted the proposition 'p' " does not
mean the same as "He uttered (or wrote) the sentence 'p' or some
equivalent" ' and suggests 'that it means in addition "He uttered a
sentence which means p" ',[3] a suggestion which is in fact inadequate
since one might utter a sentence which meant p without using it to
assert p: and in a later entry he argues that it is not true either 'that
every proposition about any particular proposition is a proposition
about instances of a sentence', or 'that every proposition about propositions in general is a proposition about instances of sentences', or 'that
if there were no instances of sentences there would be no propositions;
since even if there had never been any sentences, some propositions
might have been true and others false'.[4] There have, of course, to be
instances of sentences if any propositions are to be asserted, but this is

[1] *The Commonplace Book of G. E. Moore*, pp. 357–8.
[2] *The Philosophy of G. E. Moore* (1942), p. 545.
[3] *The Commonplace Book*, p. 360.   [4] Ibid., p. 375.

not a necessary condition of their being true or false, or even, Moore adds, of their being believed.

Moore does not notice that in so sharply separating propositions from sentences, he is faced with a problem about their identity. This is a question about which he has remarkably little to say, but his general view appears to be that in the case of any sentence which contains a token-reflexive expression, such as a tensed verb, or a demonstrative, or a personal pronoun, what proposition it expresses will be determined by the context of its utterance, in such a way that even the slightest change in context will result in a difference in the proposition expressed. For example, he says that 'If I say twice over "Caesar was murdered" the proposition which I express on each occasion is a different one',[1] on the ground that the present moment to which my use of the past tense implicitly refers is slightly different in each case. This not only leads to difficulties with respect to the logical relations between propositions, since, for example, the question whether someone who asserts that Caesar was murdered is formally contradicted by someone who says that Caesar was not murdered will depend on which of them speaks first, but it also makes the existence of a very large class of propositions dependent on the utterances of sentences, since the context of the utterance will be an essential factor in determining what proposition is expressed. It has, however, been pointed out by Professor and Mrs Kneale in their contribution to the *Essays in Retrospect* that in one of the entries in Moore's *Commonplace Book*, which was written about 1926, he says that the fact which is expressed by the sentence '*A* is occurring' is a fact of the form '*A* is timelessly simultaneous with *C*', where *C* is an event.[2] The Kneales deny that this is a satisfactory translation of what is meant by '*A* is occurring', but it seems to me to be an adequate paraphrase and it indicates a method by which any use of tensed verbs could be avoided. We have also seen, in discussing Russell's theory of descriptions, that if we demand no more than adequate paraphrases, all other token-reflexive expressions become dispensable. Moore does not himself adopt this procedure, and possibly would not have approved of it, but it is clear that he needed to adopt it if he was to maintain his view about the independence of propositions from sentences. It would also have simplified his problem about propositional identity, though it would not have solved it. For one thing, he seems to have taken the view that for two sentences to express the same proposition it was necessary that they should be

[1] *Philosophical Papers*, p. 71. [2] *The Commonplace Book*, p. 100.

synonymous, in some stronger sense than that of being logically derivable from one another: but what this stronger sense is he does not manage to define. I shall return to this question when I come to discuss his conception of philosophical analysis.

Having explained, to some extent, what he means by a proposition in the third chapter of *Some Main Problems of Philosophy*, Moore at once declares it to be certain that propositions are among the things that there are in the universe. It may, therefore, come as something of a shock to find that when he devotes himself to the analysis of belief in chapter 14 of the very same book, he reaches a conclusion which he expresses by saying that there simply are no such things as propositions, and that when, in chapter 17, he attacks the view that truths are to be identified with true propositions, he speaks of propositions as imaginary. Moore does not seem to have noticed this discrepancy at the time, but later, when he wrote the preface to the book, he remarked that there was at least a possibility that he had not contradicted himself, since it might be that when he said that there certainly were propositions he was using the sentence 'There are such things as propositions' in a different sense from that in which he was using it when he said that there were no such things. His point was that in the second case he was making the reality of propositions depend upon the correctness of a particular analysis of such sentences as 'I believe the proposition that the sun is larger than the moon', whereas in the passage in which he said that there certainly were propositions he thought it possible that he was 'using it in such a sense that the truth of what it expresses would follow from the mere fact that such expressions as "I believe the *proposition* that the sun is larger than the moon" are perfectly correct ways of expressing something which is often true'.[1]

Moore does not say what the sense is in which there being propositions is supposed to follow from the fact that sentences of the form 'I believe the proposition that so and so' can correctly be used to say something true. He can hardly be maintaining that to receive mention in a sentence which is used to express a truth is a sufficient title to reality. Perhaps, by analogy with what he says about classes, we can assume that the sense which he has in mind is that in which the reality of propositions follows from the fact that we can give examples of them.

Relying on the analogy with what Moore says about classes, we should expect the reason for his later denial that there are propositions

[1] *Some Main Problems of Philosophy*, p. xii.

to be that they are designated by incomplete symbols, but the reason which he gives is not of this kind at all. It is that he was mistaken in casting propositions as the objects of belief. His argument, though his exposition of it is elaborate, is essentially quite simple. I shall try to set it out as clearly as I can.

Moore takes as an example the false belief that anyone would be having if he believed that Moore and his audience were currently hearing the noise of a brass band. What would make this belief false, he says, would be the fact that they were not hearing any such noise, or to put it another way, the absence from the universe of the fact which would make the belief true. He then points out that this conclusion can be generalised. What makes a belief true is the presence in the universe of the fact to which it refers: what makes a belief false is the absence of this fact from the universe. If we now ask what the fact is to which a given belief refers, the answer is that it is 'the fact which has the same name as that which we have to use in naming the belief'.[1] To name a belief is to say that it is the belief that so and so, the belief that my scissors are lying on the table, the belief that unicorns exist, or whatever it may be, and the same verbal clause is used to name the fact, the fact that my scissors are lying on the table, the fact that unicorns exist, or whatever, the being or non-being of which renders the belief true or false. Moore makes it clear that he is not putting this forward as a definition of what is meant by the fact to which a belief refers: he is not suggesting that what we mean by saying that a belief is true is that the universe contains a fact which has the same name. The identity of name expresses another relation which needs to be brought to light. But for this we require an analysis of belief.

Now the analysis which Moore had hitherto accepted was, as we have seen, that belief was a special act of mind which was directed towards an objective entity, a proposition; and the proposition was supposed to exist, or perhaps we should say, to subsist, whether the belief was true or false. It follows, as Moore now remarks, that in the case of a true belief there are two objective entities to be reckoned with: the proposition which is the object of the belief and the fact which makes it true. Though they are both named by the same name as the belief, these entities are identical neither with it nor with each other: the proof that they are not identical with each other is that the proposition is present in the universe whether the belief is true or false, whereas the fact is present only if the belief is true.

[1] Ibid., p. 256.

This reduplication of entities is not regarded by Moore as a fatal objection to the theory, though he allows that it casts a suspicion against it. He thinks that the best line for an advocate of the theory to take would be to maintain that truth and falsehood were unanalysable properties of propositions and that the fact which made a given belief true simply consisted in the possession by the corresponding proposition of the property of truth. This would not be inconsistent with the definition of truth, according to which 'To say that a belief is true is to say that there *is* in the Universe *the fact* to which it refers'.[1] The sense of 'truth' in which propositions are true would, on this theory, be fundamental; and talking of the being of the fact to which a belief referred would come down to defining the truth of a belief in terms of the truth of the proposition which was its object.

Moore has two objections to this theory. He does not think that either of them is conclusive, but they are enough to make him give the theory up. The first, which is an objection only to the proposed analysis of the fact to which a true belief refers, is that he no longer finds it credible that such a fact can consist merely in the possession of some simple property by a proposition. Even if it be granted that there are propositions, their relation to facts must surely be something different from this. The second objection is more general; it puts in question the basic assumption that propositions are the objects of beliefs. In Moore's own words, 'it is that, if you consider what happens when a man entertains a false belief, it doesn't seem as if his belief consisted merely in his having a relation to some object which certainly *is*. It seems rather as if the thing he was believing, the object of his belief, were just *the* fact which certainly is *not* – which certainly is not, because his belief is false.'[2] But to say that the fact is not is only a clumsy way of saying that there is no such fact: and if there is no such fact, then no belief can have it for an object. Moore is therefore led to the conclusion that beliefs do not, in this sense, have any objects at all.

Moore develops this argument at greater length, but its point will already be clear. What determines the content of a belief is the nature of the state of affairs, or, as Moore would say, the fact, the existence or non-existence of which would render it true or false. But this state of affairs cannot be identified with a proposition, since the proposition which is cast as the object of the belief is supposed to exist equally whether the belief is true or not. Consequently, the introduction of propositions does not account for the contents of beliefs. Neither is it

---

[1] Ibid., p. 262.   [2] Ibid., p. 263.

of any assistance in arriving at a theory of truth. We can certainly predicate truth and falsehood of propositions, so long as we treat them as symbols, but in that case they gratuitously reduplicate the sentences which are used to state what is believed. If we treat them as objects, on to which beliefs are directed, we make it impossible to explain how anything comes to be true or false. Since an object, in this sense, does not refer beyond itself, the propositions simply cut off our beliefs from the actual course of events by which they are verified or falsified.

Not only do I find this argument entirely cogent, but I think that it can be extended against the attempt to cast propositions in the role of the meanings of sentences. There is, indeed, no harm in talking of propositions, so long as it is understood that this is just a convenient device for referring to what is true not only of a given sentence but of any other sentence which has the same meaning. But to conceive of the meaning of a sentence as an abstract object is not only to fail to explain how sentences are endowed with meaning, but also to misrepresent the way in which they are understood. If one supposes that understanding a sentence simply consists in apprehending an abstract entity, one will be at a loss to explain how one ever succeeds in communicating any valid information about matters of empirical fact. Once again, if the proposition is not itself a symbol, it acts not as a bridge but as a barrier between words and things. If it is a symbol, it gratuitously reduplicates the words.

This argument does perhaps afford a sufficient justification for saying that there are no such things as propositions; and, on similar grounds, for saying that there are no such things as concepts or universals. We should, however, note that in saying this we shall be giving yet another sense to this existential negation. What we shall in effect be saying is that propositions or concepts need not be taken seriously, that they are incompetent to do the work to which they have been assigned. But clearly this is not the same as saying that propositions are designated by incomplete symbols. It leaves it an open question whether all the apparent references that we make to propositions can be translated out. I am in fact of the opinion that they can at least be paraphrased out, and I have tried elsewhere[1] to sketch a theory of meaning which could secure this result. I have, however, to admit that in common with all the other attempts that I know of to achieve anything like a formal elimination of propositions, my theory encounters difficulties which I cannot claim to have entirely removed.

[1] See *The Origins of Pragmatism* (Macmillan, pp. 173–9; Freeman Cooper, pp. 162–8).

E. PROPOSITIONS AND FACTS

Moore himself seems not to have been altogether satisfied with his proof that propositions are not the objects of beliefs. At least I can find no evidence that he ever subsequently relied on the argument which I have just been summarising, and in his essay on 'Facts and Propositions', a contribution to an Aristotelian Society symposium with F. P. Ramsey, which appeared sixteen years after he delivered the lecture in which this argument is set out, he still wrote as if he thought it possible that a proposition should be what he calls 'the objective factor' in a fact of a certain sort. Since he explains that one condition for anything A to be an objective factor in a fact of the kind in question is that the fact should entail both that A is being believed and that if anything else is being believed it is contained in A, and since he goes on to say that only a proposition can satisfy this condition, and then only if it is a 'genuine entity', it is clear that in allowing this possibility he has gone back on his earlier position. To see how far he has gone back it will be necessary to examine his essay in some detail.

The first point to remark is that the facts with regard to which Moore says that he thinks it possible that they contain propositions as objective factors are facts of a peculiar sort. He defines them as facts which correspond in a certain way to another class of facts which he defines, as so often, by means of an example. The example is the fact which someone, who was at a given moment judging that Caesar was murdered, would express if he at that moment uttered the English words 'I am now judging that Caesar was murdered'. The class of facts which Moore uses this example to define consists of all those which resemble it in being correctly expressible by an English sentence of the form 'I am now judging that p'. Moore has no doubt that there are facts of this kind and he also has no doubt that they are all what he calls general facts. What he appears to mean by saying that they are general facts is that they are in some degree indeterminate. Thus, in the case of his example, he assumes that someone who judges that Caesar was murdered must be judging with regard to some description such as 'the author of *De Bello Gallico*' or 'the conqueror of Pompey' that the person who answers to this description was murdered: but certainly this information is not conveyed merely by saying 'I am now judging that Caesar was murdered'. The answer to this might appear to be that if the description in question were substituted for the word 'Caesar', as it evidently could be, the resulting sentence would still express a fact which answered to Moore's definition; but I suppose he would have replied that even this would not remove the element of generality, on the ground that there were different ways in which the description might be thought to be satisfied. Again, he assumes that when one makes a judgement one must make it with a definite amount of precision, with a particular degree of conviction, and so forth; yet none of this is stated in merely saying that one makes the judgement. Finally, he thinks it possible, in a fashion which he does not explain, that the use of the word 'I' in this context imports a further element of generality.

Now it is Moore's contention that to every general fact of this kind there corresponds one, and only one, non-general fact. The way in which it corresponds is that every one of the general facts 'is, or is equivalent to, a fact, with regard to a certain description, to the effect that there is one and only one non-general fact answering to that description';[1] the non-general fact in question is then the one which does so answer. It would seem that in order to express such a non-general fact, one would have to state, in a completely determinate way, exactly what happened on the relevant occasion to make it true that someone was then judging that Caesar was murdered or whatever it might be. Moore is, however, of the opinion that none of these non-general facts 'could possibly be expressed in any actual language', presumably on the ground that none of the sentences of any actual language which one might try to employ for the purpose would be sufficiently determinate; and he adds that 'perhaps, even none could be expressed in any possible language'.[2] It is then with these inexpressible non-general facts that Moore believed that his co-symposiast, Ramsey, was really concerned when he wrote in his paper about analysing judgements; and it is of them that he asserts that they may contain propositions among their objective factors.

There is a good deal here that is puzzling. If we consider, not the fact which someone might express by saying that he believed that Caesar was murdered, but simply the fact that Caesar was murdered, then I suppose that a case could be made out for saying that this was a general fact to which just one non-general fact corresponded. What might be meant by saying that it was a general fact would be that there were a number of different possible concrete states of affairs which would make what is expressed by the sentence 'Caesar was murdered' true;

---

[1] *Philosophical Papers*, p. 69.   [2] Ibid.

and what might be meant by saying that just one non-general fact corresponded to it would be that there was just one state of affairs which did make it true, a state of affairs which consisted in a particular man's being killed at a particular time and place by such and such other men in such and such a particular way. But if this is an example of what Moore meant by a non-general fact, I do not find it at all obvious that non-general facts are inexpressible. To avoid any difficulties that there might be in pinning down their subjects, we could attempt to cast them in such a form that the only referential expressions of which we needed to make use in stating them were expressions which referred to places and times: and it would appear possible to make these references completely precise. In order to state what occurred at the place and time, we should then need only to use predicates; and these, I take it, would be qualitative predicates standing for observable properties: they might, for example, be predicates of colour or shape. But then, in view of the fact that there are limits to our powers of sensory discrimination, there would appear to be no reason in principle why these predicates should not be wholly determinate, in the sense that all the instances in which they were satisfied were qualitatively indistinguishable in the relevant respect. It is true that one might be mistaken in supposing that the instances were qualitatively indistinguishable, but I have already argued that this is not a fatal objection to the use of such predicates. In the case of sentences which were designed to express the non-general facts which verified propositions about human actions there would, indeed, be special difficulties, since we might have to bring in predicates which were satisfied by mental images or by unspoken thoughts: but here again I see no reason in principle why a mental image should not be described with complete precision, or even an unspoken thought, to the extent that it consisted not merely in the subject's having certain propensities to speak or act in certain ways, but in some actual state of his consciousness. Of course, no series of sentences of this kind would express anything equivalent to what is expressed by such a sentence as 'Caesar was murdered'; for one thing, they would not rise to the level at which causal relations can be formulated. Nevertheless they could still constitute a completely accurate record of the particular stretch of history in virtue of which the sentence with the greater generality of meaning could be held to express a fact.

This is, however, a simpler problem than the one with which Moore presents us. As we have seen, his example of a general fact is not the fact that Caesar was murdered, but rather the fact which someone would express by saying truly with reference to a particular time that he judged at that time that Caesar was murdered; and it is in the non-general facts which correspond to general facts of this sort that he thinks himself able to distinguish objective and non-objective or at least 'not merely objective' factors. We have seen that one sufficient condition which Moore lays down for anything to be an objective factor in a fact of this sort is that it be the one and only proposition which in asserting the fact in question one is asserting to be believed. A second sufficient condition is that it be something about which the fact entails that something is being believed, in 'some sense of the word "about"'.[1] A not merely objective factor is one that may or may not satisfy one of these conditions, but in any case also enters into the fact in some other way. Thus, in Moore's view, the time at which the judgement is made is an objective factor in the non-general fact corresponding to the fact of someone's judging that Caesar was murdered, since he assumes that anyone who made such a judgement would be judging with regard to the time at which he made it that the event of Caesar's murder occurred before that time. On the other hand, the time at which the subject made the judgement would also enter into the fact in another way 'since it would also be the time, with regard to which the fact in question would be a fact to the effect that he was making that judgement *at* that time'.[2] After the same fashion, the word 'I' might refer to a factor which enters into a fact of this kind in two different ways, if the judgement is one that the subject makes about himself. Because of this, Moore thinks it advisable to define what Ramsey calls a 'mental factor', in a fact of the kind in question, in such a way that something's being a mental factor is not inconsistent with its also being an objective factor. His proposal, given that F is a fact of the appropriate sort and B a factor in F, is that 'B will be a "mental" factor in F, if and only if both (1) B is not *merely* an "objective" factor in F and also (2) B is not the time or (whatever "factor" in F corresponds to this time) *about* which F is a fact to the effect that a certain judgement is being made at that time'.[3]

Having defined mental and objective factors in this way, Moore takes it for granted that every fact of the sort he is concerned with contains mental factors and he also thinks it unquestionable that every such fact contains more than one objective factor. Unfortunately, he does not say how factors are to be individuated. Thus, if we consider such a fact as that lions exist, we do not know whether to take lions

[1] Ibid., p. 70.   [2] Ibid., p. 71.   [3] Ibid., p. 73.

A.H.

and existence as factors, or the property of being a lion and the fact that it is satisfied, or some set of properties which together make up the property of being a lion and the fact that they are conjointly satisfied. Since the judgement that lions exist could, in some sense or other of the word 'about', be said to be about any of these things, it would seem that we have a pretty free choice.

There is, however, some indication that Moore held this choice to be subject to at least one serious restriction. From what he says about propositions, in this context, it may be inferred that he was not prepared to count anything as an objective factor unless it was a genuine entity. But, in that case, so far from its being certain that the facts of which Moore is speaking always contain a plurality of objective factors, it may very well be doubted whether they need contain any objective factors at all. The sort of counter-example which I have in mind would be one in which the judgement in question did not refer to any particular period of time or to any existent things. The most obvious instance would be judgements about mythical entities, like centaurs or unicorns. It might be argued that what such judgements were really about were the stories in which these imaginary creatures figured; but the answer to this would be that one can acribe characteristics to such things as unicorns or centaurs without knowing them to be imaginary. In face of this difficulty, the easiest line for Moore to have taken would have been to say that the objective factors, in such instances, were the properties in terms of which these imaginary creatures were defined. But then what ground would he have had for saying that properties were genuine entities? Here again, Moore's failure to supply any criterion for what is to count as a genuine entity makes this question impossible to answer. All that I can say is that just as one does not explain how sentences have meaning by saying that they stand for propositions, so one does not explain how adjectival expressions have meaning by saying that they stand for properties.

Having admitted, for whatever reason, that every fact of the sort he is concerned with has more than one objective factor, Moore considers whether this admission precludes him from holding that propositions are ever the objective factors in such facts. He thinks that it would so preclude him if the principle, which he attributes to Ramsey, that there cannot be two different facts, each of which entails the other, were true: but he says that he can find no reason for believing this principle to be true, and some reason for believing it to be false. Accordingly, his tentative conclusion appears to be that in the case of any general fact which consists in someone's making a judgement, there are two corresponding non-general facts. One of them consists in the holding of some relation or relations between some not merely objective factors and a plurality of objective factors, and the other consists in the holding of some relation or relations between some not merely objective factors and a proposition. In the second case, the constituents of the proposition are also objective factors which are contained in the fact, but the fact does not, as in the first case, consist in their standing in any relation to the not merely objective factor, but only in the proposition's doing so. These two non-general facts are equivalent, in the sense that they mutually entail each other, but they are not identical.

Apart from the unclarity of the notion of an objective factor, there are two further difficulties here. The first is that Moore does not attempt to explain, still less to justify, his mysterious distinction between what a fact consists in and what it contains. The second and more serious difficulty is that he fails to give any rules for individuating facts. He seems to have had no doubt that facts, both general and non-general, were genuine entities, but at the same time no very clear idea how one fact was to be distinguished from another.

One thing which we do know is that Moore was not willing to identify facts with true propositions. His proof that they are not identical is given in an entry in the first of his notebooks, which was written in the year 1919 or thereabouts. It is shown, he says, 'by showing that "This is scarlet" is equivalent to "That this is scarlet is a fact" but is *not* equivalent to "The proposition that this is scarlet is a fact". "The proposition that this is scarlet is a fact" is nonsense, which shows that "is a fact" and "is true" are not interchangeable, although the sentences "That this is scarlet is a fact" and "That this is scarlet is true" have the same meaning.'[1] In short, the argument is that since the expressions 'is a true proposition' and 'is a fact' are not universally interchangeable, facts and true propositions cannot be identical. This would be a valid argument if its premiss were true, but the trouble is that the example, which is meant to show that the premiss is true, itself relies on the truth of the conclusion. If someone were convinced that facts were identical with true propositions, he would presumably not admit that the sentence 'The proposition that this is scarlet is a fact' was a piece of nonsense: he would accept it as an inelegant way of stating that the proposition that this is scarlet was true.

Moore's claim that his facts are not identical with true propositions

[1] *The Commonplace Book*, p. 3.

might carry more conviction if he had been able to show how they could be separately identified. I shall suggest in a moment that this can be achieved in the case of Moore's non-general facts. On the other hand, when it comes to his general facts, I am unable to see any way of identifying them except through the true propositions which they gratuitously mirror, and ultimately, therefore, through the sentences by which these propositions are expressed. To the non-general fact to which the general fact that Caesar was murdered corresponds, there also correspond, if one is to believe Moore, the general fact that the author of *De Bello Gallico* was murdered, the general fact that Caesar did not die a natural death, the general fact that a great-uncle of Augustus did not die a natural death, the general fact that either Caesar or Napoleon was murdered, the general fact that either Caesar was murdered or Napoleon was an Irishman, and countless others of similar types. What distinguishes these facts from one another is just the differences in content of the propositions with which they are severally paired, and the only purpose that is served by speaking of them is to make the point that these propositions are true. We have already had enough difficulty in attaching meaning to the thesis that propositions are real constituents of the universe; there seems even less excuse for talking as if, corresponding to every true proposition, the universe contained yet another sort of abstract entity, in the form of a general fact.

The case of non-general facts is different because here we are justified in thinking of facts, not as true propositions masquerading under a different title, but as the concrete states of affairs which make propositions true. Thus all the propositions corresponding to the so-called general facts which I have just listed are made true by the non-general fact of Caesar's dying at the particular time and place and in the particular way he did. Even here, however, Moore shows his lack of concern for Ockham's razor. He distinguishes the fact that Caesar died from the event of Caesar's death, with the implication that they are both constituents of the universe. But while it is true that facts are not identical with events, in the sense that we can say of one what we cannot significantly say of the other, the difference is no more than a difference of grammar: whichever way of speaking we find it convenient to employ, there is a sense in which the phenomena to which we are referring are the same. There is just one stretch of the world's history which Caesar's murder occupies, and whether we refer to it in terms of facts, or events, or states of affairs, or things and their attributes, or the instantiation of properties, or the satisfaction of predicates, is a matter for our convenience. There is no reason indeed why we should not draw on all these forms of vocabulary; but it is neither necessary nor profitable to reify all the entities which figure in them.

One motive which Moore may have had for upholding the reality of facts was that he thought that this was required for his correspondence theory of truth. The relation of correspondence on which this theory depends is one which is supposed to hold between a fact of the form 'A judges that p' and the fact which the p in question expresses, if it does express a fact. Moore maintains that in some uses of the word 'true', the meaning of this word can be defined by reference to this relation, and that '*all* our usages of "true" are such that a proposition expressed by the help of that word is *equivalent* to some proposition in which this relation occurs'.[1] For instance, he thinks that, in one of its meanings, ' "It is true that p" means the same as "If anyone were to believe that p, then the fact which consisted in his believing that p would correspond to a fact" '.

This theory is not objectionable in itself. It avoids the mistake into which some other correspondence theories fall of trying to cash 'correspondence' in terms of resemblance or structural similarity. All the same it achieves nothing that is not achieved more clearly and simply by the semantic schema 'S is true in L if and only if p', where it is understood that the expression which is put in the place of 'S' designates a sentence of the language L which has the same meaning as the sentence which is put in the place of 'p'. In both cases, the interesting philosophical problems still remain to be tackled. We need an informative account of meaning; we need a clear specification of the forms of sentences which are used to record the empirical states of affairs which finally determine the truth or falsity of everything that we say about the world; and we need an exact analysis of the ways in which the truth or falsity of what is expressed by sentences of other types depends upon the truth or falsity of what is expressed by sentences of this basic sort. If we had satisfactory answers to all these questions, we should, I think, be left with only a stylistic motive for speaking of propositions or of any but what Moore calls non-general facts.

[1] Ibid., p. 83.

9 The Fruits of Analysis

We have seen that Moore never admitted to thinking that the practice of philosophical analysis was the only constructive function of philosophy, although this is a conclusion which does seem to follow from the manner of his defence of common sense. He did, however, think that it was one of its important functions, and in the latter part of his career his own philosophising was increasingly concentrated upon it. It is, therefore, rather surprising that he says very little about what he takes philosophical analysis to be. Apart from some fragmentary notes for a course of lectures which he delivered in 1933–4, the only published statement of his views on this question is to be found in his fairly short reply to Professor Langford's essay on 'The Notion of Analysis in Moore's Philosophy', which appeared together in 1942 in *The Philosophy of G. E. Moore*.

The first point which Moore makes in his reply is that Professor Langford had been mistaken in supposing that he had ever conceived of philosophical analysis as being directed upon verbal expressions. He is quite clear that he has always intended to use the word 'analysis' in such a way that what can properly be said to be analysed is not a verbal expression, but a concept or a proposition. Moore also frequently speaks of analysing facts, but in this context they can be equated with true propositions. This may look like a firm commitment to the existence of abstract entities, but it need not be. The reason why Moore denies that he is concerned with the analysis of verbal expressions is that he assumes that such an analysis would have to be purely syntactical. When he says that he analyses concepts or propositions, what he is saying is that his analyses bear on what verbal expressions are used to mean. So far, therefore, as his conception of analysis goes, it would be open to him to allow that concepts and propositions were reducible to verbal expressions. We have, however, already seen that the evidence is that he did not think this to be feasible.

Not only does Moore hold that verbal expressions are not the subject of analysis, but he also holds that the statement of an analysis does not mention them. Taking as his example the analysis of the concept 'brother' in terms of the concepts 'male' and 'sibling', he says that this can be properly formulated in any of the following ways: 'The concept "being a brother" is identical with the concept "being a male sibling" ': 'The propositional function "x is brother" is identical with the propositional function "x is a male sibling" ': 'To say that a person is a brother is the same thing as to say that that person is a male sibling': and, most simply of all: 'To be a brother is the same thing as to be a male sibling'.[1] On the other hand, the analysis could not be properly expressed by saying that the phrase 'x is a brother' means the same as the phrase 'x is male and is a sibling', since in saying only that these phrases have the same meaning one is not saying what meaning they have. This argument would not apply to the suggestion, which Moore does not discuss, that the analysis could be expressed by saying that the phrase 'to be a brother' means to be a male sibling, but the objection to this would be that it is not equivalent to the formulations which Moore licenses: this can be shown by the fact that whereas a French translation of the sentence ' "To be a brother" means to be a male sibling' would have to mention the words 'to be a brother', a French translation of the sentence 'To be a brother is the same thing as to be a male sibling' would not have to mention any English words. Nevertheless Moore thinks that the proposition that to be a brother is the same thing as to be a male sibling must in some sense be about the expressions which are used in formulating it, and the reason why he thinks this is that he sees no other way of escaping the conclusion that in asserting this proposition one is merely asserting that to be a brother is the same thing as to be a brother. I shall return to this point later on.

Having distinguished the analysis of concepts from that of verbal expressions, Moore goes on to lay down five conditions which he thinks that the analysis of a concept has to satisfy if it is to be acceptable. Following Langford, he refers to the concept which is being analysed as the *analysandum* and the concept, or set of concepts, into which it is being analysed as the *analysans*. Then, his conditions are first that 'Nobody can know that the *analysandum* applies to an object without knowing that the *analysans* applies to it', secondly, that 'Nobody can verify that the *analysandum* applies without verifying that the *analysans* applies', thirdly, that 'Any expression which expresses the *analysandum*

[1] *The Philosophy of G. E. Moore*, pp. 664–5.

must be synonymous with an expression which expresses the *analysans*',[1] fourthly, that 'The expression used for the *analysans* must explicitly mention concepts which are not explicitly mentioned by the expression used for the *analysandum*', and lastly, that the expression used for the *analysans* should mention the way in which the concepts which it mentions are combined in the *analysandum*.[2]

All these conditions raise problems. The first of them appears to be inconsistent with Moore's own assumption, which figures in his defence of common sense, that we can know that the proposition which is expressed by such and such a sentence is true without knowing what is its correct analysis. Indeed, if we could not know that an object, or a state of affairs, satisfied the *analysandum*, without knowing that it satisfied the *analysans*, the search for correct analyses would never present any problem: we should know the answer before we started. It might be suggested that this condition is only meant to come into play when we have found an analysis; but even so it would be questionable. We might very well hit on a correct analysis without knowing that it was correct, or even while believing that it was not; and then we should not know that the *analysans* had the same extension as the *analysandum*. What is true, of course, is that if they do have the same extension, then in knowing of the existence of an object which satisfies the *analysandum*, we know of the existence of an object which in fact satisfies the *analysans*, but if this is all that is meant by the first condition, it is a mere consequence of the third. If we know of an object satisfying a concept which is designated by an expression E, then we know of an object satisfying the concepts which are designated by any synonyms of E, whether we know that they are synonyms of E or not.

The second condition is puzzling because it is not clear what it is meant to imply. It is obviously not true that when I verify that the *analysandum* applies to something, I must be consciously engaged in verifying that the *analysans* applies to it; for then once again the discovery of the *analysans* would present no problem. On the other hand, it is obviously true that if the *analysandum* and the *analysans* do in fact have the same extension, then what verifies the one will verify the other, whether or not one knows that this is so. But once more, this simply follows from Moore's third condition. Perhaps what he had in mind, under this heading, was that one good way to set about analysing a proposition is to ask oneself what would count as its being verified; and he may also have had in mind the fact that if one discovers or is

---

[1] Ibid., p. 663.   [2] Ibid., pp. 666–7.

able to imagine a situation to which the *analysandum* applies and a suggested *analysans* does not, then one is entitled, at any rate by his criteria, to infer that the suggested analysis is incorrect.

The main difficulty about the third criterion is that we are not supplied with any tests for synonymity. It is left to our intuition to decide whether two expressions are synonymous or not. This works well enough for cases like that of the equivalence of 'brother' with 'male sibling', where the intuitions of educated English speakers are likely to be in agreement, but it does not work at all well for cases which present some philosophical difficulty, like that of the equivalence, in which some philosophers have said that they believed, between statements about mental occurrences and statements about people's dispositions to behave in certain ways. A large part of the problem, indeed, is that such claims are made, not on the basis of linguistic intuitions, but on the basis of what one believes that there can be or what one believes that it is possible to know. Moreover, we shall see that there is a good reason to think that the requirement of synonymity is too strong, in the sense that a proposed analysis which does not satisfy it may still seem intuitively acceptable. It can even be maintained that we are not always justified in requiring so much as extensional identity. This is the position taken by Professor Goodman in his book *The Structure of Appearance*. He shows that Whitehead's definition of a point as a certain infinite class of volumes does not satisfy the criterion of extensional identity, let alone that of synonymity, since, for example, a point can also be defined as a pair of intersecting lines, and no infinite class of volumes is a pair of intersecting lines. Goodman shows also that even if we do not insist on the extensional identity of concepts, but require only that sentences mentioning the *definiendum* be systematically transformable into sentences mentioning the *definiens*, the translation of a sentence which expresses the definition itself into a sentence of a system which is based on a different but equally respectable definition may still not meet the test. Nevertheless Goodman argues, I think correctly, that this is not a sufficient ground for rejecting such a definition. If it can be shown that truth-value is preserved in the reformulation of the mathematical and physical theories which make use of points, the aim of the definition can be said to have been achieved.

The fourth and fifth of Moore's criteria could both do with further explanation. We need to be told what counts as mentioning different concepts and what counts as mentioning different ways of combining them. For instance, if using the word 'not' is mentioning the concept of negation, then it might be said that the analysis of a proposition '*p*' into 'not not-*p*' satisfied these as well as the other criteria, on condition that we explained that the two 'nots' cancelled each other out. On the other hand, it might be argued that they were not combined *in p*. But it is plain that many examples could be constructed which would leave us in a similar difficulty. Nevertheless it is reasonably clear what Moore had in mind. The concepts which are analysed are supposed both to be complex and to be commonly designated in a way which does not reveal the details of their complexity: the analysis brings these details out into the open.

But now I come to what seems to be the fundamental objection to Moore's whole account of analysis. The model provided by 'Brothers are male siblings', a proposition which no one would claim to be of the slightest philosophical interest, is almost wholly inappropriate to the way in which philosophical analysis is actually practised. I do not go so far as to say that there is no philosophical problem to which the solution could consist in the substitution for one verbal expression of another more detailed expression which is synonymous with it – for instance, it is the thesis of some moral philosophers that it is worth seeking definitions of this kind for concepts like that of 'right' or 'good' – but I am sure that there are at best very few. The nearest that one ordinarily comes to anything of this sort is the provision of a rule by which sentences containing a certain expression, or a certain type of expression, are transformed into sentences which do not contain it but do contain expressions which serve in a different way to convey the information which it helps to state. A good example of this is Moore's own transformation of sentences like 'Lions are real' into sentences like 'The property of being a lion belongs to something'. Here there is no effort to find a concept which is identical with the concept of being real: on the contrary, we have seen that Moore himself describes the result of the analysis by saying that the word 'real', in this usage, does not stand for any conception whatever: but the analysis can be said to show us what we mean by speaking of reality, at least in one of the most common ways in which we employ the term. Another obvious example is that of Russell's theory of descriptions, of which Moore himself admits, in his lecture notes, that 'it is not analysis of a concept at all'.[1] He says that Russell gives an analytic definition of a certain form of expression, but we have seen that this is inaccurate if we think of a definition as preserving identity

[1] *Lectures on Philosophy*, p. 160.

of meaning. The rigorous use of the method of transformation, laid down in the theory of descriptions results, as we found, not in translation but in paraphrase.

Although they do not meet Moore's specifications, these are at least cases in which we can be said to be concerned with the meaning of certain sorts of expressions, but there are other analytical problems where to say even so much as this would be to misrepresent what was being done. Consider, for example, the problem of personal identity. This is a problem about meaning in the sense that we have to render an account of the principles according to which the references that we ordinarily make to persons group together different series of events, but it is not to be solved by searching for synonyms or rules of transformation. We have to redescribe the facts in a way that uncovers their complexity: and we have to take into consideration not only the data available to common sense, but also the relevant scientific theories. Neither is this the sort of case in which it is at all safe to assume that our ordinary language is perfectly in order. The development of physiology, not to say para-psychology, may easily show that it needs to be modified in quite radical ways. There is, of course, a sense in which we are concerned with the use of words like the English word 'I', but it is only the trivial sense in which any review of a set of facts illustrates the use of the words which conventionally describe them. There is, after all, no great difficulty in formulating the correct rule of usage for the English word 'I': it is to be used by a speaker to refer to himself. And what does this contribute to the solution of any philosophical problem?

Much the same is to be said about the problem of analysis, which occupied Moore more than any other: that of giving a correct analysis of propositions like 'This is an inkpot', which assert the existence of common-sense physical objects. Evidently this is not a case in which we are searching for synonyms, but it might be suggested that we are looking for a rule which will enable us to transform sentences, which are used to refer to such physical objects, into sentences of a different type, which contain the same information in a more explicit way. This would, however, again be to misrepresent the problem. To begin with, as we have seen in discussing Russell's treatment of it, it is very largely a problem in the theory of knowledge. Even if one starts, as Moore does, from the position that one knows such propositions to be true, the analysis will still have to show how their truth can be known. Part of the problem will be to evaluate the assumption, which he and others have made, that we directly perceive sense-data: and if this assumption is found to be tenable, the analysis will have to show how sense-data and physical objects are related. In the end, as I see it, we shall not get a translation from one system into another, or even directions for a paraphrase, but at best an account of the way in which our talk about physical objects functions as a theory with respect to our sense-experiences. I have already, in discussing Russell's primary system, given an outline of the way in which I think this might be done. And even when this has been achieved, we have still to consider how far the common-sense view of the world can be maintained in the face of established scientific theories about the ways in which our perceptions are caused. Perhaps some light can be thrown on some of the points by an examination of the way in which English words like 'see' and 'hear' are ordinarily used, but it would be idle to hope that such an approach could take us very far. On this matter I find myself in sympathy with the concluding paragraph of the essay which Professor Broad contributed to the *Essays in Retrospect* of Moore. 'To imagine', he said, 'that a careful study of the usages, the implications, the suggestions, and the *nuances* of the ordinary speech of contemporary Englishmen could be a substitute for, or a valuable contribution towards, the solution of the philosophical problem of sense-perception, seems to me one of the strangest delusions which has ever flourished in academic circles'.[1]

This is not, in fact, a delusion from which Moore himself suffered, at least to any very serious extent. How little his belief in the truth of common-sense propositions committed him to a common-sense interpretation of them is shown by a passage from his essay 'The Nature and Reality of Objects of Perception'. He has taken as an example the proposition that 'Hen's eggs are generally laid by hens' and says that he is quite willing to allow for the moment that if this proposition is true at all, 'We must understand by "hens" and "eggs" objects very unlike what we directly observe, when we see a hen in a yard, or an egg on the breakfast-table'. 'I am willing', he continues, 'to allow the possibility that, as some Idealists would say, the proposition "Hens lay eggs" is false unless we mean by it: A certain kind of collection of spirits or monads sometimes has a certain intelligible relation to another kind of collection of spirits or monads. I am willing to allow the possibility that, as Reid and some scientists would say, the proposition "Hens lay eggs" is false, if we mean by it anything more than that:

[1] G. E. Moore: *Essays in Retrospect*, p. 203.

Certain configurations of invisible material particles sometimes have a certain spatio-temporal relation to another kind of configuration of invisible material particles. Or again, I am willing to allow, with certain other philosophers, that we must, if it is to be true, interpret this proposition as meaning that certain kinds of sensations have to certain other kinds a relation which may be expressed by saying that the one kind of sensations "lay" the other kind. Or again, as other philosophers say, the proposition "Hens lay eggs" may possibly mean: Certain sensations of mine *would*, under certain conditions, have to certain other sensations of mine a relation which may be expressed by saying that the one set would "lay" the other set. But whatever the proposition "Eggs are generally laid by hens" may *mean*, most philosophers would, I think, allow that, in some sense or other, this proposition was true'.[1]

It is true that the tone of this passage is faintly ironical, and it is also true that it was written as early as 1905–6. At a later date Moore would not have said that there was any doubt about the meaning of the proposition that hens lay eggs, though he would have said that there was a doubt about its correct analysis. Nevertheless, the knowledge which we are supposed to have of its meaning, or rather of the meaning of the sentence which expresses it, does not apparently permit us to set any very narrow limits to its interpretation. No doubt Moore was not serious in saying that hens might turn out to be collections of monads, but we shall see that he did take the representative theory of perception seriously, from which it would follow that they were 'configurations of invisible material particles', and we shall also see that he was never prepared to reject the phenomenalist theory according to which physical objects are to be identified with actual and possible sense-data. But this is to entertain a conception of analysis which is quite different from anything that could properly be understood by an investigation of conventional usage. It also shows, as I said earlier, how little is defended in Moore's defence of common sense. The plain man is given the assurance that what he believes is true: but these true beliefs may be turned by the processes of analysis not only into beliefs which he has never consciously held, but into beliefs which he probably would not accept if they were suggested to him.

---

[1] *Philosophical Studies*, pp. 64–5.

B. THE PARADOX OF ANALYSIS AND THE NATURALISTIC FALLACY

The assumption that philosophical analysis conforms to the model of 'Brothers are male siblings' has caused attention to be paid to what has been called the paradox of analysis. As formulated by Professor Langford, the paradox is that 'If the verbal expression representing the *analysandum* has the same meaning as the verbal expression representing the *analysans*, the analysis states a bare identity and is trivial; but if the two verbal expressions do not have the same meaning, the analysis is incorrect.'[1] In fact, as we have just seen, philosophical analysis has not often taken a form in which it would encounter this paradox, but the paradox is still worth discussing for its own sake, since it raises a surprisingly difficult question about the interpretation of any explicit definition.

The paradox also has an historical interest for a student of Moore's philosophy, since it embodies the main argument which he used in his *Principia Ethica* to show that good was a simple non-natural indefinable quality. His discussion of this point is somewhat clouded by the fact that he thinks that a definition, in the sense with which he is concerned, 'states what are the parts which invariably compose a certain whole',[2] and that he does not make clear in what sense he supposes that a quality can have parts, but essentially his argument is that what the word 'good' stands for cannot be identified with what is meant by any other expression, since the result of such an equation must be either trivial or false. Thus he remarks that one philosopher 'will affirm that good is pleasure, another, perhaps that good is that which is desired', and then if one contradicts the other, substituting his own definition of good, what he will be saying is that pleasure is not what is desired: and what has that, asks Moore, to do with ethics? Moore does not notice that on this view the two philosophers will not be disagreeing at all, since both will be saying that pleasure is not what is desired, but he might not have thought this detrimental to his argument. Neither will he have it that the discussion is a verbal one, about the meaning of the word 'good'. For moral philosophers are 'anxious to persuade us that what we call good is what we really ought to do'. And how absurd it would be to say 'You are to do this, because most people use a certain word to denote conduct such as this'.[3] Besides, if the word 'good' did

---

[1] *The Philosophy of G. E. Moore*, p. 323.   [2] *Principia Ethica*, p. 9.   [3] Ibid., p. 12.

stand, say, for pleasure, then in saying that pleasure was good, one would simply be saying that pleasure was pleasure. And surely this is not what is intended by someone who says that pleasure is good.

Moore goes on to argue that 'The hypothesis that disagreement about the meaning of good is disagreement with regard to the correct analysis of a given whole, may be most plainly seen to be incorrect by consideration of the fact that, whatever definition be offered, it may always be asked, with significance, of the complex so defined whether it is itself good'.[1] He takes as an example of a plausible definition the suggestion that 'To be good may mean to be that which we desire to desire'.[2] But now let A be something that we think good. Then we can significantly ask 'Is it good to desire to desire A?' But evidently, Moore argues, this is not equivalent to asking 'Do we desire to desire to desire to desire A?' Consequently, the suggested definition must be incorrect: and a similar argument could be used against other definition of this general type.

Since the philosophers against whom he is arguing had mostly tried to identify good with some natural property, like that of being pleasurable, Moore speaks of the mistake which he thinks that these philosophers have made as that of committing the naturalistic fallacy. In *Principia Ethica*, he makes this accusation cover several different charges which he does not there distinguish. He does, however, distinguish them in a preface which he began to draft about the year 1920 for a second edition of the book, but did not publish. He there admits to having confused 'the three entirely different propositions: (1) "So and so is identifying Good with some property other than Good": (2) "So and so is identifying Good with some *analysable* property": and (3) "So and so is identifying Good with some *natural or metaphysical* property" '[3] and to having attributed the commission of the naturalistic fallacy to anybody to whom any one of these three different propositions applied. Dr Lewy, from whose contribution to the *Essays in Retrospect* I have obtained this information, relates that Moore went on to say 'that if he still wished to use the term "naturalistic fallacy" he would define it as follows: " 'So and so is committing the naturalistic fallacy' means 'He is *either* confusing Good with a natural or metaphysical property, *or* holding it to be identical with such a property, *or* making an inference *based* upon such a confusion' " '.[4] And since Moore thought that the term 'committing a fallacy' should

[1] Ibid., p. 15.   [2] Ibid.   [3] G. E. Moore: *Essays in Retrospect*, p. 296.
[4] Ibid., p.297

properly be restricted to the making of invalid inferences, he added that in employing it as he did 'he was using it in an extended, and perhaps improper, sense'.[1]

This last point is unimportant. The question is whether someone who holds a view which is covered by Moore's emended definition of the naturalistic fallacy is bound to be making any mistake at all. I think that he may be and that the reason why he may be is to be found in Moore's saying, or rather implying, that the fact, if it were a fact, that the word 'good' was correctly used to refer to some natural property of an action would not carry the implication that the action was worthy to be done. In short, the argument echoes Hume's saying that 'ought' is not derivable from 'is'. From the premiss that 'good' is a normative word, the conclusion is drawn that it must be a mistake to try to give it any purely descriptive meaning. On this view, Moore himself was guilty of an extension of the naturalistic fallacy when, having satisfied himself that 'good' could not stand for any natural quality, he inferred that it stood for a non-natural one. Quite apart from any difficulty that there may be about the very notion of a non-natural quality, the proper conclusion of this argument was that 'good', not being a descriptive term, did not stand for any quality at all.

In his reply to his critics in *The Philosophy of G. E. Moore*, Moore shows some willingness to accept this conclusion. He says that he is inclined to think that words like 'good', 'right', 'wrong', 'ought', 'duty', in their ethical uses are 'not the names of characteristics at all',[2] but that he is also inclined to think that this is not so, and that he does not know which way he is inclined most strongly. This question has been much debated by moral philosophers in recent years, and various attempts have been made to show that normative statements can be deduced from statements about what Hume called matters of fact. For instance, it has been argued that from the fact that someone, in a given set of circumstances, utters the words 'I promise to repay the money', it follows that he ought to repay the money. I can only say here that I do not find these arguments convincing. In the case of promising, it seems obvious that the conclusion does not follow, without the additional normative premiss that when by the utterance of certain words one has caused people to rely on one's performing a certain action, one ought not to disappoint them.

This is not, however, a question which Moore discusses any further, and it is not my intention to stray at this point into moral philosophy.

[1] Ibid.   [2] *The Philosophy of G. E. Moore*, p. 654.

What I am now concerned with is the fact that the argument in which Moore follows Hume is the only one of those that he advances in the first chapter of *Principia Ethica* which has any strong claim to validity. The others all prove too much. If we came to accept them, we should have to conclude not only that good was indefinable but that no explicit definition could be given of any term whatever.

But this is to say only that Moore's arguments raise the paradox of analysis. We have it on Lewy's authority that Moore himself came to think that whatever might be the complete solution of the paradox, 'It was essential to hold that [for example] to be a brother *is* to be a male sibling and that yet the proposition "To be a brother is to be a male sibling" is *not* identical with the proposition "To be a male sibling is to be a male sibling".'[1] If one makes use of Frege's distinction between sense and reference, one can obtain this result by holding that the expressions 'to be a brother' and 'to be a male sibling' denote the same attribute but have different senses. From the fact that they have different senses, it can be held to follow that the substitution of one for the other in the sentence 'To be a brother is to be a male sibling' results in the expression of a different proposition. We have, however, seen, when discussing Russell's criticism of Frege, that there are difficulties in this approach; and in any event we need some further explanation of the fact that one proposition is trivial and the other not.

In this connection, two points seem clear to me. The first of them is that the proposition that to be a brother is to be a male sibling is not to be identified with any proposition about English words. This is proved by the fact, to which I have already referred, that the proposition could equally well be expressed in another language, where it would become obvious that no English words were being mentioned. And the second point is that even though the proposition is not about words, it is only because of the information which the expression of it in some language incidentally gives about the words which are used to express it that the proposition is of any interest. To say that to be a brother is to be a male sibling is not to *say* anything about the use of the English word 'brother' or any other word; but what one learns from the statement *is* a fact about the correct use of the English word 'brother' or the French word 'frère' or the German word 'Bruder' or whatever, according to the language in which the proposition is expressed. The problem then is to try to reconcile these two points. The best suggestion that I can make is that a proposition like 'To be a brother is to be a

<hr />

[1] G. E. Moore: *Essays in Retrospect*, p. 302.

male sibling' should be regarded as a schema from which a set of linguistic propositions about the use, in the relevant sense, of the English word 'brother', or the use of the corresponding words, if they exist, in other languages, can be derived. Of course it can be said of any true proposition '*S* is *P*' that what one learns from it, incidentally, is that the expression which is used to designate *P* applies to anything which is designated by the expression which is used to designate *S*; but a distinction has to be drawn between the case where we take it for granted that the use of the expressions which we are employing is known, and the purpose of our utterance is to give some factual information about the things to which they must be taken to refer, and the case where, although we speak in a way that would be appropriate if the use of our expressions were being taken to be known, the point of what we say is just to impart this knowledge.

C. THE ROLE OF SENSE-DATA

I have said that the problem of philosophical analysis to which Moore devoted the most attention throughout his career was that of finding the correct analysis of propositions about material objects like 'This is a hand' or 'That is the sun', and that he never came, or believed that he came, at all close to solving it. As he said in his essay 'A Defence of Common Sense', the only things about it which ever seemed quite certain to him were, first, that when he knows or judges such a proposition to be true 'there is always some sense-datum about which the proposition in question is a proposition – some sense-datum which is *a* subject (and, in a certain sense, the principal or ultimate subject) of the proposition in question', and secondly, 'that, nevertheless, *what* I am knowing or judging to be true about this sense-datum is not (in general), that it is *itself* a hand, or a dog, or the sun, etc., etc., as the case may be'.[1] As to what we are then judging, Moore thought that there were three possible theories, between which he was unable to decide, though we shall see that he eventually rejected one of them. The first theory, which is the one that he eventually rejected, is that what we are judging, and what we know when we know a proposition of this sort to be true, is that the sense-datum is identical with part of the surface of the material object in question. The second theory is that we know or

[1] *Philosophical Papers*, p. 54.

judge there to be some relation R such that some unique thing, or set of things, which is identical with part of the surface of the material object in question, has the relation R to this sense-datum. Most philosophers who have adopted this type of theory have taken R to be some causal relation, but Moore says that the only view of this kind which seems to him to have any plausibility is that 'R is an ultimate and unanalysable relation'.[1] And the third theory is the phenomenalist theory which Mill summarised by saying that things are permanent possibilities of sensation. On this view, to know, for example, that this is a hand is to know that under the appropriate conditions one would perceive other sense-data which are related to this one in certain specific ways.

But before we consider what Moore has to say about these different theories, we must examine the point from which he approaches them. Is it really certain that when one uses a sentence like 'This is a hand' to mean what one ordinarily would mean by it, one is speaking about some sense-datum? Is it even true? The first step towards answering these questions must be to try to see exactly what Moore meant by a sense-datum.

So far as I can discover, the first occasion on which he used the term was in the lectures which constitute *Some Main Problems of Philosophy*, though in his earlier essay on 'The Nature and Reality of Objects of Perception', he had used the term 'sense-content' with what appears to be the same intention. His method of introducing sense-data in *Some Main Problems of Philosophy* was to hold up a white envelope before his audience and explain to them that when they saw the envelope they were directly apprehending sense-data. The sense-datum which he himself saw was, he said 'a whitish patch of colour, of a particular size and shape'.[2] On several occasions in these lectures he spoke of the colour, size and shape, that is to say of the sensible qualities of the patch, as being themselves sense-data, but this is at variance with his standard usage which is to treat sense-data as particulars, and therefore, in such a case, to apply the term 'sense-datum' only to the coloured patch and not to its sensible qualities. This is the only visual illustration that he gives in *Some Main Problems*, by way of introducing sense-data, but he also speaks of hearing a sound and feeling a toothache as cases of direct apprehension and adds that 'all these things – the whitish colour, the sound and the ache – are sense-data'.[3]

The fact that he gives a toothache as an example of a sense-datum

[1] Ibid., p. 56.   [2] *Some Main Problems of Philosophy*, p. 32.   [3] Ibid.

may suggest that Moore conceives of sense-data as things of which the
esse is *percipi*, and this is an inference which one might also draw from
the fact that one of his favourite examples of a sense-datum, in his
later writings, is that of an after-image. Nevertheless, Moore refuses to
characterise them in this way, because it would be inconsistent with
the possibility, which he wishes to leave open, that some sense-data
are identical with parts of the surfaces of material objects. But then the
effect of leaving this possibility open is that it remains unclear what
sense-data are supposed to be.

The most determined effort which Moore made to explain exactly
what he did mean by a sense-datum is to be found in his reply to his
critics in *The Philosophy of G. E. Moore*.[1] Having taken as an example a
situation in which a person 'is seeing his right hand as well as something
else',[2] he says that this person 'must be having a direct visual field
which contains at least two objects', and he explains that he regards this
as a logical entailment. He holds it to be 'part of the very meaning of
the assertion that a person is seeing his own right hand as well as
something else that he has a direct visual field containing at least two
objects';[3] and he refers to these objects, which are directly seen, as
examples of what he means by sense-data. He then goes on to explain
that the sense of the word 'see', in which constituents of the direct
visual field may be said to be seen, is the 'visual variety' of direct
apprehension, and that the objects of the other varieties of direct apprehension are also to be counted as sense-data, according to his usage
of the term. The mere fact that an object is directly apprehended is a
sufficient condition for it to be a sense-datum. Moore does not, however, say that it is a necessary condition, because he still does not wish
to commit himself to the proposition that sense-data cannot exist
unperceived. In saying that it is a sufficient condition, he forgets that
he has also spoken of abstract entities, like propositions, as being
directly apprehended. But perhaps he could have said that the sense
in which abstract entities are directly apprehended is different from that
in which sense-data are.

Before we go further, it may be well to ask why Moore finds it
necessary to stipulate that the person who is seeing his right hand must
also be seeing something else, if it be only a black background. The

---

[1] The following passage is a slightly emended version of a passage in an essay called 'The
Terminology of Sense-data' which I published in *Mind* in 1945. It is reprinted in my
Philosophical Essays.

[2] *The Philosophy of G. E. Moore*, pp. 630–1.   [3] Ibid., p. 631.

answer appears to be that he has in mind the directions which he gave for 'picking out' a sense-datum in his essay 'A Defence of Common Sense'. Using the same example of someone's looking at his own right hand, he there says that the person 'will be able to pick out something (and unless he is seeing double, *only* one thing) with regard to which he will see that it is, at first sight, a natural view to take that that thing is identical, not, indeed, with his whole right hand, but with that part of the surface which he is actually seeing, but will also (on a little reflection) be able to see that it is doubtful whether it can be identical with the part of the surface of his hand in question. Things *of the sort'*, Moore continues, '(in a certain respect) of which this thing is, which he sees in looking at his hand, and with regard to which he can understand how some philosophers should have supposed it to *be* the part of the surface of his hand which he is seeing, while others have supposed that it can't be, are what I mean by "sense-data".'[1] This passage had been criticised by Professor Bouwsma in his contribution to *The Philosophy of G. E. Moore*, and among the questions which he raised about it were the questions what the sense-datum was supposed to be picked out from, and what was then left. Moore's answer to these questions was that it was picked out from the subject's direct visual field, and that what was left was the remainder of this field: and it was to make this answer possible that he insisted, in his revision of his example, that the person who was seeing his own right hand must also be seeing something else.

But here surely he allowed Professor Bouwsma to lead him astray. If the problem were merely that of distinguishing a visual sense-datum of a person's hand from other visual sense-data, there would be a point in contrasting this sense-datum with other elements of the subject's direct visual field. But what Moore was trying to provide was a method of identifying sense-data in general and not merely of distinguishing one sense-datum from another. And this being so, the description of a process which consists in concentrating upon one element of a direct visual field is not at all helpful; for if the person to whom one is trying to teach the meaning of the word 'sense-datum' does not understand what is meant by a 'direct visual field', he will not be any the wiser; and if he does understand this, it is sufficient to tell him that a visual sense-datum is a constituent of a direct visual field, without the complication of a selective process which turns out to be a process of discriminating between sense-data. Indeed, if he is able to identify any

[1] *Philosophical Papers*, p. 54.

object as one that he is directly seeing, in the sense intended, the question whether it occupies the whole or only a part of his visual field is obviously irrelevant.

It looks, then, as if Moore has been misled here by his own metaphor of 'picking out'. For it suggests that sense-data can be distinguished from physical objects in the way that one physical object, or one sense-datum, can be distinguished from another: as one might give directions for selecting one out of a row of books, or distinguishing in a tune the sound of a particular note. But such directions would be of no use to those whom Moore is trying to enlighten. For their position must be assumed to be, not that they do not know what special sort of sense-data they are required to fix on, but that they do not know what sense-data are in general: so that their natural response to the directions which Moore gives would be to look for some physical object which was related to their hand in the peculiar way that Moore describes, and having failed to find one, to doubt the existence of sense-data. And this was, in fact, the line which Bouwsma followed. No doubt, in his case, the misunderstanding was something of a pretence. But the point which it illustrates is valid.

We are thrown back, then, for our understanding of what Moore means by a sense-datum, on our ability to understand his use of expressions like 'directly see'. Now these are technical terms, at least in the way that Moore uses them, and one would, therefore, expect him to give some precise and comprehensive rules for their use. He fails, however, to do this, again for the reason that he does not want to prejudge the question whether sense-data are ever identical with parts of the surfaces of material objects. All that he will commit himself to saying is that sense-data cannot be perceived otherwise than directly, and that from the fact that a sense-datum is directly perceived, it follows logically that it exists.

In my essay on 'The Terminology of Sense-data', from which I have reproduced my criticism of Moore's reply to Bouwsma, I argued that even this rather slender commitment precluded Moore from holding that sense-data were ever identical with parts of the surfaces of material objects. My argument, which was not well put, was that it was not self-contradictory to say of a physical entity that it was seen but did not exist, but that it would be self-contradictory, in Moore's usage, to say this of a sense-datum. Moore replied to me in an appendix to the second edition of *The Philosophy of G. E. Moore* and argued that while it was true that there was a sense of the word 'see' in which, for example, Shakespeare could be said to have represented Macbeth as seeing a dagger which did not exist, this dagger which did not exist was not a physical entity. This is a good answer to what I had actually said, but I still think that the point which I was trying to make was sound. It can be put more succinctly by saying that in the statement form 'A saw x, which did not exist', 'x' can significantly be replaced by a description which, if it were satisfied, would be a description of a physical entity, whereas it cannot significantly be replaced by a description which, if it were satisfied, would be a description of a sense-datum: and I think that this fact is sufficient to show that sense-data, in Moore's usage of the term, cannot be identified with physical entities.

I do not, however, need to pursue this point, as in the last paper which he published, an essay on 'Visual Sense-data' which appeared in *British Philosophy in the Mid-Century* in 1956, Moore himself finally decided that he had been 'mistaken in supposing that, in the case of "seeing" an opaque object, where in "seeing" it you are seeing only one visual sense-datum, the sense-datum can possibly be identical with that part of the opaque object's surface which you are seeing'.[1] He had always realised that if the possibility of such an identity was to be maintained, it would have to be admitted that sense-data could seem to have properties that they did not really have: this followed from the fact that sense-data which belonged to the same physical surface at the same time might be qualitatively incompatible, and that there could be no reason for identifying one of them with a part of the surface which would not be a reason for identifying the others with it also. Moore, however, had thought it to be possible, as he put it in his essay on 'Some Judgements of Perception', 'that the sense-datum which corresponds to a penny, which I am seeing obliquely, is not really perceived to *be* different in shape from that which corresponded to the penny, when I was straight in front of it, but is only perceived to *seem* different – that all that is perceived is that the one *seems* elliptical and the other circular'; and that the same applied in other cases even to the extent 'that the sense-datum presented when I touch this finger is not perceived to *be* different in any way from that presented to me when I see it, but only to *seem* so – that I do not perceive the one to be coloured and the other not to be so, but only that the one *seems* coloured and the other not'.[2] This was to meet the objection that a tactual and visual

[1] *British Philosophy in the Mid-Century*, ed. C. A. Mace, p. 210.
[2] *Philosophical Studies*, p. 245.

sense-datum cannot both be identical with the same part of the surface of a material object since they are not identical with one another. Moore said at the time that he made these suggestions that he was not sure that they were not nonsensical, and nearly forty years later he was at last able to convince himself that they were nonsensical.

What Moore at all times failed to see was that the answer to such a question as whether a sense-datum could seem to have properties that it did not really have was not something that he had to discover but rather something that he had to decide. There being no established usage for the term 'sense-datum', or for expressions like 'directly see', it was incumbent on him to lay down rules from which it would follow either that a sense-datum could or that it could not exist unperceived, and either that it could or that it could not seem to have properties that it did not really have. So long as he failed to lay down the necessary rules, such questions remained unanswerable: there was no basis on which an answer to them could be given. This was, indeed, a point that I tried to make in my essay 'On the Terminology of Sense-data', and Moore's reply to it, in the appendix to *The Philosophy of G. E. Moore*, was that there was a basis for an answer in the ordinary use of sentences like 'This is an inkpot'. He thought it to be certain that such a sentence was used to assert the existence of two objects, an inkpot and one that he called a sense-datum, and that what it asserted of them was that there was just one inkpot which stood in the relation R to this sense-datum, the problem being to discover the nature of the relation R. Later on, in his essay on 'Visual Sense-data', he took me to task for saddling him with the view that the demonstrative 'this' as used in the sentence 'This is an inkpot' denoted a sense-datum: and indeed a more accurate account of his view would be that what denoted a sense-datum was not the demonstrative 'this' as used in the sentence 'This is an inkpot', but the demonstrative 'this' as used in the sentence to which he thinks that 'This is an inkpot' is equivalent; the sentence 'There is just one inkpot which stands in the relation R to this'. But now it is simply not true that reflection on the ordinary use of sentences like 'This is an inkpot' will uncover any such demonstrative as that which occurs in Moore's expansion of this sentence, still less elicit the properties of the object which Moore takes it to denote. As we saw when discussing Russell's theory of descriptions, the function of demonstratives like 'this' is not to name objects but to serve as aids to orientation. In the example given, it directs attention to an object which the speaker then identifies, or misidentifies, as an inkpot. In a case of hallucination, where the object to which the speaker intends to draw attention does not exist, the demonstrative still performs a function by directing attention to the place where the object is believed to be: I do not strongly object to anyone's saying that it denotes this place, but I think it more correct to say that it does not, in such a case, denote anything at all. What Moore is doing, in his formulation of the sentences which are his first approximation to the analysis of sentences like 'This is an inkpot', is to use demonstratives, in a way they are not ordinarily used, as logically proper names: and then he has to postulate objects for these names to denote. Apart from the assumption that these logically proper names are involved in our ordinary use of demonstratives, which will be found to make trouble for Moore to the point of preventing him from taking his analysis of propositions like 'This is an inkpot' any further, this is a legitimate procedure. So long as the technical term which one is introducing is coherent and can be shown to have application, the only question is whether its introduction serves a useful purpose, and in this instance it does. But then one is called upon to give directions for its use, which are sufficient to show that these conditions are satisfied.

In the case of sense-data I have no doubt that they can be satisfied. As I have explained elsewhere,[1] it is possible to define a class of sentences which express what I call experiential propositions, the mark of an experiential proposition being that it records the presence of a sensory pattern, without carrying any implication about the status of this pattern, or about the existence or character of anything else whatever. These propositions fall short of being incorrigible in that the identification of a pattern is subject to revision, but if there is revision, it is the revision by the speaker of his own decree. It is out of such materials that I showed that Russell's primary system of sensibilia was capable of being constructed, and following Russell's later view and borrowing also from Nelson Goodman's *The Structure of Appearance*, I conceive of the objects to which my experiential propositions refer as complexes of qualities, rather than particulars in which the qualities inhere, and speak of them as sense-qualia rather than as sense-data. The reason for this change of locution is not only to make the point that my primitive data are qualities but also to avoid the suggestion, which the term 'sense-datum' has acquired a tendency to convey, that they are private entities. As I explained when discussing Russell's system, the question of

[1] See *The Origins of Pragmatism*, pp. 303-21, and 'Has Austin Refuted the Sense-datum Theory?', in *Metaphysics and Common Sense*.

privacy or publicity does not arise at this stage. I do, however, assign
to sense-qualia the function which Moore assigned to sense-data of
supplying the basis of all our judgements of perception. The way in
which I should put it would be that it is impossible for any proposition
to the effect that someone is perceiving a physical object to be true,
without its being the case that some experiential proposition is true;
and if this is granted, then the case for the introduction of some such
concept as that of the sense-datum is that we need to be able to formulate experiential propositions in order to analyse our judgements of
perception, at least to the extent of bringing out the features of our
experience which sustain our conception of the physical world.

D. THE ANALYSIS OF PROPOSITIONS ABOUT MATERIAL OBJECTS

For Moore, as we have seen, the problem of analysing judgements of
perception was that of discovering exactly what we are saying about
the sense-datum which is, in his view, 'the principal or ultimate
subject' of the proposition, when we assert a proposition like 'This is
a hand' or 'That is the sun'.[1] The theory which attracted him most was
that the sense-datum is identical with part of the surface of the material
object in question, but he never could overcome the objection that this
would require sense-data to seem to have properties that they did not
really have and eventually, as I said, rejected the theory for this reason.

This left him, as he saw it, only with the alternatives of phenomenalism and one form or other of what, in the notes for a course of lectures
which he delivered in 1928-9, he calls the 'Representative Theory of
Perception'. He remarks in these notes that for the representative
theory to be true it is necessary that there be a relation between a
sense-datum and the 'corresponding' physical object, which is first of
all such that we can know for certain that it relates these two terms
uniquely, and secondly such that it is plausible to suppose that, when
we make such a judgement as 'that this is a hand', we are making a
judgement about this relation, to the effect that it does uniquely hold
between the two terms in question. He then goes on to say that it is
generally assumed by philosophers who hold this type of theory, that
this relation must be a causal one, but points out that it is very difficult

[1] *Philosophical Papers*, p. 54.

to specify a causal relation which satisfies his first condition. There is no doubt that when one perceives a physical object, the object is among the causes of the perception, but this leaves us with the problem of differentiating it from the other causes, in purely causal terms, since to differentiate it as the one among the causes which was also the thing perceived would obviously be circular. Moore considers a suggestion made by Broad in his book on *Scientific Thought* that the object can be distinguished as the only relatively permanent causal condition which is common and peculiar to a series of actual and possible sense-data of which the sense-datum in question is a member, and says of it that it seems to him the only causal analysis of perceptual statements that might just possibly be true. He has, however, five objections to it which make him very doubtful whether it can be true. The first three of them, which are objections to every causal theory, are: (1) that while it is certain that when I perceive a physical object, my perception of it is caused by events on its surface, it is not at all certain that my sense-datum is, at least in the way required, since the state of my nervous system would be sufficient to produce this sense-datum even if the physical object did not exist; (2) that it is very doubtful whether the fact which a child comes to know when he first learns the truth of a proposition like 'This is a hand' is 'a fact which includes as a part that it has a cause';[1] and (3) that the proposition that the sense-datum has the physical object in question as one of its causes does not seem to be a tautology, which it would have to be if the physical object were itself identified only as one of the causes of the sense-datum. In addition, Moore has two objections to Broad's version of the causal theory, the first of them being (4) that it seems very doubtful whether our observation of the ways in which a series of sense-data are related to one another can be sufficient by itself to give us good reason to believe, still less to enable us to know, that they have a common external cause, and the second being (5) that it seems very doubtful whether the inclusion of hypothetical sense-data in the series does not presuppose a knowledge of physical objects.

Of these objections it is the implications of the third and fourth that seem to me decisive. It is surely obvious that if we are to have any good reason to believe that our experiences are caused, in the relevant way, by physical objects, we must be able to know independently that the physical objects in question exist; and this means that there must be some other way of identifying physical objects than as the causes of

[1] *Lectures on Philosophy*, p. 101.

our experiences. This argument applies not only to the causal theory
in its traditional form, where physical objects are represented as unobserved causes of sense-data, a theory which, in discussing Russell's
version of it, I have already shown to be objectionable on other grounds.
It applies also to the modern version of the theory in which it is
blended with naïve realism. A strong case can, indeed, be put for
making it a necessary condition for any physical object to be perceived
that the occurrence of the perception should be causally dependent
upon the action of the object; but this condition can be introduced only
at a relatively advanced level. It presupposes that a system of physical
objects should already have been constructed. But this entails that we
can speak of perceiving a physical object in a more primitive sense
which involves nothing more than the projection of sense qualia: and
in this sense no causal condition can be included.

If the causal analysis is, therefore, to be rejected, one may try to fall
back on what we have seen that Moore regarded, in his 'Defence of
Common Sense', as the only form of the representative theory that
seemed to him then to have any plausibility: the theory that the
relation which a sense-datum has to the corresponding physical object
is unique and unanalysable. But apart from the fact that this hardly
deserves to be called a theory, it fails to explain how we can know that
physical objects exist. As Moore points out in his lecture notes, it is
not as if we observed physical objects alongside sense-data and then
discovered that this unanalysable relation held between them. The
theory has to be that in apprehending a sense-datum we sometimes
know intuitively that there is just one physical object, with such and
such properties, which has this relation to it: and though Moore does
not go so far as to rule this suggestion out entirely, he rightly finds it
rather too much to swallow.

We are left then with phenomenalism. Professor Braithwaite tells
us, in the biography of Moore which he contributes to the *Essays in
Retrospect*, that in Moore's 'Cambridge lectures in the middle thirties,
phenomenalism received a far more favourable treatment than might
have been expected',[1] but there is no very detailed treatment of it in
Moore's published writings and what there is appears mainly un-
favourable. In an essay on 'The Status of Sense-data' which appeared
in the *Proceedings of the Aristotelian Society* in 1913–14, and is reprinted
in his *Philosophical Studies*, he does say that 'The great recommendation
of this view seems to me to be that it enables us to see, more clearly

---

[1] G. E. Moore: *Essays in Retrospect*, p. 23.

than any other view can, how our knowledge of physical propositions can be based on our experiences of sensibles',[1] but there and elsewhere he finds objections to it which he cannot overcome. As summarised in his 'Defence of Common Sense', these objections are first that the sensory equivalent of propositions like 'This is a hand' will have to include propositions which refer not to actual sense-data but to those that would be sensed if certain conditions were fulfilled and that it is very doubtful if these conditions can be stated without reference to physical objects; secondly, that it is doubtful if we can discover a set of relations between sense-data which will be such that in knowing that a given sense-datum belongs to a particular physical object, we know that it stands in this relation to other sense-data; and thirdly, that the sense which would be given, in this theory, to saying that a physical object is round or square, 'would necessarily be utterly different from that in which our sense-data sensibly appear to us to be "round" or "square" '.[2]

I do not think that any of these objections is decisive, but I also think, for reasons which I have given elsewhere,[3] that the programme of translating sentences which express propositions about physical objects into sentences which express only propositions about sense-data cannot be carried through. And if this programme cannot be carried through, then none of the three types of theory which Moore regarded as the only serious candidates for supplying the correct analysis of propositions like 'This is a hand' turns out to be successful.

But now I want to suggest that the reason why Moore could not find a satisfactory theory was that he was setting himself an impossible task. The assumption from which he started was, as we have seen, that the ultimate subject of a judgement of perception was always some sense-datum, and the question to which he vainly sought an answer was exactly what we are saying about a sense-datum when we assert such a proposition as that this is a hand. But if I am right in what I said earlier about our ordinary use of demonstratives, the correct answer may be that in asserting a proposition of this kind we are not saying anything at all about a sense-datum. I do indeed believe that it is possible to construct a physical system on the basis of sense-qualia, and in discussing Russell's logical atomism I have given some indication of the way in which I think it can be done. But from this it does not

---

[1] *Philosophical Studies*, p. 190.   [2] *Philosophical Papers*, p. 58.
[3] See my essay on 'Phenomenalism', in *Philosophical Essays*, and *The Problem of Knowledge*, chap. III.

follow that the statements of the physical system can be translated into sensory statements, any more than the statements of theoretical physics can be translated into the physical observation statements by which the theory is supported. Neither does it follow that, when speaking at the physical level, I am still referring to a sense-quale, even if the physical object of which I am speaking is finally identified by the use of a demonstrative. It is of course possible to designate a sense-quale and ask how it is related to the physical object to which it corresponds. And then, if one has been able to show in general how standardised percepts are converted into physical objects, the correct answer may just be that it is one of a group of sense-qualia out of which the relevant standardised percept can be abstracted.

If this answer is correct, it shows that Moore was following a sound philosophical instinct in his reluctance to give up the theory that sense-data are sometimes identical with parts of the surfaces of physical objects. This is, indeed, not true as it stands. If, as I believe, the physical object is an idealisation, no sense-quale, or group of sense-qualia, can be identical with any part of it. It may, however, contain an element of truth, in the sense that the physical object is an idealisation *of* sense-qualia, and that it is from sense-qualia which we take as typical that it directly derives its perceptual properties. This is a less ambitious result than that at which Moore was aiming, but it may be the best that is attainable.

At the end of his reply to his critics in *The Philosophy of G. E. Moore*, Moore admitted to being 'an unsatisfactory answerer',[1] and said that part of the reason why he had not solved many of the problems which he wished to solve might be that he had set about them in the wrong way. I have argued that this may be true of the problem, which occupied him more than any other, of finding the correct analysis of judgements of perception. I think also that the reason why he concentrated so much upon this problem was not just that it set a difficult and intricate analytical exercise, but rather that it had a very important bearing on the theory of knowledge. Not that he ever wavered in his conviction that he knew the truth of the common-sense propositions which he claimed to know, but he felt that this claim could do with the support which a correct analysis of judgements of perception might provide. And in general, though it cannot be said of him, as I believe that it can of Russell, that he was interested in analysis only as a method of justification, he was less concerned with questions of meaning than with

[1] *The Philosophy of G. E. Moore*, p. 677.

the question what can be known and how it can be known. So while there is some excuse for those who look upon him as an exponent of ordinary-language philosophy, they are doing him an injustice. It is a still more serious mistake to bracket Moore with the later Wittgenstein. Though we have seen that he differed from Russell in many ways, he agreed with him in thinking that philosophical problems are genuine and that they are capable of being solved.

Index

I

Tautology, 88–9, 93
Time
  phenomenal and physical, 46
  reality of, 188
  Russell's construction of, 62–4
TRINITY COLLEGE, CAMBRIDGE, 5, 6, 138–40
Truth
  coherence theory of, 190
  correspondence theory of, 105–8, 219
  idealist theory of, 155, 190
  Moore's theories of, 187, 189, 219
  Russell's theories of, 9, 80, 82–3, 98, 100, 103, 105–9
Types, Russell's theory of, 23–6

Unit classes, 21
Universals
  Moore's theory of, ix, 195–202
  nominalist view of, 71, 73, 184–5

Russell's belief in the existence of, 17
Russell's view of their relation to particulars, 15, 69–77, 196, 201
regarded by Russell as objects of acquaintance, 13, 38
Unobservable objects, 13, 109, 124–5

VOLTAIRE, 7

WARD, James, 140
WEBB, Beatrice, 6
WEBB, Sydney, 6
WEITZ, Morris, 10
WELLS, H. G., 6
WISDOM, John, 139, 179
WITTGENSTEIN, L., 10, 12, 16, 48, 54, 64, 84, 88–9, 92, 104, 106, 140, 142, 245
WOOLF, Leonard, 137
WOOLF, Virginia, 137